PRAISE FOR *BUIL~~DING~~*
TOP-PERFORMING

CW00740615

As we move away from the heroic leader towards distributed leadership, operating in complex, dynamic systems, leaders need to be able to curate and craft team performance, like a conductor or a premiership coach. *Building Top Performing Teams* is written by two highly experienced practitioners, who bring their insights from practice, and blend this with the emerging science on team performance to create a book for our time. This is an ideal read for team coaches, consultants and leaders concerned with creating work relationships which deliver more than the sum of their parts

Professor Jonathan Passmore, Director Henley Centre for Coaching, Henley Business School

Grounded is a word that springs to mind when I think of the potency of this book. As a new and burgeoning practice, Team Coaching – what it is and how it works – still eludes many. This book clearly situates the discipline and rightly positions it amongst the many modalities that support team efficacy. The authors ground us in the literature over the first three chapters which in and of itself is no mean task but the effect on the reader is comfort. I know where I am. They then share their own proprietary model that underpins their work with teams in an incredibly accessible manner, littering the pages with ideas/examples/ exercises all generously shared. This book is a re-read, over and over again. You will feel extraordinarily guided as you move through your own practice or work with teams with this book as your companion.

Tara Nolan, MCC, founder and host of the *Game of Teams* podcast

Never before have teams been so important to our future as the problems of the world today will only be solved by greater collaboration and teamwork. This new work is a welcome contribution to the literature on teams. Whether you are a leader, team coach or facilitator, this is packed full of useful tools and techniques that will expand and enrich your team development toolkit.

Georgina Woudstra, MCC & Allard de Jong, PCC, Team Coaching Studio Directors and Faculty

If you're looking for a comprehensive overview of team coaching that balances theory and practice, then look no further. Widdowson and Barbour have created a thorough overview of the doing and being of team coaching structured around important team topics. Whether you are an aspirant or experienced team coach, this book has something to offer you.

Dr Declan Woods, CEO, teamGenie® and Global Head, Team Coaching Standards and Accreditation, Association for Coaching (AC).

Widdowson and Barbour have delivered a powerful and practical guide for team coaches to help them connect more deeply with their 'way of being' as a coach and with the teams they are coaching. This is an important book for team coaches supporting teams on their journey to transformational performance.

Mike Sharrock, Chief Executive Officer, British Paralympic Association

If you want a comprehensive companion of current thinking and practical applications to unlock the collective power of teams this book is it.

Carissa Bub PCC, Executive Leadership Coach, host of the *Team Coaching Zone* podcast

Lucy and Paul's guide to team coaching is my blueprint for creating top team performance. It builds upon the critical team foundations of purpose, identity, values and beliefs. I have applied the knowledge and experience shared in this book across my organization, and it has delivered continuous improvement and outstanding results for our business, our customers, our many other stakeholders, and in the lives of the inspired and motivated members of my wonderful team.

John MacArthur FREng FEI, Vice President Group Carbon, Shell

This is a compelling and important contribution to the team coaching literature that is extremely clear and easy to follow. There is a genuine appreciation for value and importance of supervision as an integral element to support the team coach.

Dr Alison Hodge, EMCC Master Practitioner, Executive Coach and Coaching Supervisor

Any executive looking to transform their team in these ever-challenging times will get tremendous insight and practical guidance from this book. Its clear and accessible content, based on both academic principles and practical team coaching experience of the authors, will become required reading for all those looking to lead or coach teams in how to go to the next level of performance and effectiveness. Not only will a team benefit itself from engaging in the authors' coaching model to create the 'team edge', but the effectiveness of *other* teams in the organization that interact with that team will also improve as a result.

Jeremy Barton, General Counsel, KPMG LLP (UK)

Building Top-Performing Teams

A practical guide to team coaching to improve collaboration and drive organizational success

Lucy Widdowson
Paul J Barbour

KoganPage

First published in Great Britain and the United States in 2021 by Kogan Page Limited

2nd Floor, 45 Gee Street	122 W 27th St, 10th Floor	4737/23 Ansari Road
London	New York, NY 10001	Daryaganj
EC1V 3RS	USA	New Delhi 110002
United Kingdom		India

www.koganpage.com

Kogan Page books are printed on paper from sustainable forests.

ISBNs

Hardback	978 1 78966 678 6
Paperback	978 1 78966 676 2
Ebook	978 1 78966 677 9

British Library Cataloguing-in-Publication Data

A CIP record for this book is available from the British Library.

Library of Congress Control Number

2020948770

Typeset by Integra Software Services, Pondicherry
Print production managed by Jellyfish
Printed and bound by 4edge Limited, UK

CONTENTS

Foreword xi
Acknowledgements xiv

01 Introduction: Why the world needs top-performing teams and the argument for team coaching 1

The importance of teams 1

What is a team and how do teams differ from groups? 2

The challenge with teams 3

Team coaching in relation to other forms of team development and intervention 4

Defining team coaching 7

What type of teams can team coaching benefit? 11

Does team coaching work? 13

Moving towards an empirically tested and validated theory of team coaching 15

Our purpose and approach in writing this book 16

How to use this book 16

02 Beyond tools and techniques: Why is a team coach's 'way of being' so important? 19

Who can be a team coach? 19

The professionalization of coaching 19

The role of the leader in team coaching 20

Team coaching competencies: the 'Being, Doing and Knowing' of team coaching 22

Core coaching competencies: the 'doing' of team coaching 23

Foundation knowledge: the 'knowing' dimension of team coaching 26

Beyond tools and techniques: the 'being' of a team coach 30

Towards team coaching mastery 39

03   Team coaching frameworks, models and approaches: Introducing the 'Creating the Team Edge' framework 41

Keeping frameworks, models and approaches in perspective 41

Team coaches' views on frameworks, models and approaches 43

Review of frameworks, models and approaches 45

Exploring the 'Creating the Team Edge' framework (Widdowson, 2017) 46

Useful questions for team coaches to consider when reflecting on team coaching frameworks, models and approaches 50

04   The purpose-driven team: Why does being purpose-driven matter so much? 61

Defining purpose 61

The psychology behind purpose 62

The importance of purpose for organizations 65

Developing a team purpose 68

The challenges of team purpose 72

Tools and techniques for developing team purpose 74

05   Team identity: Why is team identity so important? 85

Defining identity 85

The psychology behind identity 86

The importance of identity for organizations 87

Developing team identity 88

The challenges of team identity 92

Tools and techniques for developing team identity 97

06   Team values and beliefs: Why are team values and beliefs so important? 108

Defining values and beliefs 108

The psychology behind values and beliefs 109

The importance of values and beliefs for organizations 111

Developing team values and beliefs 113

The challenges of team values and beliefs 118

Tools and techniques for developing team values and beliefs 120

07   **Team awareness: Why is it important to develop awareness both within and beyond a team?** 133
Defining awareness 133
The psychology behind awareness 134
Considerations for awareness in organizations 139
Developing team awareness 140
The challenges of team awareness 146
Tools and techniques for developing team awareness 147

08   **Team relatedness: Why is building trust and connection so important?** 161
Defining relatedness 161
The psychology behind relatedness 163
The importance of relatedness in organizations 167
Developing team relatedness 168
The challenges of team relatedness 174
Tools and techniques for developing team relatedness 177

09   **Team ways of working: How can teams keep reinventing how they work together?** 190
Defining ways of working 190
The psychology behind ways of working 190
The importance of ways of working for organizations 193
Developing team ways of working 197
The challenges of team ways of working 207
Tools and techniques for developing team ways of working 209

10   **Team transformation: What do teams need to do to become transformational?** 222
Defining transformation 222
The psychology behind transformation 222
The importance of transformation for organizations 226
Developing team transformation 227
The challenges of team transformation 236
Tools and techniques for developing team transformation 237

11   Conclusion: What does the future require of team coaching? 250

Imagining the future 250

The urgent need for collaboration 250

The power of deeper connection 253

The changing nature of work 255

The development and the professionalization of team coaching 257

Final thoughts 259

References 260

Index 277

FOREWORD

We live in the times of a great transition when not only every team, not only every organization, but the whole of humanity is having to evolve and develop in response to our changing world.

I have written extensively over the last twenty years about how individual heroic leadership in organizations no longer works. The world in which organizations operate is too complex and changing too fast for one individual CEO to be the only point of integration for an organization, while their fellow executives just focus on their own functions. In *Leadership Team Coaching: Developing collective transformational leadership* (Kogan Page, 2017) I showed how leadership teams, at every level, could become more than the sum of their parts. This is not something that changes overnight but is a development journey that takes commitment and support. This is where skilled team coaches have a critical role to play. Team coaching is currently the fastest growing part of the coaching profession, but the world still needs many more team coaches, who can work systemically, connecting depth change at the individual, team, function, organization and wider eco-system levels.

All evolution is co-evolution. Species and ecological niches evolve in dynamic relationship with each other. All learning and development is relational. Individuals develop through relationships with their family, teams and communities. Teams develop in dynamic relationship with the wider organization and beyond to their stakeholder systems of customers, suppliers, investors, employees, communities where they operate and the 'more-than-human' wider ecology.

Gone are the days when team building was just about getting team members to know each other and have good interpersonal relationships, or helping leadership teams sit in expensive hotel rooms, dreaming up their vision and mission. As I have written elsewhere, it is the purpose that creates the team, not the team that creates the purpose. The purpose precedes the team. If there was not a purpose to respond to and fulfil, you would not need the team or the organization. Much of the research on team effectiveness shows that having a shared purpose that requires collaboration is the most critical requirement for any team. Lucy and Paul show not only why teams need to be purpose-led, but how teams can be helped to discover and develop a clear co-owned purpose that aligns all their efforts.

In the fourth edition of *Leadership Team Coaching* (which Kogan Page will be bringing out in 2021) I write about how organizations and teams, in order to be future-fit need to be purpose-led; stakeholder-centric; environmentally learning; teaming across boundaries; and agilely networked. Arguably the only competitive advantage that any organization of whatever sector can have, is its ability to learn faster than the world around us is changing. Yet, we humans are by nature animals that respond to what is proximal in space and time. We knew there was going to be a global pandemic. The World Health Authority and the Gates Foundation had been telling us for years that it was not a matter of 'if' but of 'when' it would happen. But most governments totally ignored the warnings, focusing instead on immediate issues, they knew how to handle, or that would win the popularity with the electorate. It was not until the coronavirus was overwhelming the health service of a neighbouring country, or affecting someone the politicians knew, that action was taken, often all too late. We have known for over forty years that humanity is driving the world towards ecological collapse and a climate emergency, but turned a blind eye, seeing it as somebody else's problem to solve, or something for the future, or too complex and difficult, or with a blind faith in technology to solve it for us.

Leadership and management teams need to be able to simultaneously focus on running the business of today, innovating for tomorrow and future foresight of preparing for what is coming over the horizon. This is more than any individual can manage, especially as it needs to be combined with partnering with an increasingly complex web of stakeholder relationships that may be spread across many countries, different sectors and varied cultures.

The world is crying out for a shift in human consciousness. One that can adapt to a world of nearly 8 billion people, who are digitally interconnected. A world of the Anthropocene where all life on this earth is impacted by human behaviour. A world where climate crisis, loss of biodiversity, soil erosion, growing human inequality, human prejudice and problem cantered thinking are all interconnected. No longer can we solve problems one at a time for the challenges lie in the connections not in the parts. Coaching has made a great contribution over the last 40 years in helping individual leaders move from 'IQ' to 'EQ' from intellectual cognitive intelligence to also having emotional and relational intelligence. Now the challenge is to help collective leadership move from 'I' Q to 'We Q', from individual egocentric intelligence, to collective eco-centric leadership.

This requires teams that can think together, and generate new learning, insight, and action, between them. Teams that do not spend their meetings just exchanging pre-cooked thoughts but cooking new thinking that none of them could have thought alone. Lucy and Paul show how 'We need to re-structure work around teams to enable more rapid, flexible, and adaptive responses to the unexpected.' They also provide team coaches with some very clear and useful tools for helping teams develop their 'We Q' – tools for moving beyond groupthink and consensus, to surfacing their assumptions and challenging them.

I welcome this important new edition to the growing literature on how to coach and develop teams and hope it will not only help many team coaches but also team leaders and team members in finding their own pathways to becoming highly effective teams that create beneficial value for all their stakeholders.

Peter Hawkins
Renewal Associates
Barrow Castle, Rush Hill, Bath BA2 2QR
www.renewalassociates.co.uk

ACKNOWLEDGEMENTS

In the same way that teams are never just about the team itself, there are so many individuals and teams that have journeyed alongside us as a core team of two. We are deeply grateful to everyone who has inspired, supported and collaborated with us in the writing of *Building Top-Performing Teams*.

Specifically, we would like to acknowledge the pioneers in team coaching. There are so many we could mention. However, we would especially like to acknowledge the influence of Peter Hawkins and David Clutterbuck, for their relentless thinking, continual challenge and prolific writing in the service of advancing the field of team coaching and its influence. We are deeply grateful to Peter Hawkins for writing the foreword for this book.

Henley Business School, where we each completed an MSc in Coaching and Behavioural Change, also requires special mention. At Henley, we were taught to appreciate the eclectic nature of coaching, the importance of an evidence-based approach and the need to embrace paradox and critically analyse. We are grateful for our wonderful MSc cohort who we now consider friends, as well as members of the Henley team, who have been part of our journey, especially Jonathan Passmore, Rebecca Jones, Dorota Bourne, Christina Van Newburgh and Alison Hardingham.

This book is the result of our combined 50 years-plus experience of leading and working with individual coachees and teams. Thank you to each of these teams and our clients. We trust that we have honoured each of you in the words that we have written.

Special thanks to the team at Kogan Page, especially Lucy Carter and Anne-Marie Heeney for believing in this book and their brilliant support, challenge and patience.

Thanks from Lucy to

Heidrick and Struggles for providing probably the most challenging and yet supportive team coach development programme. This taught me the importance of building psychological safety and then being brave to challenge.

The International Coach Federation for allowing me to share my knowledge and passion of team coaching in co-leading the initial research on team coach competencies, representing UK ICF in developing these globally and for providing the opportunity to lead team coaching for the UK ICF chapter.

This book would not have been possible without the amazing support of family, friends and colleagues. So many to mention, my previous partners at

Performance Edge, many talented team coaches I partner with and I would like to specifically mention my colleagues Gail Lineham, Kate Oldridge who along with Paul provided immense support during writing this book when serious illness and bereavement impacted my family. Thank you so much.

My heartfelt thanks to my family, Keith, Alex, Joe and Sophie, for their love, patience, support and encouragement throughout and in particular for their understanding when I said I was on another Zoom call writing with Paul! I couldn't have done it without you!

Finally, thanks to my mum who always supported me, inspired me with her thirst for knowledge and always made me feel I was good enough. I wish you were here to share this final part of the journey with me.

Thanks from Paul to

Kerry Group PLC, my second home for 20 years. So much of my thinking has been shaped by my experience of leading in one of Ireland's greatest corporate success stories. We always had a deep awareness that we could do so much more by working together than apart and that our work had meaning and purpose.

To those that I collaborate with, in my work. While I cannot name everybody, I would like to thank John F Kelly (FXL Executive Solutions), Alex Lazarus (Lazarus and Maverick) and Nicole Sorrell (Lumina Learning). I thank you each for your inspiration, encouragement and unwavering belief in me.

My family system, friends and community. My experience as a child of the Northern Ireland troubles has shaped my views on the need for humans to collaborate. I'm thankful to my loving family and friends for influencing who I am as a person. I would especially like to thank my family Rhonda, Chloe, Hollie and Carrie for their love, support and encouragement during the writing of this book. My contribution to this book would not have happened without each of you! Thank you with love.

Finally from us both

Besides thanking people, we are also grateful for the creative process and transformational experience that is writing a book. Little did we know when we started to write that our purpose for the book – *to help teams within and across organizations collaborate better, to create meaningful lasting change* – would change us. We both feel richer for our time working with each other, for our discussions as we wrestled with the balance between evidence-based research and our own experience, and for the weight of purpose, in writing a book that we believe can make a difference. We are also deeply grateful to everyone who has chosen to read this book and make it part of their team coaching journey. Thank you all.

Introduction   01

Why the world needs top-performing teams and the argument for team coaching

The importance of teams

Working with others is at the very heart of our human experience. Human history can be considered a story of how people have worked together in groups to explore, achieve and conquer (Kozlowski and Ilgen, 2006). It would be a pessimistic view of humankind not to marvel at what we have accomplished and continue to accomplish when working together. It has been suggested that being in and learning to cooperate in groups is at the root of not only our business success but 'of all our achievements as a species' (Thornton, 2016: 4). While we need to work in groups to survive and achieve, being in a group is also considered essential to our mental fulfilment (Bion, 1961). As humans, we need groups to be mentally fulfilled, physically survive and to achieve things together that we could never achieve apart.

Despite the human need to be in and work in groups, it has been suggested that western philosophical tradition has celebrated the individual as the key to change (O'Connor and Cavanagh, 2016). This focus on the individual has been evident in how work was historically designed. It has been suggested by Kozlowski and Ilgen (2006) that the modern idea of work in the late 19th and early 20th centuries is largely a story of work as a collection of individual jobs; however, this story has changed as global forces have forced organizations to 'restructure work around teams, to enable more rapid, flexible, and adaptive responses to the unexpected' (p. 77). Despite the restructuring of work around teams, individual leadership development still dominates, including the growth of executive coaching. The focus on team development is often resigned to organizational values that eulogize the virtue of the teamwork in name only, corporate conferences where well-intentioned motivational speakers share insights from team conquests, and enforced attendance at the often-dreaded team building event. More sustainable attempts to develop teams is evidenced through the growing popularity of 'high-performance team' programmes and the focus of this book, team coaching.

It has been suggested that there has been a move away from the idea of a 'heroic leader', towards an increased focus on teams and the wider system (Lanz, 2016; Whittington, 2016). Agreeing with this view, Hawkins (2014) has suggested teams have greater potential than individuals to rise to the growing challenges facing organizations. To meet these challenges, he has recommended a shift in focus towards 'highly effective leadership teams' (p. 22). While we agree with each of these sentiments, we would argue that the enormity of the task facing humankind, given the growing global population, the ecological crisis, the risk of global pandemics, the demand for continued economic growth, political instability, the global battle between liberal and conservative values and the continued impact of technological advancement mean that heroic leaders will still be important and top-performing teams will be even more essential. It is our intention that this book will contribute to the important work of teams, at all levels in organizations.

What is a team and how do teams differ from groups?

The word team is widely and often loosely used, with many teams being a team in name only. So what constitutes a team and how do they differ from groups? Katzenbach and Smith (1993a: 45) suggest a team is 'a small number of people with complementary skills who are committed to a common purpose, performance goals, and approach for which they hold themselves mutually accountable.' This commitment to a common purpose and performance goals, they argue, is the specific way that a team differs from a group. Nevertheless, as highlighted by Forsyth (2014), while some definitions of a group emphasize the need for a shared purpose or goal, most agree that a group is 'two or more individuals who are connected by and within social relationships' (p. 4).

For the purposes of writing this book, we are a team of two. However, this book would never have been written without the support of our families, the publisher and many other stakeholders. No team operates in a vacuum, a point captured by Thornton (2016) who has stated that 'a team has an explicit shared purpose and/or task, usually in a broader organizational context' (p. 11). A comprehensive definition, that can serve as a checklist to ascertain if a team is indeed a team, has been proposed by Kozlowski and Ilgen (2006), who have suggested that a team should, among other aspects: include two or more individuals who possess one or more common goals; exhibit interdependencies with respect to workflow, goals, and outcomes; and be embedded together in an encompassing organizational system, with boundaries and linkages to the broader system context and task environment.

The challenge with teams

While teams are vital to organizational performance, research shows that many teams are not high performing. For example, Wageman *et al* (2008: 12) in their study of 120 senior leadership teams discovered that only 21 per cent of the teams could be described as performing to an outstanding level, with 37 per cent mediocre and 42 per cent considered poor performers. More recently, Price and Toye (2017: 49–51), in their analysis of 3,000 teams, reported that only 13 per cent were operating at the highest-performing level, in what they refer to as accelerating, with 28.5 per cent advancing, 31 per cent steady, 19.5 per cent lagging and 8 per cent derailing. Interestingly, they also found that teams at director level and above performed worse, with only 9 per cent considered accelerating, compared to 15 per cent accelerating at below director level. Also of interest was their finding that the closer a team is to the customer, the more likely it is to be accelerating. Importantly, they also recorded that teams at the highest level of performance had, on average, an economic impact 22.8 per cent higher than that of derailing teams.

The widespread preoccupation in society with individualism would appear to be a key issue as to why teams don't perform better. Supporting this view, Kozlowski and Ilgen (2006) have powerfully stated that 'given the centrality of work teams, it is more than a bit remarkable that we have a strong individual-centric perspective in the western world. We school our children as individuals. We hire, train, and reward employees as individuals. And yet we have great faith that individuals thrown together into a team with little thought devoted to team composition, training and development, and leadership will be effective and successful' (p. 115).

We believe that team coaching can help ease the tension between individualism and the team. With this in mind, this book has been written to benefit not only team coaches, but anyone who leads, is part of or works with a team.

Team coaching in relation to other forms of team development and intervention

Given the growth of team coaching, it is not surprising that there is a debate about how team coaching differs from other team interventions. While the debate is important, the subsequent confusion is not helpful to purchasers of team coaching. An example of this was apparent during a workshop we hosted at Henley Business School in the autumn of 2019, where a delegate shared that having been both a vendor and a supplier, she and many others remained 'muddled' as to the question 'what is team coaching?'

Before discussing and proposing our definition of team coaching, we believe it is helpful to understand it in relation to other forms of team development and intervention. It's important to note, though, that there remains little agreement on *how* team coaching is different from other team interventions (Lawrence and Whyte, 2017). Highlighting the confusion, Megginson (2013), when writing the foreword for the 2013 Ridler Report, stated that 'a challenging finding (for me) is the clear evidence for the growth of what people call 'team coaching'. For sceptics like me, who are not even convinced that such a process differs significantly from action learning, team building and other established interventions, the sharp question raised by the report is, 'Do you want to get on board, or will you risk missing the bus?" (p. 2). With demand for team coaching continuing to grow, we agree with Jones *et al* (2019) on the need for differentiating and defining team coaching.

The following sections will discuss three areas of intervention, which in our experience are often confused with team coaching: group coaching, including action learning sets/learning groups; team building; and facilitation, including process consultancy.

Group coaching (including action learning sets/ learning groups)

It has been suggested that group coaching attends to the coaching of individuals within a group, whereas in team coaching, the client is considered to be the whole team (Hawkins, 2017). Helpfully, the same author has highlighted that action learning differs from group coaching, due to its focus on the challenge presented. Similarly, when discussing the difference between learning groups and teams, Thornton (2016) has noted that in learning groups, the group goal is individual learning, compared to team coaching, where common learning goals are important. She further observes that while individual learning still takes place during team coaching, it takes place in 'the service of the team achieving its shared purpose' (p.11).

While these statements help differentiate group coaching (including action learning sets/learning groups) from team coaching, what may complicate the reality of practice is the discovery by Lawrence and Whyte (2017) that some team coaches adapt the action learning process for use in their team coaching work.

Team building

Team building has been described as interventions designed to improve 'effectiveness in working together by confronting and resolving problems' (Boss, 1983: 66). Kriek and Venter (2009) have similarly suggested that team building tends to focus on interpersonal relationships and improved productivity or improved alignment with an organization's goals. In addition, they highlight that team-building interventions typically consist of a one-day (or potentially more) intervention, with examples including: interventions based on fun and enjoyment (eg paintballing); interventions that simulate workplace dynamics (eg an obstacle course); assessment-based interventions (eg personality assessments); and problem-solving activities (eg experiential games).

In a challenge to the benefits of team building, Clutterbuck (2007) suggested that the 'efficacy of team building is mixed at best' (p. 108), and that while it does appear to improve relationships between team members, this does not necessarily translate into longer-term performance improvement. Several reasons are suggested for the lack of long-term impact, two of which include: the potential long intervals between team-building activities, punctuated by normal working patterns; and the potential for deeper behavioural or interpersonal issues only being temporarily addressed.

Personally, we both have positive recollections of organizing and being part of team-building events but despite this, the events were normally 'one-off' interventions that took place at infrequent intervals and our experience was that improvements in performance were short-lived and not sustained. In contrast to the ideal of 'one-off' interventions, we agree with the view expressed by Jones *et al* (2019) that team coaching is considered to typically take place over a series of sessions. It has been proposed that team building should be viewed as 'any process used to help a team in the early stages of team development' (Hawkins, 2017: 72). It is therefore clear that while a team-building event may be useful as part of an overall team coaching intervention, it is not team coaching.

Facilitation (including process consultancy)

Clutterbuck (2007) is clear that whilst a coach may at times use facilitation skills, the difference between team coaching and team facilitation is important. A team facilitator provides external dialogue management to help a team reach decisions, whereas a team coach is concerned with empowering the team to manage their own dialogue. He also reflected on how similarities with aspects of facilitation can result in team coaching being depicted as 'a sub-genre of a coaching style of facilitation, or alternatively, a facilitative style of coaching' (Clutterbuck, 2014, p. 281).

Hawkins (2014) has attempted to bring clarity by considering team facilitation as part of a continuum of team coaching. Alongside team facilitation, where the coach is mainly focused on helping the team manage their team processes, the other parts of the continuum include: team performance coaching, where the focus is on both team processes and performance; leadership team coaching, where the focus is on the collective leadership; and finally transformational leadership team coaching, where the coach is working with the team to help them transform the business. Another perspective has been proposed by Hastings and Pennington (2019) who, from their study of experienced external team coaches, noted that the pragmatic approach described by team coaches included, at times, taking on more of a facilitator role, especially when creating a coaching space.

Another area worth exploring is process consultancy. Schein (1988) has defined process consultancy as 'a set of activities on the part of the consultant that help the client to perceive, understand, and act upon the process events that occur in the client's environment' (p. 34). To do this work best, Schein (1990) suggests a 'facilitative' style of consulting. In addition, he calls for consulting to learn from psychotherapy, social work, teaching and coaching, in prioritizing the relationship with the client as central to the work. Hawkins (2017) considers process consulting as a form of facilitation in which the consultant helps the team to review and reflect upon the task process. He suggests that team coaching is likely to use less of a diagnostic type language and better balance a problem and appreciative focus, by exploring what is and isn't working well. Nevertheless, he suggests that team coaching has much to learn from process consultancy where the consultant is described as walking 'alongside the client, in a spirit of partnership, facilitation and co-inquiry' (Hawkins, 2017: 73).

In summary, while it is important to differentiate and define team coaching, we would caution against team coaching undermining one of its key strengths: its ability while using a coaching approach to draw upon multiple disciplines and approaches.

Defining team coaching

There is almost universal agreement that team coaching is a relatively new concept that lacks consistency of definition, practice and empirical evidence (Clutterbuck, 2014; Jones *et al*, 2019; O'Connor and Cavanagh, 2016). Before defining team coaching, it is useful to consider how practising team coaches work. To this end, Lawrence and Whyte (2017) interviewed 36 team coaches, to explore what practitioners do. They concluded that team coaching is essentially about the process. Five approaches to the process were discovered, none of them mutually exclusive and each relied upon to differing degrees: task, relational, developmental, dialogic and broad systemic. In addition, they discovered four main methodologies used by team coaches, again each to differing degrees: educational, behavioural, action learning and planned vs emergent approaches. Similarly, Hastings and Pennington (2019), from their study of team coaches, reported a focus by team coaches on 'the interpersonal relationships, relational dynamics and systemic context of the team, rather than an explicit focus on task performance' (p. 184).

Different team coaching definitions have highlighted the importance of:

- a common goal, group collaboration and performance, and individual performance (Thornton, 2016);
- team learning to increase collective capability and the application of coaching principles (Clutterbuck, 2014);
- thinking 'systemically' and not just within the confines of the team (Hawkins, 2017);
- partnering with a team in a relationship over time (Clutterbuck, 2020).

Jones *et al* (2019) described team coaching as 'practice-led' and 'pre-theory' and have suggested that without an agreed definition of team coaching, it will be difficult for the literature to develop. In what they described as the 'first systematic exploration of a definition of team coaching in relation to alternative team interventions' (Jones *et al*, 2019: 62) they reviewed 15 team coaching definitions published since 2000, and analysed the responses from 410 web-based interviews. They have defined team coaching as:

a team-based learning and development intervention that considers the team to be a system and is applied collectively to the team as a whole. The focus of team coaching is on team performance and the achievement of a common or shared team goal. Team learning is empowered via specific team coaching activities for self and team reflection, which is facilitated by the team coach(es) through the application of coaching techniques such as impactful, reflective questioning which raises awareness, builds trusting relationships and improves communication. A team coach does not provide advice or solutions to the team. Rather, team coaching requires advanced coaching skills from the coach such as considering multiple perspectives simultaneously and observing and interpreting dynamic interactions and is typically provided over a series of sessions rather than as a one-off intervention (p. 73).

We welcome this definition by Jones *et al* (2019) as an important base from which team coaching theory can be developed. Following much discussion, our own definition of team coaching is as follows:

Team coaching helps teams work together, with others and within their wider environment, to create lasting change by developing safe and trusting relationships, better ways of working and new thinking, so that they maximize their collective potential, purpose and performance goals.

Our definition includes seven key elements, as follows:

Team coaching

It may appear obvious to state that team coaching should have coaching activities and a coaching philosophy at its heart. It is our experience that most purchasers of team coaching are already well versed in what coaching activities entail. However, given the difficulty of working with group dynamics, the complexity of the challenges facing teams and the influence of multiple stakeholders, team coaching is both different and more demanding than individual coaching. Team coaching should be carried out by a suitably qualified internal or external coaching practitioner. In Chapter 2 we will propose an adaptation to Renshaw and Alexander's (2005) 'Being, Doing and Relating' coaching model, by proposing that a team coach should focus on: doing, the core coaching capabilities; knowing, specific areas of knowledge important for team coaches; and being, the importance of being able to connect deeply, to display confidence while retaining a sense of vulnerability, to have courage 'in the moment', and to continue to learn. Who exactly should be a team coach is an important question that we will address in Chapter 2.

Helps teams work together, with others and within their wider environment

At the most basic level, team members need to be able to work with each other. However, simply working with each other is not enough. Organizations are made up of a collection of teams that need to be able to work together. The importance of this principle is presented in the book *Team of Teams: New rules of engagement for a complex world* by McChrystal *et al* (2015). In the foreword of the book, Isaacson commented that, to triumph in this more complex world, organizations need to change and 'this involves breaking down silos, working across divisions, and mastering the flexible response that comes from true teamwork and collaboration' (p. vii). In addition, a team will only fully succeed if it is aware of, understands, acknowledges, interacts with, and ultimately serves the stakeholders in its wider environment. Coaching that embraces the wider system (systemic coaching) has been defined as 'that which acknowledges, illuminates and releases the system dynamics so each element can function with ease. It is coaching that prioritizes the system' (Whittington, 2016: 37). Chapter 7 will discuss creating self-awareness, team awareness and awareness within the context of teams' internal and external environment.

To create lasting change

Team coaching should help a team to reach a place where they no longer require the team coach. A place where the team itself embeds a new way of being, doing and knowing. However, to create lasting change takes time. From our experience, individual coaches rarely contract for one, two or even three coaching sessions, with five to six sessions being more representative of the average. Regarding team coaching, irrespective of the number of sessions or the format in which the coaching takes place, team coaches need to partner with their client on a journey. Most journeys worth taking involve multiple destinations and stops.

By developing safe and trusting relationships

As will become evident as you read this book, it is our view that it is only by being in robust, healthy and trusting relationships that humans can feel safe enough to individually and collectively flourish. Hawkins (2017) points out that while humans may never be able to put absolute trust in each other, it is about trusting each other enough to disclose their mistrust. It's about creating enough psychological safety that everyone feels safe to contribute and challenge. It's about teams where low-level conflict is generative and creative, not destructive and demoralizing. It's about teams where support comes before the challenge and feedback is given with permission and purity of intent towards another. Chapter 8 will propose a model for developing team relatedness.

Better ways of working

While at times the team coach may step into what Hauser (2014) describes as the advisor role, the role of the team coach is not to be an expert in ways of working, but to be an expert in helping the team develop awareness, as well as create solutions that improve how they do their work. These solutions may involve bringing in a subject matter expert (eg agile expertise, process consultant). Within the context of how the team works together, internally in the organization and the external environment, the solutions might include: creating better ways to make team decisions; a radical rethink about how the team meets; and reviewing the team internal and external processes and rhythm (for example, this could involve adopting agile methodologies to move outside siloed ways of working). Chapter 9 will explore how team coaching can help teams develop their ways of working.

New thinking

Individual learning and development have been confirmed as key effectiveness outcomes for individuals receiving one-to-one coaching in the workplace (Jones *et al*, 2016). We are of the view that team coaching offers a unique opportunity for learning to take place at an individual and collective level. Thornton (2016: 30), writing in the context of groups and teams, has commented that 'in order to learn, we must encounter something new, something different to our previous experience, that at a profound level, momentarily disorients us'. A team coach can create a safe space where team members can take learning risks they are unlikely to take elsewhere. A team coach can help a team to develop new thinking about how they: create and innovate together; embrace inclusion and diversity, including diversity of thought; take team well-being seriously, both mental and physical; and learn together and support each other in that learning. Chapter 10 will explore how teams can transform their thinking and learn together.

Maximize their collective potential, purpose and performance goals

The aim of any team coaching intervention should be to help a team perform in alignment with its collective purpose and work in service to its stakeholders. However, a team purpose without collective performance goals is like navigating without a map. The team must be clear on what its collective output should be. The team should be aware of what it can achieve by working together, that it could not achieve as a group of individuals. Chapters 4, 5 and 6 will explore the team purpose, identity, and values and beliefs, required as a base, from which a team can work towards maximizing their collective potential.

What type of teams can team coaching benefit?

It is our view that while team coaching has the potential to benefit any team, not every team will be ready for team coaching. Some initial questions worth considering include:

- Is this, in fact, a real team?
- How could team coaching potentially serve this team and its key stakeholders?
- Is team coaching the right form of intervention or should something else be considered?
- Does the proposed intervention best use the available team coaching resource?
- Is the context right for a team coaching intervention? (eg team and organizational readiness, practical matters – see Chapter 3)
- For team coaching to take place, is the composition of the team correct?

The design of a team coaching intervention will be greatly influenced by the type of team. Hawkins (2017: 125–26) has proposed the typical criteria used to classify teams, which include:

- **Duration** (eg project, stable or temporary teams).
- **Function** (eg sales, marketing, finance).

- **Customer** (eg X account team, Y account team).
- **Geographic spread** (eg dispersed, regional, national, international, virtual).
- **Position in the hierarchy** (eg board, leadership, front line).
- **Model of operating** (eg executive decision making, advisory, consultative, reporting).
- **Leadership style** (eg manager-led, self-managing).

Within the literature, there may be no agreement on an exact list of types of teams; however, there is an agreement that teams are multi-faceted and multidimensional. Offering an alternative on the very term team, Edmondson (2012), in her book *Teaming*, distinguishes between a team as a noun, being 'an established, fixed group of people cooperating in pursuit of a common goal or purpose' compared to teaming as a verb, a dynamic activity that 'is largely determined by the mindset and practices of teamwork, not by the design and structures of effective teams' (p. 13). Edmondson gives the example of a hospital emergency department, where a team can quickly form at a moment's notice, potentially without knowing each other's names. Another important term in the context of teams is 'agile'. Agile has been described as a way of organizing teams to work in an iterative, incremental, and highly collaborative manner (Thong, 2018). Hawkins (2017) has combined the terms teaming and agile to propose 'agile teaming', which he describes as 'quickly forming (and ending) teams as needed to achieve project-based commissions' that are 'helped by using agile methodology' (p. 349). Chapter 9 will explore how adopting an agile mindset and methods can benefit how a team goes about its work.

The teams we are most commonly asked to work with include:

- executive teams and boards;
- senior leadership teams (normally led by a member of an executive team);
- functional teams (sometimes includes multiple sub-teams);
- cross-functional teams (sometimes includes multiple sub-teams).

In addition, we are noticing an increased interest from teams that can best be described as:

- networks of teams (team of teams);
- dispersed teams (teams that never or rarely meet in person and operate virtually);

- joint account and client teams (normally consist of personnel from multiple functions in service of an agreed joint purpose and goals);
- temporary teams (applying the principles of team coaching in fast-changing environments);
- project teams (complementing already established project team methodologies).

Irrespective of the type of team, there are forces both expected and unexpected, which will continue to shape how teams work. An example of an unexpected force was the impact of the COVID-19 pandemic in 2020 when a sudden requirement for employees to work at home resulted in many organizations rethinking their approach to remote working. Remote working will be discussed in Chapter 9. An example of an expected force is the ongoing advancement of technology, for example, 5G, fibre-optic broadband, IoT (internet of things), AI (artificial intelligence) and AR (augmented reality). We believe that team coaching needs to disrupt itself and that those team coaches who are innovative in how they integrate technology into their work will lead the future of how team coaching develops (Chapter 11 will discuss the implications and opportunities of technology for team coaches).

Does team coaching work?

The Ridler Report (2016) noted that while team coaching accounted for 9 per cent of total coaching, some 76 per cent of the organizations surveyed expected to increase their use of team coaching over the next two years. Lawrence and Whyte (2017) have estimated that about a third of organizations use team coaching. While not denying the growth of team coaching and its importance in coaching, this in itself is not evidence that team coaching is effective.

Jones *et al* (2019), while highlighting the contribution of Hackman and Wageman's (2005) Theory of Team Coaching, with its focus on coaching provided by either the team leader or group members, have suggested that it was 'not sufficiently inclusive for capturing the range of team coaching scenarios that occur in practice. Further, the model is yet to be empirically tested or validated.' They went on to state that, 'in the absence of any alternative models or frameworks on team coaching per se, the field of team coaching could thus be described as pre-theory' (p. 64). While team coaching effectiveness studies to date may lack the robustness of empirical testing or validation, there are numerous studies that highlight the benefits of team coaching.

Some of these include:

- Wageman *et al* (2008) conducted research with more than 120 teams. They identified six conditions that impact team effectiveness, with team coaching being one of these conditions. In addition, they discovered that 'outstanding teams had significantly more coaching, both from leaders and from one another, than did mediocre and struggling teams' (p. 160).

- Anderson *et al*'s (2008) study with Caterpillar's North American Commercial Division leadership teams. It reported that senior leadership teams which underwent a team coaching programme, as part of a wider culture transformation programme, reported an improvement in the overall effectiveness of their teams.

- 'HCI & ICF: Building a Coaching Culture for Change Management Report' (Filipkowski *et al*, 2018) highlighted a link between team coaching and the effectiveness of change management interventions.

- Peters and Carr's (2013) case study entitled 'The experience of team coaching: A dual case study', based on two Canadian leadership teams, reported on improved collaboration, improved relationships, personal learning benefits, communication and participation improvements, as well as other positive impacts beyond the team.

Inspiration for this book comes from our experience of positive team coaching outcomes in multiple organizations. Additional inspiration is the research by Widdowson (2018), regarding the effectiveness of her 'Creating the Team Edge' framework on team effectiveness and performance within a leading UK retailer. The study involved in-depth interviews of five team leaders, whose teams each went through a 'Creating the Team Edge' coaching programme. In addition, six team coaches who had run a number of team coaching programmes across the same organization were interviewed. The findings indicated that the team coaching intervention improved performance and effectiveness both for the team itself and at a wider organizational level (ie for teams reporting into and those working alongside). The study highlighted three main contributing factors to the improved performance (Widdowson, 2018). First, the teams worked on collectively creating a purpose and agreeing on why they existed. This enabled the teams to ensure that their values and beliefs (behaviours), identity and strategic objectives were aligned to the purpose. Second, by creating a feeling of psychological safety, teams were able to be more open and honest, show vulnerability and give robust feedback. Finally, it was perceived that the team coaching process resulted in improvements in both individual and team learning, as the team shared knowledge and best practice with each other. The 'Creating the Team Edge' framework will be used to inform the key areas of discussion in Chapters 4 to 10.

Moving towards an empirically tested and validated theory of team coaching

In what was described as the first systemic examination of the effectiveness of individual coaching in the workplace, Jones *et al* (2016) concluded that individual coaching is effective in delivering individual learning and development and improvements in performance and results for organizations. They suggested that their findings provide 'an evidence base from which practitioners can draw confidence' (p. 270). A valid question to ask is, will team coaching effectiveness have to wait as long to be empirically tested or validated?

It has been estimated that team coaching is 20 years behind individual coaching (Hawkins, 2017). While this may be true, we would agree with the view that 'team coaching is catching up fast' (Lanz, 2016: 313). In addition, we believe team coaching will not have to wait as long as its successful forebearer to be empirically validated, specifically in the context of organizations. It has been proposed that the next important step for team coaching is the development of a comprehensive theory of team coaching that can provide a series of testable propositions to guide the research into team coaching effectiveness (Jones *et al,* 2019). Hastings and Pennington (2019) have alluded to the same point.

It is our view that team coaching demand will continue to grow, irrespective of the absence of validated effectiveness studies. Nevertheless, such evidence would be a welcome confidence boost and underpin what team coaches are already experiencing. That is, team coaching is on a journey to become one of the most powerful forms of team intervention, which significantly benefits teams, organizations and the wider organizational environment. We are hopeful that this book can contribute to that journey.

Our purpose and approach in writing this book

Our purpose as a team in writing this book is *to help teams within and across organizations collaborate better, to create meaningful lasting change.* At every stage, we have worked as a core team of two with an amazing network of support, as mentioned earlier in this introduction. The very writing of this book has been a team coaching journey in itself, as together we have created something we could not have completed apart. Together we have lived out the principles we have written about, through both the good and the more challenging periods.

In our work as authors and team coaches, we adopt an evidence-based approach. The evidence in this book is drawn from the developing literature on team coaching and other disciplines, such as team effectiveness, group therapy and individual coaching. We are also privileged to have worked together in making a joint contribution to the discipline of team coaching (Widdowson *et al*, 2020; Widdowson and Barbour, 2020) and separately to both team coaching (Widdowson, 2018) and conflict resolution (Barbour and Bourne, 2020). However, what brings us the most joy is the exchange between theory and practice. Together we bring a combined 60 years of experience as leaders and executive and team coaches. As we reflect on our experience throughout this book, both of us are indebted to the individuals we have led and coached, as well as to the teams we have been part of, both through leading and team coaching.

How to use this book

Chapters 1–3

Following this introductory chapter, Chapter 2 – Beyond tools and techniques – discusses our views on what it takes to be a team coach. Chapter 3 – Team coaching frameworks, models and approaches – introduces readers to the 'Creating the Team Edge' framework that includes a model of team effectiveness and an approach that can be used by team coaches.

Chapters 4–10

These chapters discuss the seven characteristics of team effectiveness as outlined in the 'Creating the Team Edge' framework. The book discusses team purpose (Chapter 4), team identity (Chapter 5), team values and beliefs (Chapter 6), team awareness (Chapter 7), team relatedness (Chapter 8), team ways of working (Chapter 9) and team transformation (Chapter 10). In Chapters 4 to 10, the following structure will be used to explore each characteristic:

- definition of the characteristic;
- the psychology behind the characteristic;
- the importance of the characteristic in organizations;
- developing the characteristic in teams;
- the challenges of the characteristic in teams;
- tools and techniques for developing the characteristic in teams;
- reflective questions regarding the characteristic.

The 42 tools and techniques (six per chapter) presented in Chapters 4–10 can each be used in person or virtually. For the tools and techniques, we are grateful to the community of team coaches trained in the 'Creating the Team Edge' framework, as well as input from other team coaching colleagues. Where we have presented or adapted a tool or technique from another source, we have endeavoured to reference the originator. Despite our best efforts, in some cases, this has not been possible. These instances have been highlighted.

Importantly, for the spirit of how we would like the tools and techniques to be used, the following guidance appears before the tools and techniques in each chapter.

Using tools and techniques

When applying these tools and techniques, it is essential that the team coach or leader builds connection and psychological safety first. The tools and techniques are offered as a support and guide, that when used should feel natural and in 'flow', with the process and steps behind the tools remaining effectively invisible.

Using reflective questions

Reflective questions are used throughout the book to help you to think about what you do currently and to consider how you can apply learnings to your role as a team coach or a leader.

Stories

Throughout this book, we have shared stories that demonstrate the various concepts in action. For these stories, we are grateful to both the individuals and the teams that have inspired them and the team coaching colleagues we worked alongside during some of these memorable experiences. The stories, while each true, have been told in a non-attributable way. If any part of this book should inspire your own team coaching or leadership story, we would be delighted to hear about your experiences.

Chapter 11

In our conclusion, we present our views about the future of team coaching.

Reflective questions on team coaching

- Consider a brilliant team you have worked in:
  - o What made it brilliant?
  - o How effective was that team?
  - o What were the team's main accomplishments?
- Do you have the right people in your team? If you aren't confident that you do, what changes do you need to make?
- What does team coaching mean to you?
- What does team coaching mean to your organization?
- Consider what your team can deliver that individual team members can't achieve on their own.

Beyond tools and techniques 02

Why is a team coach's 'way of being' so important?

Who can be a team coach?

In Chapter 1 we stated that 'team coaching should have coaching activities and a coaching philosophy at its heart'. Therefore, at the most basic level, a team coach should be a professional coach. However, as this chapter will discuss, being a competent one-to-one coach is not enough. We will argue that there are important areas that a team coach needs to be knowledgeable on, that may be useful to coaches who practise with individuals, but are not essential for them. In addition, we will propose that there is a 'way of being', that, though important for all coaches, is essential for anyone wanting to practise as a team coach. We are not precluding non-coaches from using ideas outlined in this book, and we state that 'at the most basic level, a team coach needs to be a coach'. Team coaching ideas and methodologies, used effectively, could benefit the work of most experienced team leaders or organizational consultants. Nevertheless, if team coaching is to develop to its full potential, who can be a team coach needs to be considered carefully.

The professionalization of coaching

First, let us reflect on the status of professional coaching. Grant writing in 2007 commented that 'coaching is an industry and not a profession, there are no barriers to entry, no regulation, no government-sanctioned accreditation or qualification process and no clear authority to be a coach'. He further highlights that 'following a few days' training and the payment of a suitable fee, one can become a Certified Master Coach' (Grant, 2007: 27). The concern about the ease at which a person can claim to be a coach is shared among professional coaches, with 'untrained individuals' being highlighted as the greatest obstacle in research conducted by the International Coach Federation (ICF, 2016). It has been suggested that as coaching emerges into a profession, commissioners of coaching will expect coaches to hold a master's or equivalent qualification (Hain *et al*, 2011) as those who buy in coaching services are becoming more demanding. Mann (2015), author and principal researcher of the 6th Ridler Report, highlighted that the sponsors of coaching requiring accreditation had increased from 54 per cent in 2013 to 68 per cent in 2015. The increasingly professional nature of coaching is welcome and we are confident that team coaching can learn lessons from its journey.

Who is considered a coach?

Given the changes to client expectations, it's interesting to consider the ICF study that estimated that there are 64,100 professional coaches globally who exist along a coaching continuum. At one side of the continuum are an estimated 53,300 (83 per cent) coach practitioners, made up of both external and internal coaches. At the other side of the continuum are an estimated 10,900 (17 per cent) managers, leaders, and human resource and talent development professionals, who use coaching skills in their day-to-day work (ICF, 2016). While there are no figures on the number of coaches who team coach, we would suggest that team coaches will continue to emerge from this growing body of coach practitioners and managers/leaders who use coaching skills.

The role of the leader in team coaching

Should a team leader or manager be the team coach of their own team?

From our experience as team members, team leaders and team coaches we are clear that leaders play an essential role in a team's effectiveness. It has been suggested that frontline managers are important to a team's effectiveness due to their discretion in determining team structure, their influence on team rewards and information, and their role in determining team direction (Wageman, 2001). As well as being important to the effectiveness of a team, they are equally important to the success of any team coaching intervention. This view is supported by the findings of Lawrence and Whyte (2017) who concluded that 'aside from contracting, it is important for the coach to be convinced as to the genuine commitment of the leader to the process' (p. 105). They noted from their research many stories of team coaching interventions that did not work as a result of unsupportive leader behaviours.

While the full support of the team leader during any team coaching intervention is essential, another key area to consider is, should a team leader or manager be the team coach of their own team? In the context of individual coaching, it has been suggested that 'there exists a power relationship between line managers and their subordinates, which is absent in the helping relationship a coachee would have with an independent coach' (Jones *et al*, 2016: 251). While implicit in the work of Hackman and Wageman (2005) that the same people can effectively operate as a team leader and coach, we remain unconvinced that it represents the most effective approach. Challenging the assumption that a team leader can effectively operate as the team coach, Mathieu *et al* (2008: 453) pose the following questions:

- Do we know if people can easily transform from the leadership role to a coaching role?
- Are those two skill sets likely to reside in the same people, and are they willing and able to transform their behaviours as necessary?
- Are formal leaders the best source of coaching, or might a third party better fulfil that role?
- Finally, will team members readily accept their leader as their coach?

While recognizing this is an area that requires research, we would suggest that a team leader, even if a trained and experienced team coach, could better serve their organization by acting as a team coach for teams they do not lead.

Should a team coach be external or internal?

Jones *et al* (2016), when reviewing the literature on coaching effectiveness in the workplace, hypothesized that external coaches would have a greater impact on outcomes. However, while issuing a note of caution given the low number of studies that used internal coaches, they discovered that 'although coaching by both internal and external coaches was beneficial for learning and performance, the effects of coaching by internal coaches had a stronger effect compared to external coaches' (p. 269). In our own experience, team leaders and internal team coaches that we have trained in a number of organizations have reported positive shifts in performance from the team coaching programmes they have run.

While specific team coaching research on this area would be helpful, we are of the view that the development of internal team coaches, who can independently coach teams across their organizations, will be essential if team coaching is to fully realize its potential.

Team coaching competencies: the 'Being, Doing and Knowing' of team coaching

Our experience of team coaching would lead us to agree with Jones *et al* (2019) that coaching a group of individuals, all at the same time, is more complex than coaching on a one-to-one basis and that team coaching requires a level of advanced coaching skills.

A useful perspective when discussing evidence-based practice and team coaching competencies could be Drake's (2009) reference to four domains of knowledge in coaching: personal (self-knowledge), contextual, professional, and foundational. Another perspective is Hawkins and Smith's (2013) 3 Cs of competencies, capabilities and capacities. However, after much discussion, we have decided to adapt Renshaw and Alexander's (2005) 'Being, Doing and Relating' coaching model, to 'Being, Doing and Knowing', with the 'being' element placed centrally within the model (see Figure 2.1). In our adaption, Renshaw and Alexander's 'Relating' is incorporated with our definition of 'Being'.

Drake's 'professional' domain can be aligned with the 'doing' element, the 'contextual' and 'foundational' domains with the 'knowing' element and finally, the 'personal (self-knowledge)' domain with the 'being' element. Hawkins and Smith's 3 Cs of competencies, capabilities and capacities are slightly more difficult to map against 'Being, Doing and Knowing', with the exception of capacities, which has been described as representing 'one's being, rather than one's doing' (p. 247).

It is our view that the 'Being, Doing and Knowing' of team coaching is essential for those who want to be team coaches professionally, as well as those who wish to practise elements of team coaching within their role, eg team leaders.

Figure 2.1 The 'Being, Doing and Knowing' model of team coaching competency

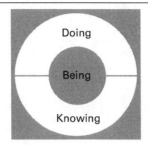

Core coaching competencies: the 'doing' of team coaching

As discussed earlier, the purchasers of coaching services will increasingly demand that a coach should be accredited. It is therefore important that the providers of coach training, including team coach training, offer routes towards accreditation by the main coaching bodies. Despite this statement, we recognize that until team coaching competencies are established, team coaching training providers will have to use coaching competencies, developed with the coaching of individuals in mind (see Table 2.1). We would suggest that an important foundation for any team coach is competency in coaching individuals. We would also propose that whatever team coaching competencies are agreed in the future, they should build upon the coaching competencies already established.

Coaching competencies, while applicable to team coaching in the broader sense, require further consideration to be fully applicable to team coaching. To consider this further, we have summarized the current competencies (excluding the additional competencies presented by the Association for Coaching (AC) for executive coaching) of the International Coach Federation (ICF, 2019), AC (2012) and the European Mentoring & Coaching Council (EMCC, 2015) into the following eight categories:

- ethical practice;
- coaching mindset and presence;
- continued professional development (CPD);
- contracting (coaching agreements);
- developing a trusting relationship;
- creating awareness and insight;
- effective communication;
- client growth and momentum.

Table 2.1   Coaching competencies of the ICF, AC and EMCC

ICF (2019)	AC (2012)	EMCC (2015)
1. Demonstrates ethical practice	1. Meeting ethical, legal and professional guidelines	1. Understanding self
2. Embodies a coaching mindset	2. Establishing the coaching agreement and outcomes	2. Commitment to self- development
3. Establishes and maintains agreements	3. Establishing a trust-based relationship with the client	3. Managing the contract
4. Cultivates trust and safety	4. Managing self and maintaining coaching presence	4. Building the relationship
5. Maintains presence	5. Communicating effectively	5. Enabling insight and learning
6. Listens actively	6. Raising awareness and insight	6. Outcome and action orientation
7. Evokes awareness	7. Designing strategies and actions	7. Use of models and techniques
8. Facilitates client growth	8. Maintaining forward momentum and evaluation	8. Evaluation
	9. Undertaking continuous coach development	
	10. Working within the organizational context	
	11. Understanding leadership issues	
	12. Working in partnership with the organization	

Considering team coaching under these eight categories, some areas specific to team coaching could include:

- Ethical practice:
  - o It is important for the team to agree what confidentiality means for their interactions with each other (eg peer coaching) and others (eg stakeholders) during the team coaching intervention.

- Coaching mindset and presence:
  - o On many occasions, a team coach will be coaching in partnership with other team coaches. While a collective coaching mindset is not required, the coaches should be broadly aligned philosophically. In addition, they should agree on how disagreements will be surfaced and managed authentically, 'in the moment'. By how they work with each other, team coaches are in an excellent position to role-model a peer-to-peer relationship.
  - o A team coach should be mindful of their own energy levels and potential decreases in presence, particularly during coaching engagements that last several hours.
- Continued professional development (CPD):
  - o There are significant differences between the ongoing development journey of a team coach and a coach who works with individuals. The following section entitled 'Foundation knowledge: the 'knowing' dimension to team coaching' will discuss some of these.
- Contracting (coaching agreements):
  - o The team coach needs to ensure the team and other relevant stakeholders are aware that, as the team coaching interventions progress, the team coach will look for opportunities to step back and let the team, in effect, coach itself.
- Developing a trusting relationship:
  - o The team coach needs to consider how they will create and maintain their relationship with the team, while also attending to individual relationships, in a way that does not undermine the relationship with the team.
  - o The team coach needs to be aware of the invisible forces of group dynamics, which can both undermine and strengthen relationships.
- Creating awareness and insight:
  - o The team coach should, where they judge it beneficial, consider using an existing team diagnostic tool or other methodologies co-created with the team, to develop team awareness.
- Effective communication:
  - o The team coach should embody and role-model listening at an individual, team, organizational and wider environmental/systemic level.
  - o When two team coaches work together, they should practise deeper listening to introduce perspectives that could be missed by a single team coach.

- Client growth and momentum:
  - o The team coach should help cultivate a team climate, to ensure learning and growth take place.

While this may not be an exhaustive list, it illustrates the need for focus to be placed on team coaching competencies.

Foundation knowledge: the 'knowing' dimension of team coaching

While there may be some overlap with core team coaching competencies, we have highlighted nine areas of knowledge (see Figure 2.2) that we believe are essential for team coaches and those who want to practise elements of team coaching within their role to consider. Although this list is by no means exhaustive, we believe it represents keys areas of knowledge for a team coach, which we will now briefly consider.

Figure 2.2 Important areas of knowledge for team coaches

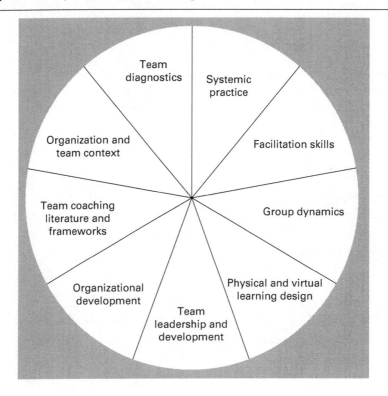

Systemic practice

The discipline of systemic coaching has been described as 'coaching that prioritizes the system' (Whittington, 2016: 37). Essentially it is coaching that deals with the wider system and adapts the coaching to address issues at every level, including that of the individual (Cavanagh, 2006). Hawkins and Smith (2013: 75) have observed that while the coaching of individuals has grown exponentially over the last 30 years, 'equally important but far less documented in the literature, is the coaching of teams, organizations and whole systems'. A team coach must learn how to practise systemically. Indeed, it has been stated that 'it is the system's insight that makes team and group coaching possible' (O'Connor and Cavanagh, 2016: 488).

Facilitation skills

As discussed in Chapter 1, while team coaching is distinct from facilitation, a team coach should be able to step into facilitation mode when required. Heron (1999) has suggested six dimensions and three modes that should be considered when facilitating. The six dimensions are planning, meaning, confronting, feeling, structuring and valuing. The three modes are hierarchical, co-operative and autonomous. While facilitation training is important, practice is essential. In our experience, developing advanced facilitation skills, for both working in person and virtually, is also essential.

Group dynamics

It is our view that team coaches must develop their knowledge of group dynamics. Group dynamics has been defined as 'all the invisible and emotional forces and communications between individuals in a group, which lead groups to behave in much more extreme ways than any of the individuals would have done on their own' (Hardingham et al, 2004: 168). Thornton (2016) in her influential book *Group and Team Coaching* has commented on the importance of group theory. The literature on group dynamics discusses both conscious and directly observable factors, such as the style of interaction, handling difficult conversations, challenge and conflict, and team defensive mechanisms, as well as the more hidden aspects, such as the unconscious aspects of group life (Bion, 1961; Lewin, 1947; Menzies Lyth, 1989; Gillette and McCollom, 1990).

Physical and virtual learning design

In our experience, a team coaching programme is likely to consist of a multidimensional and integrated learning and development approach, consisting of a series of interventions. Jones *et al* (2019: 73) in their definition of team coaching stated that interventions are 'typically provided over a series of sessions rather than a one-off intervention'. When designing these interventions there are several areas a team coach needs to consider. These can include a pre-team coaching stage, involving meeting with the key stakeholders and the team leader to understand the organizational context; financial metrics; objectives for the programme and important information about the team and the system in which they operate. Following this there is likely to be a diagnostic stage, which may include the use of a team diagnostic or 360 questionnaire and, for example, one-to-one interviews with team members, stakeholders and customers. The team coaching programme itself is likely to consist of a series of module-style team workshops, which can take place either face to face, virtually or using a hybrid of each. In our experience of team coaching virtually, team coaches need to be comfortable using multiple virtual platforms and their various features (eg virtual whiteboards, annotation, breakout rooms, screen sharing, polls). Also, the team coach needs to apply maximum creativity to their design (eg each tool and technique in Chapters 4 to 10 can be used in a virtual setting), as well as give detailed consideration to practical matters (eg the length of a session, technical and connectivity aspects). The workshops are likely to include self and team reflection exercises, as well as exercises to reach decisions and agree commitments and actions. Throughout the team coaching journey, interventions are often supported by one-to-one coaching, observation of the team at work and sharing of knowledge and learning materials. It is therefore essential that the team coach has knowledge of how to design and develop multidimensional physical and virtual learning interventions.

Team leadership and development

At an open workshop we hosted at Henley Business School in the autumn of 2019, one delegate asked a pertinent question. 'Surely,' they asked, 'does a team coach not need to have experience of leading and developing teams?' We answered that while it would be ideal, people who have worked and helped develop teams in non-leadership roles should not be excluded. Furthermore, we stated that what is essential is having extensive experience in being part of a team that you have played important roles in developing. It is our view that a team coach should be someone who over many years has demonstrated a genuine interest in how teams develop and has played an active role to improve the teams they were part of. Put simply, team coaches should enjoy being a part of teams and should be intrigued by how they work and don't work.

Organizational development

Cummings and Worley (1997) consider organizational development to be about a system-wide application of behavioural science knowledge to the planned development and reinforcement of organizational practices (strategies, structure, processes etc), to improve an organization's effectiveness. From our own experience of team coaching, we believe it is important that a team coach has experience of organizational development, either in the capacity of a leader, manager or a more specialist organizational development role.

Team coaching literature and frameworks

Lawrence and Whyte (2017), from their study of 36 team coaches, concluded that 'the general lesson appears to be less around adopting a specific approach, as to be confident in adopting an approach that the coach understands and has confidence in' (p. 105). We are of the view that team coaching's eclectic nature is part of its strength. However, to be eclectic in how you practise, it is essential to understand different perspectives. For a team coach, this means having a knowledge of team effectiveness theory and team coaching literature, the differences between individual versus collective development, and multiple team coaching frameworks, models and approaches.

Organization and team context

Whitmore (2009) emphasized that experience in an area or technical knowledge are not requirements to coach and indeed can be a drawback. While we agree with this sentiment, it is essential that a team coach learns as much about the organization as possible, including their financial situation and outlook, and the context in which the team operates. It is important that the team coach takes into account these factors when designing the team coaching programme, and through their language and actions can demonstrate this knowledge to the team and its stakeholders. While a broad range of organizational experience will be beneficial, even more important may be a mindset that is genuinely curious and enthused about the client's world.

Team diagnostics

A team coach should be practised in methods that can help team members develop self-awareness, and help the team become more aware of itself, other teams and their wider environment. This could involve methodologies to develop awareness that are co-created with the team, off-the-shelf individual and team diagnostic tools, or a mixture of both. While we do not wish to be prescriptive about which methodologies a team coach should use, we believe it is important that a team coach is able to communicate to clients how they will safely develop a team's awareness.

Beyond tools and techniques: the 'being' of a team coach

While much has been written about the importance of a coach's 'way of being' (Renshaw and Alexander, 2005; Hurley and Staggs, 2012; Hawkins and Smith, 2013; Hawkins, 2014; Van Nieuwerburgh, 2017; Hullinger and DiGirolamo, 2018, Widdowson et al, 2020, Widdowson and Barbour, 2020), most writers have focused on what characterizes a coach's 'way of being', rather than defining it. We will be taking a similar approach. The words of Rogers (1961: 103) when discussing client-centred therapy seem appropriate, when he stated, 'we are talking here about something at an experiential level – a phenomenon which is not easily put into words, and which, if apprehended only at the verbal level, is by the very fact, already distorted.'

At the very heart of our competency model is the 'Being' element of a team coach. In Chapter 1 we described it as the importance of a team coach's ability 'to connect deeply, to display confidence while retaining a sense of vulnerability, to have courage "in the moment", and to continue to learn'. We have termed these four characteristics as the 4 Cs of Being: connection, confidence, courage and continuing (see Figure 2.3). The following sections will discuss each characteristic, with the main focus placed on what we believe to be the most important characteristic – connection.

Figure 2.3 The 4 Cs of Being

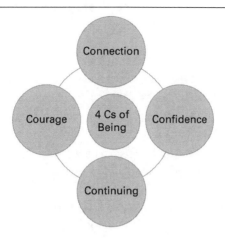

Connection

It is clear that a team coach must be able to connect deeply, build trust and create a feeling of safety with each individual and the team collectively, both at the same time. The importance of safety has been highlighted by Hastings and Pennington (2019) who suggested that for team coaching to be productive, team members have to 'feel safe, or at least be willing to be vulnerable' (p. 184). While team coaching may be lacking in empirical research, a wealth of research exists about the importance of building connection during individual and group therapy. While coaching is not therapy, it is therapeutic in nature, with Bossons *et al* (2012: 3) observing that coaching is 'probably the only non-therapeutic relationship' where the full attention is given to the other person. Importantly, large-scale studies on executive and workplace coaching have demonstrated that the strength of the working alliance, as viewed through the eyes of the coachee, is a key ingredient of coaching effectiveness (De Haan *et al,* 2016, 2019). The same research has also highlighted the need for further studies to consider the coaching of groups.

Rogers (1995) in his book *A Way of Being* suggests that in therapy, an individual needs to be shown empathy (listened to and understood), genuineness (openness and self-disclosure on behalf of the therapist) and acceptance (considered with unconditional positive regard). Empirical research has confirmed the importance of each of these elements. We are confident that the empirical research from individual and group therapy can help team coaches better understand connecting with others.

> ### Story: The power of unconditional positive regard
> Contributor: Paul
>
> Some 18 months after the end of a coaching intervention, a coachee shared how the introduction to unconditional positive regard had had a transformative impact on how he connected with others.
>
> The coachee had been having a difficult relationship with his boss. He explained how as a result of the coaching, he had started to remind himself, 'I don't know what is causing my boss to be the way she is in this moment, but I will hold her in positive regard and remain curious.' The relationship transformed. I hypothesized with the coachee that he had potentially stopped overthinking about what his boss was thinking and had replaced his frustration with a gentle curiosity. I further suggested that at a deeper level both parties had let their defensive barriers drop enough to discover a deeper sense of value in each other.
>
> It would be naive to suggest that we can solve all disputes in this way; however, holding others in more positive and curious regard would be a good start.

Summarizing empirical research by the American Psychological Division 29 (Division of Psychotherapy), Norcross (2010) outlines a list of relationship elements judged to be most effective in therapy. The elements that were found to have the strongest correlation to successful outcomes included empathy, the alliance (strength of the relationship), cohesion (in groups), and goal consensus and collaboration. Table 2.2 describes each of these elements and proposes questions that we believe can help review how well each of us develops relationships at an individual and team level.

Other relationship elements with a positive correlation to successful therapeutic outcomes, albeit with a less compelling body of research, included positive regard, congruence/genuineness, feedback, repair of alliance ruptures, self-disclosure, management of countertransference, and the quality of relational interpretations. Table 2.3 describes each of these elements and proposes questions that we believe can help review how well each of us develops relationships at an individual and team level.

Table 2.2 The key applications for team coaching from empirical research on therapeutic relationships

Relationship elements with the strongest correlation to successful therapeutic outcomes (Norcross, 2010)	Useful questions for building relationships at an individual and team level
Empathy "Involves entering the private, perceptual world of the other" and "communicating that understanding back to the client in ways that can be received and appreciated" (p. 118).	• How well do you really listen (*listening like they are the most important person in the world*)? • Do you listen to the whole person (*beyond their words*)? • How well do you sensitively communicate back your understanding of how you think the other person is feeling (*feeling with another*)?
Alliance "The quality and strength of the collaborative relationship" (p. 120)	• How strong is your emotional bond to the other person? • What can you do to strengthen it? • What could be getting in the way of a stronger bond?
Cohesion (in groups) "The forces that cause members to remain in the group" (p. 121)	• How do you help the team develop cohesion? • What do you do that decreases team cohesion? • What could you do more of to develop team cohesion?
Goal Consensus and Collaboration "The therapist and client journey together toward a mutual destination" (p. 122)	• Does the relationship have a joint overriding purpose from which goals can be derived? • What do you want to achieve together that you cannot do separately? • What would success for this relationship look like?

Adapted from Norcross (2010: 118–25)

Table 2.3 Other applications for team coaching from empirical research on therapeutic relationships

Other relationship elements that have a correlation to successful therapeutic outcomes (Norcross, 2010)	Useful questions for building relationships at an individual and team level
Positive Regard "Is characterized as warm acceptance of the client's experience without conditions" (p.123)	• Whatever your view of the other person, can you let yourself feel positive regard towards them? For example, "attitudes of warmth, caring, liking, interest, respect?" (Rogers, 1967: 52).
Congruence/Genuineness "The therapist's personal integration in the relationship and the therapist's capacity to communicate his or her personhood to the client" (p. 123)	• What aspects of your true self are you not bringing to some relationships? • How can you show more of your true self?
Feedback Feedback on the "client's behaviour or the effects of that behaviour" (p. 124)	• How can you ensure you have positive intention when giving feedback? • How willing are you to give feedback? • How well does your feedback address the behaviour and its impact?
Repair of Alliance Ruptures An alliance rupture is "a tension or breakdown in the collaborative relationship" (p. 124)	• What do you notice about your approach to repairing relationships? • How can you improve in this area?
Self-Disclosure Appropriate and infrequent "therapist statements and behaviours that reveal something personal" (p. 124)	• How do you show an appropriate level of vulnerability?
Management of Countertransference "Reactions in which the unresolved conflicts of the psychotherapist, usually but not always unconscious, are involved" (p. 125)	• How do you know when your own emotions are getting in the way of the relationship? • What are your reflections on how well you manage your emotions in the moment?
Quality of the Relational Interpretations Bringing "material to consciousness" (p. 125)	• How well do you spot connections/themes and bring these to awareness in a psychologically safe, non-judgemental and respectful manner?

Adapted from Norcross (2010: 118–25)

Our own discussions on this empirical research have resulted in two areas that we believe warrant further discussion in the context of connection. First, the result of how this empirical research has been presented highlights a group of relationship elements found to have a stronger evidential base (Table 2.2) than the other elements (Table 2.3). This has caused us to reflect on how we use the popular support versus challenge model. Common usage of the support versus challenge model (adapted from the work of Sanford (2017) which was first published in 1966) would imply that individuals need an equal amount of support and challenge, to maximize their growth and development. However, we have repeatedly witnessed, both in our leadership careers and our work as team coaches, that when the challenge comes before support, it can negatively impact connection and the work itself. This is particularly pertinent for team coaches, as the team coach when challenging a team is, in effect, also presenting a challenge at an individual level.

The second area to highlight from Table 2.2 is the importance of cohesion (in groups). Team coaches need to be able to build relationships at multiple levels. An important piece of empirical research from group therapy is the Burlingame et al (2011) meta-analysis of 40 studies that demonstrated that as group cohesion (togetherness) increases, client outcomes improve. Cohesion in this context includes the group members' relationships to and perception of the group leader, particularly regarding their competence, genuineness and warmth, as well as the group members' relationships with each other and the group as a whole. Inspired by the same findings, Norcross (2010) has highlighted six principles a group therapist needs to embody, to foster group cohesiveness and improved group outcomes. Table 2.4 highlights each principle and how we believe each of these can be applicable for team coaches.

Confidence

The confidence of 'Being' for a team coach is about:

- **Being confident, but not under-confident or overconfident.** It's about having an assured sense of self that does not fear showing vulnerability. It is about having a gracious presence and being able to say to yourself, 'everything I've done in my life has led me to this moment working with this team, and I feel privileged and honoured to do so.' It's about valuing our own uniqueness and innate inner wisdom, or as Alison Hardingham, a tutor on our MSc in Coaching and Behavioural Change and a role model to both of us, would say, it's about:

Table 2.4 The applications for team coaches from empirical research on developing group cohesiveness in therapy

Creating cohesion in group therapy (Norcross, 2010: 121)	Applications of each principle for team coaches
Carry out pre-group preparation that sets expectations, ground rules, and outlines what effective participation would look like	Pre-intervention interviews with each participant to ascertain current status of team, outline programme, get feedback and detail expectations regarding each member's participation
Establish clarity regarding group processes early in the sessions	Give clarity at the initial sessions regarding the processes and structure of the team coaching intervention
Model real-time observations, guide effective interpersonal feedback, and keep a moderate level of control and connection	Courageously and in real-time, point out what you observe, guide team members when giving each other feedback and retain a moderate level of control and connection with the team
Carefully give timely feedback. Ensure it is mainly positive at the start and balanced between positive and negative in later sessions. Ensure the recipient is open and ready for it	Carefully give feedback 'in the moment' or as soon after as possible. At all times consider the readiness and openness of team members to feedback. Contract clearly with the team on the level of expected feedback. They may value robust feedback from the outset
Manage one's own emotional presence within the group and appreciate the relationships taking place at an individual level, as well as each group member's experience of the leader's manner of relating	Carefully manage your emotional presence within the group and tend to relationships with individuals and the team as a collective, while also being cognizant of how the team members experience your manner of relating at an individual and team level
Facilitate group members' emotional expression, how others respond to that expression and the shared meaning from such expressions	Provide a safe space (container) where team members' emotions can be expressed, responded to and a shared meaning attached

Adapted from Norcross (2010: 121)

o 'falling back in love with yourself';

o 'coming home to who you truly are';

o 'coaching from a place of who you are'; and

o 'not changing who you are, but how you are in certain situations'.

In summary, it is about finding inner contentment, owning and celebrating our own unique story, avoiding unhelpful comparisons with others, not overthinking what we perceive others to be thinking and projecting ourselves powerfully and graciously into the world. Heron (1999: 224) has described personal power as 'the ability to be empowered by one's own inner resources, the wellspring within, and the ability thereby to elicit empowerment in others'. He further describes it as 'rather like the original light of the soul taking charge of its earthly location and its human relationships'.

- **Owning our anxieties and ego.** Working from this place of inner contentment, a peace-like serenity, on a consistent basis, is nearly impossible. Lawrence and Whyte (2017) have commented that 'effective team coaches need to manage their egos and be open to learning. The coach may need to get used to years of never feeling completely confident and capable' (p. 105).

Courage

The courage of 'Being' for a team coach is about:

- **Serving the team by being truly present with the individuals, team and their environment.** A team coach needs to submerge themselves and be fully present in the work of the team. Similarly, Thornton (2016) discusses the need for the team coach to 'temporarily inhabit' (p. 83) the team's world.

- **Becoming your own instrument and responding 'in the moment' when appropriate.** Rogers (1961: 61) when discussing congruence, describes it as when 'the feelings the therapist is experiencing are available to him, available to his awareness, and he is able to live these feelings, be them, and be able to communicate them if appropriate'. It is about having the courage to use how you are feeling in the moment, as valuable information to share and help the team reflect and learn. It's about *becoming comfortable with discomfort.* We regularly use the metaphor that team coaching is like juggling. Your focus is on each of the individual balls (team members) and on keeping all the balls in the air (the team). At the same time, you are constantly looking out for unexpected balls from both inside (organizational factors) and outside the room (the wider environment). Occasionally, you will get hit (sidelined or triggered), but it is important to have the courage to stay present 'in the moment' (in the moment reflection), to pick up the balls (responding instead of reacting) and to take regular counsel with the circus master (supervision). Some of the phrases used by Hurley and Staggs (2012) in their archetypal practices model help illustrate the type of courage we are referring to. Phrases such as fearless engagement, illuminating truth, surfing the wave, staying in the fire, uplifting the treasure, and eating the dark and bitter rind.

- **Planning professionally and then being at ease with letting it go.** Lawrence and Whyte (2017) quote one of the interviewees in their research, who commented, 'I prepare a lot,' and 'then I just step back and let it go' (p. 105). A team coach must be able to be flexible and have the self-ease to let go when they judge it to be the right moment. This means knowing when to step back and allow the team to do their own work. It is about becoming comfortable about becoming invisible for the purposes of the team coaching work.

- **Taking calculated risks to develop and learn.** It has been suggested that 'if coaches are courageous and committed in forging a new path, they may find their way home to their highest selves, doing for themselves what they do so well for others' (Drake, 2008: 24). We would both agree that some of our most effective work as team coaches is when we have had the courage of our convictions, to challenge and say what would normally remain unsaid. On occasion, you can feel the release of tension in a room, when the truth is spoken. The ability to challenge freely requires both courage and deep connection with the coachees.

Continuing

The continuing of 'Being' for a team coach is about:

- **Appreciating that we will never be the finished article and that's perfectly ok.** From our experience as coaches and team coaches there is always more to learn. Being a team coach should be approached as a lifetime journey and not a destination.

- **Being committed to self-reflection and self-discovery.** In our view, a team coach needs to engage in regular reflective practice, generating insights that lead to new awareness and self-discovery. The importance of reflective practice in developing a coach's way of being has also been highlighted by Van Nieuwerburgh (2017).

- Understanding our need for support and challenge, particularly the importance of coaching supervision from a supervisor experienced in team coaching. Clutterbuck and Megginson (2012) have suggested that few coaches seem to have embraced supervision as a core activity, with many viewing it as a 'tick-box' exercise. Given the complexity of team coaching, supervision is essential (we each partake in both individual and group supervision and consider it a critical part of our journey as team coaches). We agree with Hawkins (2012: 286) that 'supervision can help take supervisees to their learning edge, confront their limiting beliefs and mindsets, and grow their emotional and ethical capacity to more effectively engage with their clients'.

Towards team coaching mastery

'The qualities that make for mastery can often feel mysterious and elusive as we seek to attain the heights in our chosen field' (Hurley and Staggs, 2012: 289). We would argue that these words describe why it is so difficult to accurately define 'mastery' in coaching. To us, mastery is a journey and not a linear process. Nevertheless, we have developed the 'Being, Doing and Knowing' model of team coaching development (Figure 2.4) that we believe is helpful for team coaches to reflect on. It is important to point out that at any moment a team coach may be in one or more of the developing, professional, relational or transformational quadrants. What is important is not where they are, but the commitment to the journey.

Figure 2.4 The 'Being, Doing and Knowing' model of team coaching development

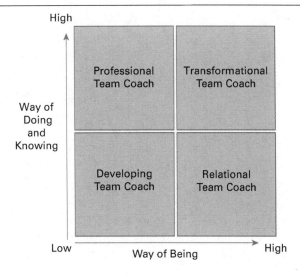

Regarding the development journey, Passmore (2014) has commented that 'for the master coach, mastery is a journey that can enhance their service to their clients, but is also one of pleasure and enjoyment as they learn, develop and grow' (p. 12). We trust that this book can help team coaches on that journey.

Reflective questions

- How do you want to be known as a team coach?
- If you are a team leader or manager, what aspects of the 'Being, Doing and Knowing' of team coaching would be useful in your work?
- When reflecting on 'Being, Doing and Knowing', where are your:
  o Strengths?
  o Areas of development?
- How can you build upon your strengths?
- What can you do to develop further as a team coach?
- Upon reviewing the 'Being, Doing and Knowing' model of team coaching development:
  o Where do you think you spend most of your time?
  o How aligned is this with what you would like it to be?
  o What does this insight mean for your development as a team coach?

Team coaching frameworks, models and approaches

03

Introducing the 'Creating the Team Edge' framework

Keeping frameworks, models and approaches in perspective

We shared our view in Chapter 2 about how important a team coach's 'way of being' or 'being' is. Coupled with this, the rest of this book will present a framework, model, approach and tools to use when working with teams.

We know from our experience as leaders, coaches and team coaches that without genuine connection, the true potential of any exchange is lost to mistrust, defensiveness and fear. This exchange includes, in our view, the use of any team coaching framework, model, approach or tool. Our view is supported by scientific studies from the work of therapists, both individual and group. As suggested in Chapter 2, while coaching is not therapy, it is therapeutic in nature and we believe team coaching can learn much from this research base. The following percentages and contributing factors on what results in good outcomes in therapy have been proposed:

- 40 per cent extra-therapeutic factors;
- 30 per cent the relationship;
- 15 per cent model or technique;
- 15 per cent hope, expectancy and the 'placebo effect'(Miller *et al*, 1997).

Referring to the same research base, two things are obvious from the reflections of Hubble *et al* (2010). Firstly, while there may be debate over the exact percentages, the direction of travel is clear. They noted that 'depending on which study is cited, the amount of change attributable to the alliance is five to seven times greater than that of specific models or techniques' (Hubble *et al*, 2010: 37), with alliance defined as 'the quality and strength of the collaborative relationship' (Norcross, 2010: 120). Secondly, the factors are interlinked. Hubble *et al* (2010) suggested that 'models achieve their effects in large part, if not completely, through the activation and operation of placebo, hope, and expectancy' (p. 36) and further stated that 'models and techniques work best when they engage and inspire the participants' (p. 37).

From this analysis, we would stress that team coaches not only need to connect, but they also need to connect in a way that engages and inspires teams. In addition, they need to create hope, that by journeying together with the team coach, the team can and will become more effective. Interestingly for team coaches, the same research has noted that 'little or no correlation exists between the length of the treatment and the strength of the alliance' (Hubble *et al*, 2010: 37). In effect, the idea of developing connection over time is somewhat misleading and not useful. This aligns with our experience, that coachees can sense a team coach's 'being' immediately. Unsurprisingly to us as coaches, the importance of the working alliance in coaching has been confirmed as a key ingredient of coaching effectiveness (De Haan *et al*, 2016, 2019). We look forward to seeing future research that we are confident will confirm the importance of the working alliance to team coaching effectiveness.

We believe that the framework, model, approach and tools presented in this book can benefit team coaches, but only if they first attend to the 'being' element of what it means to be a team coach. The same could also be written about leaders.

Story: The power of 'being'
Contributors: Lucy and Paul

We were both participants in a group supervision session made up of members from our MSc in Coaching and Behavioural Change cohort. Over lunch, with this book never far from our minds, we started to explore which guest speaker's 'way of being' had the most impact on the group. While various names were suggested, one name was mentioned most often:

Nancy Kline, creator of *Time to Think* (Kline, 1999, 2015) had left a lasting impact in terms of her 'way of being'.

Reflecting on what Nancy did using the 4 Cs of Being model (Chapter 2, Figure 2.3) reveals the following:

Connection: The first thing Nancy did was to express sincere gratitude for being invited to work with the group, followed by deep gratitude towards the Henley tutor in the room. This was more than work; it was a calling and she expressed a sense of privilege in receiving a full day in our busy schedule to share her work with us. Next, Nancy said she wished to get everyone's voice in the room, based on her belief that 'until you've spoken you haven't arrived'. She asked each of us to share one phrase or short sentence of whatever was on our minds. She listened to everyone individually, thanking us each for our contribution. Her attention and appreciation of each person's words and presence were clear.

Confidence: Nancy then shared the story of how she had come to be working in this area and the role that her childhood and key members of her family had played. She revealed the impact of her work in leading organizations. She was confident, but at the same time displayed a sense of vulnerability and thankfulness.

Continuing: Nancy's enthusiasm for working with people, despite doing it for some years, had not waned. It was as if she viewed each person she worked with as a teacher, from whom she would learn something new.

Courage: One of her demonstrations involved the courage of only asking three questions during a 45-minute coaching session.

In summary, it is our view that Nancy's 'way of being' enabled a deeper level of exploration and openness.

Team coaches' views on frameworks, models and approaches

One way of looking at the use of frameworks and models in coaching is through the lens of coaching maturity. We both recall our early days as coaches, with an over-reliance on the use of models. We recall that as we gained experience, the models became a guest to our coaching work but never the work itself. This is how we would like the model, approach and tools presented in this book to be used. Clutterbuck and Megginson (2012) captured the essence of this thinking when they proposed four levels of a coach's maturity: (1) models-based, (2) process-based, (3) philosophy or discipline-based and (4) system eclectic. The system eclectic proposes a number of critical questions to the coach. These include:

- Are both parties relaxed enough to allow the issue and solution to emerge in whatever way it will?
- Do I need to use any technique or process at all?
- If I do, what does the client context tell me about how to select from the wide choice available to me?

In further expanding on the 'system eclectic' level, Clutterbuck and Megginson (2012) highlight the importance of a personal philosophy of coaching that includes: a sense of being that is based on reflection; understanding the business context; permission to do less talking; meaningful use of supervision; commitment to personal development; an awareness of boundaries; a sense of progression as a coach; knowing who to best work with; conception of a fully functioning person (based on Rogers, 1961); and allowing time for maturity to take place. In addition to the areas we have already discussed in Chapter 2, we hope that the frameworks and models presented in this book will further support the work of the team coach or leader when working with teams.

So how are practising team coaches using models, approaches and tools at present? Lawrence and Whyte (2017), in their interviews with 36 team coaches, concluded that 'the general lesson appears to be less around adopting a specific approach, as to be confident in adopting an approach that the coach understands and has confidence in' (Lawrence and Whyte, 2017: 105).

In summary, our view is aligned with the words of Thornton (2016) who, when discussing the use of the conceptual frameworks and models, would appear to offer wise advice, when she stated that 'models have their uses, if we remember they offer a starting point, not an end point' (p. 123) and that team coaches need to rely on their judgement and experience when picking an instrument. She further noted that 'in coaching teams, all tools require an artisan, or perhaps at times an artist' (p. 123). We look forward to hearing stories of how team coaches have applied their artistry to some of the ideas presented in this book.

Review of frameworks, models and approaches

Before introducing the 'Creating the Team Edge' framework, model and approach, it is useful to recognize the work of some key influencers in this area. These include:

- **Hackman and Wageman (2005); Wageman *et al* (2008)**
  - o Proposed six conditions for senior leadership team effectiveness: the essentials of (1) a real team, (2) a team purpose, and (3) the right people, as well as the enablers of (1) a solid team structure, (2) a supportive organizational context, and (3) competent team coaching (Wageman *et al,* 2008).

- **Clutterbuck (2007, 2014, 2019, 2020)**
  - o Suggested that for a team to be high performing, it needs to focus on tasks, relationships and team learning, without over-focusing on one area at the expense of the other.
  - o Proposed a team coaching model called PERILL, which stands for (P) purpose and motivation, (E) external processes, systems and structures, (R) relationships, (I) internal processes, systems and structures, (L) learning and (L) leadership.

- **Thornton (2010, 2016, 2019)**
  - o Focused on how psychoanalytic and systemic theories and approaches can be applied to work with groups, teams and whole organizations.

- **Hawkins (2011, 2014, 2017, 2019)**
  - o Proposed five disciplines of successful team practice. These include commissioning, clarifying, co-creating, connecting and core learning.
  - o Proposed the CID-CLEAR model of team coaching process, which stands for (C) contract 1, (I) inquiry, (D) diagnosis and design, followed by (C) contract 2, (L) listening, (E) exploring and experimenting, (A) action, and (R) review and evaluation.
  - o Recent emphasis on Eco-Systemic Team coaching and a 'team of teams' approach.

- **Peters and Carr (2013, 2019)**
  - o Outlined six main components proposed in order of (1) assessment, (2) coaching for team design, (3) team launch, (4) individual coaching, (5) ongoing team coaching, and (6) review learning and successes.

- o The High-Performance Team Coaching (HPTC) System proposes that there are three times in a team's cycle when coaching has the greatest impact including (1) team new beginning (define and initiate), (2) midpoint (review and realign) and (3) ending (reassess and integrate).

- Hauser (2014, 2018)
  - o The 'Shape-shifting model' identified four different coach behaviours which are linked with intended outcomes. These include the (1) advisor (2) educator (3) catalyser, and (4) assimilator.
  - o Also proposed three phases linked to different coach behaviours, including the beginning (advisor), middle (educator, catalyser) and the end (assimilator).

Exploring the 'Creating the Team Edge' framework (Widdowson, 2017)

Following over 25 years of experience leading and working with teams and extensive research into the characteristics of high-performing teams, the 'Creating the Team Edge' framework was developed by Lucy Widdowson in 2015, while she was a partner in Performance Edge Partners Limited. Lucy would like to acknowledge the contribution and input of her previous colleagues Glenn Wallis, David Pilbeam and Sharon Sands. Since 2015, Lucy has continued to further develop and research the 'Creating the Team Edge' framework at Performance Edge Partners Limited, culminating in this book with Paul.

The framework consists of a team effectiveness model with seven characteristics (see Figure 3.1), a suggested team coaching approach (see Table 3.1) and a 360-team diagnostic. The suggested approach is indicative only of what we consider best practice. The first three stages – contracting, diagnostics and co-design – result in a unique team coaching intervention. The outcomes from these exploratory phases will determine which parts of the team effectiveness model receive the most focus in stages four, five and six, including how many team coaching interventions will take place and in what format.

The level of detail in the final evaluation stage will be determined by what is agreed during contracting and re-contracting engagements. Other key elements of the suggested approach that run in parallel to the actual team coaching intervention include the practicalities of how the team coaching intervention will take place, the role of one-to-one coaching, and agreement

Table 3.1 'Creating the Team Edge' suggested team coaching approach

Stage 1 Pre-team coaching	Stage 2 Interviews and team diagnostic	Stage 3 Co-design team coaching	Stage 4 Workshop1	Stage 5 Workshop 2	Stage 6 Workshop 3 +	Stage 7 Evaluation
Establish team coaching need	1-2-1 with each team member and selected stakeholders	Co-design and agree team coaching journey using feedback from interviews and team diagnostic	*Example areas:* building relationships, team purpose, identity, values and beliefs	*Example areas:* team awareness, relatedness and ways of working	*Example areas:* team transformation and additional workshops as per re-contracting	Review (can repeat diagnostic)
Establish team coaching readiness	Team members and selected stakeholders complete team diagnostic					Evaluation
Initial contracting with key stakeholders and team leader						Return on Investment
	Issue pre-reading and links to online resources					

Intervention format: mixture of face-to-face and virtual workshops, sharing of materials, 1-2-1 coaching, peer coaching, re-contracting meetings.
1-2-1 coaching: ideally for each team member and at a minimum the team leader and selected team members based on identified team development needs.
Team observation: as per agreement. Can take place at any agreed point during the team coaching intervention.

SOURCE Adapted from Widdowson (2017)

Figure 3.1   'Creating the Team Edge' model

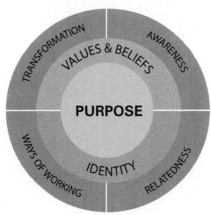

on any team observations. It is worth noting that the one-to-one coaching, while it may address multiple issues, takes place in the context of developing the team's effectiveness.

As highlighted in Chapter 1:

> the study involved in-depth interviews of five team leaders, whose teams each went through a 'Creating the Team Edge' coaching programme. In addition, six team coaches, who had all run team coaching programmes in the same organization using the 'Creating the Team Edge' framework, were interviewed. The findings indicated that the team coaching intervention improved performance and effectiveness both for the team itself and at a wider organizational level (ie for teams reporting into and those working alongside).

Chapter 1 further highlighted the three main contributing factors to the improved performance:

1 'The teams worked on collectively creating a purpose and agreeing why they exist. This enabled the teams to ensure that their values and beliefs (behaviours), identity and strategic objectives were aligned to the purpose.

2 By creating a feeling of psychological safety, teams were able to be more open and honest, show vulnerability and give robust feedback.

3 It was perceived that the team coaching process resulted in improvements in both individual and team learning, as the team shared knowledge and best practice with each other.'

In summarizing her study, Widdowson (2018) concluded that 'the framework was viewed as providing a useful and simple model to support practitioners, leaders and teams to become more effective'. In addition, she discovered two main opportunities to improve and refine the framework, based on practitioner feedback. Firstly, regarding the 'identity' characteristic in the team coaching effectiveness model, she noted that 'while some practitioners felt very positive regarding this aspect, others reported some confusion experienced by team members'. This issue has been addressed by developing methods to better explain team identity, through exploring individual identity, as well as developing tools to help practitioners explore the characteristic. Secondly, it was highlighted that 'to further support practitioners, there is an opportunity to develop more tools and approaches that team leaders and coaches can use in practice'. We are delighted that this book will help answer this need.

Chapters 4 to 10 will explore the seven characteristics of team effectiveness, in the following order: purpose (Chapter 4); identity (Chapter 5); values and beliefs (Chapter 6); awareness (Chapter 7); relatedness (Chapter 8); ways of working (Chapter 9); and transformation (Chapter 10). Table 3.2 provides a brief description of each characteristic.

Table 3.2 'Creating the Team Edge': Seven characteristics and descriptions

Characteristic	Description
Purpose	A statement of why the team exists. The purpose statement captures the spirit of the team working together to uniquely contribute towards the goals of its own organization, its stakeholders and the wider system. The statement only has weight when accompanied by collective performance goals.
Identity	The team works on developing their unique identity. The identity binds them together and constantly reinforces the team's positive mindset, energy and motivation. The team identity will be recognized and admired by both those inside and outside the team.
Values and beliefs	Values and beliefs in teams provide a sense of what is right and wrong. The team explores and agrees on the culture it desires and the values, standards and behaviours that will underpin the team's efforts. Belief in the team's purpose, identity and values are essential for the team to fully perform.

(continued)

Table 3.2   (Continued)

Characteristic	Description
Awareness	Teams increase their awareness and consciousness of each other's strengths and personal preferences, and how to leverage them for the benefit of the team as a whole. The team also develops an awareness of how it interacts with its wider stakeholders and system.
Relatedness	Teams develop their sense of unity and build mutual trust, support and understanding. Teams invest time in open and honest conversations to work more closely together and build strong relationships within the wider organization.
Ways of working	The team invests time in setting up the best systems and processes to enable its members to make confident and effective decisions. The team works on improving the structure of meetings and how it engages with others, in order to deliver concrete outcomes.
Transformation	Teams explore ways to challenge their performance and look for opportunities to test their abilities. The team rigorously reviews its plans, and applies innovative ways to think differently to ensure that the team members are always improving, learning and supporting each other's development.

SOURCE Widdowson and Barbour (2019)

Useful questions for team coaches to consider when reflecting on team coaching frameworks, models and approaches

Do I need to use a team coaching framework, model or approach?

As stated earlier in this chapter, 'team coaches should be open to using whatever the emerging situation requires, in a real, live environment, rather than being tied to any one particular methodology' (Hastings and Pennington, 2019: 183). Nevertheless, it is important that a team coach can explain their overriding team coaching philosophy and approach, especially during the contracting stage. We believe team coaching frameworks, models or approaches have an important role to play in the development of team coaching as a discipline and for the scaling of team coaching interventions. However, not before a team coach attends to the 'being' element of what it means to team coach.

Does it matter where a team is on its developmental journey?

Yes, it matters, but there are different approaches open to team coaches when considering a team's development journey. Tuckman's (1965) literature review suggested groups transition through four sequential phases of forming, norming, storming and performing, with a final stage, adjourning (Tuckman and Jensen, 1977). In contrast, Gersick (1988) presented an alternative perspective, with a focus on the importance of mid-way points in the group's life. Gersick's (1988, 1989) influence can be seen in the work of Hackman and Wageman (2005) and Peters and Carr (2013) with their emphasis on beginnings, midpoints and endings.

We believe that each team will have its own unique development story that should be explored. This is aligned to the findings of Lawrence and Whyte (2017), who found in their interviews with 36 team coaches that team coaches are more likely to ask teams to reflect on their history and share stories about the team's development, rather than explicitly using developmental frameworks.

How does contracting for team coaching differ from one-to-one coaching?

As with one-to-one coaching, clear contracting at the start and throughout the coaching intervention is essential. However, it is here that a lot of the similarities cease. The complexity of team coaching interventions presents multiple opportunities for inadequate contracting to derail an intervention. It is not surprising that Lawrence and Whyte (2017), when investigating what were the main lessons learned and challenges faced by coaches new to team coaching, recorded that 'interviewees mentioned the importance of contracting most often' (p. 104). We consider the key differences when contracting for one-to-one and team coaching to be:

One-to-one coach contracting

- Relationship required with sponsor, coachee and potentially the coachee's line manager.
- Line manager likely to have agreed level of involvement.
- Defined organizational process in procuring executive coaching.
- Diagnostics can be useful but not always necessary.
- General acceptance of the average number of coaching sessions and average duration of each.
- Ethical considerations mainly focused on a few individuals.
- One coach for each coachee.

Team coach contracting

- Relationship required with sponsor, team leader and every team member.
- Team leader needs to be intricately involved at all stages.
- Lack of a team coaching procuring process and experience.
- Team diagnostics likely to play a more important role.
- No clarity or acceptance on the average number of team coaching sessions and average duration of each. In addition, each team coaching intervention will need to be uniquely designed based on the identified needs of the team.
- Can be more difficult to get 'buy-in' to multiple sessions, due to time requirement and a higher level of total investment.
- Ethical considerations take on a more complex dimension (team members and multiple stakeholders).
- Potential involvement of multiple team coaches in one intervention.
- Agreement about whether one-to-one coaching will be included.

What are the benefits and drawbacks of partnering with another team coach?

Benefits of partnering with another team coach

- One coach can 'hold the room' and the other coach can observe the group dynamics, the behaviours of team members and the impact (this is equally as important if working virtually).
- Opportunity to use different styles and approaches.
- Contingency planning and cover.
- Increased creativity regarding intervention design and re-contracting during the intervention.
- Joint problem solving.
- Opportunity to role-model the positive behaviours of the coaches to the coachees, including how they handle differences.
- Increased time to focus on coachees (eg during breakout exercises, one-to-one conversations).
- More access points for coachees to build a relationship with the team coaches.
- Give each other feedback, positive and developmental.
- A second set of eyes 'in the room'.
- Practice working in and being a top-performing team.

Drawbacks to partnering with another team coach

- Higher investment levels required by the client/organization.
- Risk of over-complicating a team coaching intervention for coachees (eg contrasting styles and/or 'way of being').
- Potential for confusion in managing the overall client relationship.
- Unhealthy conflict and tension, if coaches are not philosophically aligned.

Story: Working with difference and diversity when partnering with a team coach
Contributor: Lucy

In almost every team coaching programme, I partner with another team coach. It enables one team coach to 'hold the room' and the other to focus on group dynamics. It allows the team coaches to share what they see is happening in the team, re-contract if need be with the team and then flex and adapt the programme to meet whatever is presenting itself in the room. However, despite the clear benefits, partnering with a team coach can at times be challenging.

On one particular team coaching programme, I was paired with a team coach whom I hadn't worked with before. During our pre-contracting call, it was evident that my partner was an experienced team coach who I would value working with, but we had very different strengths and styles. Although determined to make this work, I did wonder how we would work together in practice.

By contracting and re-contracting clearly about our roles and how we would work together before and during the programme, we found that our styles complemented one another very well. For this particular programme, my focus was on more of the emerging and experiential aspects and my partner's on the use of models and the process. This proved to be an ideal combination, bringing different and yet complementing styles and focus together. As a result, the team made some major shifts in their connection, clarity of purpose, open and honest conversations, decision making and ultimately their effectiveness both within the team and with their stakeholders. This was a great reminder for me that leveraging difference and diversity can be very helpful when partnering with another team coach.

What is the ideal team size for team coaching and how does this relate to the number of team coaches required?

Burlingame *et al* (2011) have confirmed from studies on group therapy that group cohesion (togetherness), which has been positively correlated with successful outcomes, is strongest when groups are composed of between five and nine members. Research by Wageman *et al* (2008) found that of the six conditions for senior leadership team effectiveness, a solid team structure, of which team size is a key component, had the greatest determining effect on which teams were outstanding. They commented, 'we have seldom seen teams of more than eight or nine members operating as true decision-making leadership teams' (p. 19).

Realistically, a team coach may not have a direct input into the size of the team they are asked to work with; however, they should recommend the number of team coaches required. Whenever possible, we are of the view that two team coaches should be in the room, one to 'hold the room' and the other to observe behaviours and group dynamics. We have on several occasions had two team coaches working with a team of six.

Team coaches must exercise caution when asked to work with a team that they consider to be too large. Indeed, it has been stated that working with larger groups, of between 10 and 25 people, 'is not a venture for the inexperienced or untrained' (Thornton, 2016: 108). We agree with this point. Nevertheless, without taking away from the challenge of working with larger teams, we have both been involved in effectively coaching teams of over 25 people, as part of a team coaching pair and even a coaching trio, on occasion. If team coaches find themselves working with larger teams, we would strongly recommend they identify subgroups and find ways for the subgroups to benefit from the team coaching. Also, the team coach needs to ensure they have enough support in the room and attend to all the areas we have highlighted, such as contracting and connecting, to name but two. If team coaching virtually, a second team coach is recommended, irrespective of the team size.

How long should a team coaching intervention last?

As stated in our definition of team coaching in Chapter 1, we believe that team coaching is about creating 'lasting change'. In our experience, this implies involvement with a team over time. It requires team coaches to be courageous in their contracting with each key stakeholder, including team members, about the commitment required (investment, time and effort). Agreeing with this position, Thornton (2016) has commented that 'team coaching, like all coaching, must also take place over time' (p. 120). Jones *et al* (2019: 73) have also observed that 'team coaching is typically provided over a series of sessions rather than as a one-off intervention'. In studies from group therapy, Burlingame *et al* (2011) found that group cohesion (togetherness) was at its strongest when there were more than 12 group sessions.

Jones *et al* (2019) noted a discrepancy between participant opinion that team coaching is a longer-term intervention and data that reported that only 1.6 coaching sessions took place. This would suggest that there is often a difference between the length of intervention desired or needed and what an organization can, or is willing to, invest. Nevertheless, the average number of sessions and the duration (approximately 2.5 hours) reported both appear extremely low, based on our own experience. It is clear that this is an area that could benefit from further research.

What questions should you ask to check if the team and client are ready for team coaching?

Some example questions that could be useful during a pre-contracting or contracting meeting include:

Past-focused questions

- What is the team's history in the context of the organization?
- What journey has led to team coaching?
- What previous team development interventions have taken place?

Present-focused questions

- Where is the team on their development journey, eg new, reforming or in need of transformation?
- What work do the team members do together (their collective output) and what work do they do when apart?
- What role does the team play in the overall organization (formal and informal)?
- What internal and external stakeholders do the team serve and how well are they doing this?
- What other teams, internally and externally, does the team rely on to get its collective work done?
- How is the team structured? (number of personnel, location, key roles)
- How is the team performing and what metrics are used to measure progress?
- How are members of the team performing?
- How is the team led (officially and unofficially)?
- How much autonomy does the team leader and the team have?
- How closely aligned is the team to the organization's purpose, vision and values?
- How is the team spoken about by others (internally and externally)?
- How is the team remunerated, eg for individual and/or collective output?
- What gets in the way of the team acting collectively (eg remuneration, KPIs, structure)?

- Who from the organization is sponsoring this team's coaching intervention and how does it complement or not complement other development interventions within the organization?
- What does the team (including the team leader) know about the proposed team coaching intervention and how do they feel about it?

Future-focused questions

- Outside of commercial objectives, what is the ultimate purpose of the team?
- What does the future need from this team?
- How open are the team to engage with other teams, as part of a team coaching intervention?
- How open are the team to engage with key stakeholders as part of the team coaching intervention?
- Who could stop the team from being successful and why?
- How important is this team to the success of the organization?
- What are the future aspirations for the development of coaching capability for the team, the team leader and the organization?

Do you need to use a team diagnostic?

We believe it is important to carry out some form of a team diagnostic. For major team coaching interventions, the more ways in which you can generate awareness about the team, the more beneficial this will be (see Chapter 7). Table 3.3 highlights, in order of preference, our view of how diagnostic tools and techniques could be prioritized when team coaching. The team coach must keep asking, what best serves this coaching intervention?

Do you need to carry out one-to-one interviews before starting the team coaching?

As evidenced by our prioritization in Table 3.3, we would strongly recommend contracting for one-to-one interviews, with both team members and key stakeholders. Key benefits of the interviews include connecting, explaining, questioning, clarifying, capturing concerns and discussing the next steps regarding the team coaching journey. Thornton (2016), agreeing with their

Table 3.3   Prioritizing team diagnostic tools and techniques

In order of preference	Team diagnostic tools and techniques
1	**Full** one-to-one interviews with each team member and selected stakeholders, followed by a team 360 diagnostic
2	Team 360 diagnostic, followed by **short** one-to-one interviews with each team member and selected stakeholders
3	Team 360 diagnostic, followed by short one-to-one interviews with a **representative sample** of team members and selected stakeholders
4	Team 360 diagnostic **or** one-to-one interviews (full, short or representative sample)
5	**After prioritizing 1–4,** use of individual psychometric assessments

importance, has highlighted how individual goals may differ and has described it as 'prudent to interview all members of the team individually before embarking on working with them together' (p. 120). Interviews with team leaders, team members and key stakeholders each have a different emphasis, as follows:

Team leader interviews

Suggested areas of focus for the interview include: the continuance of the contracting conversation including expectations, objectives and how you will work together; the team's development history; the context of the team; the team's composition; the team's effectiveness by probing on the clarity of team purpose, identity, value and beliefs, awareness, relatedness, ways of working and transformation; and, importantly, their role as a leader.

Team member interviews

While the interview would include a similar structure and areas of probing, as outlined for the team leader, a key difference would be questions specifically about the team leader. It is also important to retain confidentiality and ensure that you use information in a way that is non-attributable to any one team member, unless you have contracted otherwise.

Team stakeholder interviews

A similar line of inquiry can be used, as with the team member interviews. Again, it is important to contract clearly with the key stakeholders on confidentiality and agree what can be discussed openly with the team, what needs to be held in confidence and what can only be used in a non-attributable manner.

Do you need to use a 360 team diagnostic tool?

After one-to-one interviews, we consider a team 360 diagnostic as a key awareness-raising tool that should be prioritized by team coaches. The challenge is to carry out a diagnostic exercise while not adversely impacting the team's relationship with the team coaching journey and the team coach. In particularly sensitive team coaching interventions, it may be appropriate to leave the diagnostic until there is agreement with the team.

Part of the suggested team coaching approach for 'Creating the Team Edge' is a 42-question (six questions per characteristic) diagnostic tool. Completed by the team members and agreed stakeholders, the results provide an initial insight into the team's strengths and priority areas. Responses are grouped and reported on anonymously, except for agreed individual responders. The information captured and insights generated are particularly useful for co-designing the team coaching journey and for encouraging dialogue during the early stages of the team coaching intervention. The diagnostic can be repeated mid-way and at the end, as part of an evaluation exercise. In addition, it can be useful to repeat parts of the diagnostic at multiple stages. For example, repeating the six questions of the relatedness characteristic is an excellent way to track the team's journey with psychological safety.

Given the findings of Kluger and DeNisi (1996) that one-third of feedback interventions decreased performance, the experience and judgement of the team coach regarding the use of a diagnostic is essential. Chapter 7 on awareness will further explore ways to develop team and stakeholder awareness that is safe, generative and insightful.

Do you need to use a psychometric tool to increase individual self-awareness?

While there are multiple ways a team coach can develop individual self-awareness, in our experience, the use of a well-validated psychometric tool can be extremely powerful in developing individual and team awareness. Nevertheless, they must be introduced in a way that complements and does not distract from the team coaching. Using the prioritization suggested in Table 3.3 can help team coaches to decide when they should and shouldn't use a psychometric tool. Important considerations include the length of time required for a professional debrief, which for many leading psychometrics requires a full day.

Reflective questions

- What models of team effectiveness do you use?
- What has worked well and why?
- What hasn't worked well and why?
- Think about a team you worked in that you felt was high performing. What was it that worked in this team?
- From your experience, what do you think are the characteristics of a high-performing team?

The purpose-driven team

04

Why does being purpose-driven matter so much?

Defining purpose

Aristotle believed that everything, whether created by human endeavour or nature, has an inherent purpose, a reason for being the way it is. The *Oxford Dictionary* defines purpose as 'the reason for which something is done or created or for which something exists'. In essence, knowing the purpose of a person or thing is about knowing or finding the 'why' behind its reason for existence.

Story: Finding team purpose on Mother's Day
Contributor: Paul

The moment the bedroom door eases open, it all starts to feel a bit like Christmas. My three daughters have made their yearly pilgrimage to the kitchen and prepared the most amazing feast of culinary breakfast delights. As the children trundle into the bedroom, happiness radiates as a mother feels the love of her children.

For my part, even though I'm not the direct recipient of this act of love, I take delight in watching my daughters, without direction from anyone but themselves, take initiative and overcome the normal sibling squabbles to create what is, for a short time only, a high-performing team that delivers collectively.

It is now clear to me that over the years, they have been demonstrating the power of a COMMON PURPOSE! A heartfelt desire *to delight their mother and demonstrate their undying love.*

> Unfortunately, this high-performing team ceases to operate when it comes to doing the dishes. Thankfully, my purpose as a father, *to love unconditionally and always be there for my daughters*, results in me joyfully clearing up their mess. The power of purpose.

This story clearly illustrates the benefits of having an agreed purpose, even when it may not have been purposefully articulated. We believe that getting purposeful about purpose is crucial in helping teams to:

- connect emotionally on a task;
- feel the meaning behind their actions;
- work collaboratively;
- work out differences;
- think beyond self;
- support each other;
- demonstrate initiative;
- be creative;
- learn new skills together;
- take calculated risks;
- create excitement;
- deliver collectively on a goal.

Discussing purpose more generally, Renshaw (2018) has proposed that purpose helps people find meaning, have clarity of identity, be themselves, connect with others, find energy, inspire others, develop winning teams and create business differentiation.

The psychology behind purpose

The why of purpose

Understanding 'why' we do what we do, versus 'what' and 'how' we do it, can help us to find a deeper level of connection in life. Spunt *et al* (2010) differentiate sitting down on a chair (the how) from falling into a chair (the why). If you were asked to think about 'how' you physically sit down, you would start to picture the movements required to successfully transition from upright to sitting. In contrast, if you were asked to think about 'why' you would fall into a chair, you are likely to think about your deeper unconscious intentions and motives. Sinek (2009), using his 'Golden Circle', illustrates the role of 'why' in human behaviour. At the centre of the 'Golden Circle' is the 'why' we do things and 'how' we choose to do them, both of which he links to the older limbic brain, responsible for feelings, trusting and making 'in the moment' decisions. On the outside of the 'Golden Circle' is the 'what' level, linked to our more recently developed neocortex, associated with rational and analytical thought, as well as language.

An important part of the limbic brain is the amygdalas, commonly referred to in the singular as the amygdala. The amygdala plays a key role in helping us confront (fight), escape (flight) or stay still (freeze) as we encounter real or perceived threats. However, it is so much more. It is influential in 'love, bonding, sexual behaviour, anger, aggression and fear' and it also has the role 'to attach emotional significance to situations or objects and to form emotional memories' (Pittman and Karle, 2015: 3).

It is evident that purpose, our 'why', mainly connects at an emotional level, whether that is moving towards (eg bonding), away (eg real or perceived threat) or a mixture of both. With this in mind, Sinek (2009) has suggested that to drive behaviour, communication needs to start at the 'why' level and not the more factual and rational 'what' level.

Finding meaning and purpose in the everyday

A study of 28 hospital cleaners, each with the same job description, found that the cleaners who viewed their role as a calling developed ways to make their work feel more meaningful. They also viewed their role as critical in healing patients (Dutton *et al*, 2000).

Furthermore, research demonstrates a positive link between believing what you do is important and quality of your output. McGregor and Doshi (2015) highlight a study where the groups that had significance attached to their work produced better results, despite earning less money, than the other groups that had no meaning attached to their work.

The life-giving power of purpose

The life-giving power of purpose is illustrated by the Austrian psychiatrist Viktor Frankl, who, whilst a prisoner in Nazi concentration camps, imagined himself on a platform in comfortable surroundings giving a lecture on the psychology of a concentration camp. He believed he had more to contribute to the world. He describes sensing when people had given up and the inevitable physical and mental decline that followed. To Frankl, having a purpose was the difference between choosing life or death (Frankl, 2004).

The link between purpose, motivation, values, goals and well-being

Ryan and Deci (2000) have suggested that 'from birth onward, humans, in their healthiest states, are active, inquisitive, curious, and playful creatures, displaying a ubiquitous readiness to learn and explore, and they do not require extraneous incentives to do so' (p. 56). The importance of intrinsic motivation has been highlighted by McGregor and Doshi (2015), who have outlined six main reasons why people work. These included play, purpose and potential, which are considered intrinsic causes of increased motivation and performance. This is in contrast to emotional pressure, economic reasons and inertia, which are considered extrinsic reasons that tend to hurt performance. In the context of this research, play is linked to being motivated by the actual work itself; purpose is linked to the alignment of an individual's values to the values of the organization; and potential is linked to opportunities for an individual to grow and develop. Their research also revealed that having a sales commission that encourages an employee to act in a way that is contrary to their values can act as a demotivator, with the opposite effect also true. Similarly, people who pursue goals that are in alignment with their interests and values will make more effort and will have a greater chance of achieving them (Linley *et al*, 2010). It has also been demonstrated that people's well-being improves when they pursue goals they are interested in (Sheldon *et al*, 2004).

The need for a common purpose to unite

Deci and Ryan (2004) advocate that humans have an innate need to relate to others. However, without intervention, people have a natural tendency to relate more to those with whom they feel safest. As humans, we move towards certain individuals, our in-group(s). In contrast, we tend to move away from those we believe to be a threat, our out-group(s). Hills (2016) has suggested that a useful tactic to overcome this most human of tendencies is 'to create a common goal across workgroups so that people believe they have the same purpose and interests. Common goals form common in-groups' (p. 95).

The importance of purpose for organizations

What is a purpose-driven organization?

It has been suggested that very few companies clearly articulate why they do what they do, with the 'why' being described not in terms of making money, which is a result, but rather as a 'purpose, cause or belief' (Sinek, 2009: 39). The stakeholders of an organization need to know not only where it is going (vision) but why (purpose) they should be part of the journey.

Most organizations make some form of statement about who they are and what they are trying to achieve; however, there appears to be little consistency in literature and practice as to what constitutes a purpose, vision and mission, with each being used interchangeably. Table 4.1 illustrates what we would consider strong statements of purpose and the various ways each has been described by their organization.

Hawkins (2017) has suggested the mission as an overarching framework. He proposes a 'Model for the organization mission' which includes purpose, strategy, values, vision, and standards and behaviours. Table 4.2 illustrates how we differentiate organizational purpose from vision and what we consider to be the desirable features and benefits of each.

Table 4.1   Examples of organizational purpose statements

Organization	Purpose stated/identified	How referred to by the organization
EY	Building a better working world	Purpose
Cancer Research UK	Together we will beat cancer	Purpose
Virgin Group	Changing business for good	Purpose
Tesco	Serving shoppers a little better every day	Purpose
Nando's	To simply create memorable experiences for everyone who has a bit (or a lot) of Nando's in their life	Our main aim

(*continued*)

Table 4.1   (Continued)

Organization	Purpose stated/identified	How referred to by the organization
Microsoft	To empower every person and every organization on the planet to achieve more	Mission
IKEA	To create a better everyday life for the many people	Vision
The Body Shop	To Enrich Not Exploit. It's in our hands	Our commitment
Tesla	To accelerate the world's transition to sustainable energy	Mission
Uber	We ignite opportunity by setting the world in motion	Mission

The benefits of being a purpose-driven organization

Collins and Porras (2005) demonstrated that between 1926 and 1990 visionary companies, who had a purpose greater than shareholder value, not only generated long-term financial results but had also woven themselves into the fabric of society. More recently, in a report entitled 'The Business Case for Purpose' (2015), a team from *Harvard Business Review* and EY's Beacon institute reported from a survey of 474 executives that purpose-driven companies make more money, have more engaged employees, have more loyal customers and are better at innovation and delivering on transformational change. They went on to state that 'it seems easier to win the game when you care about the game' (p. 4). Despite this compelling argument for purpose-driven companies, only 46 per cent of those surveyed believed their company had a strong sense of purpose, with a further 44 per cent stating that their company was trying to develop one.

The drive towards being a purpose-driven organization appears to be gathering momentum, as was evidenced in 2019. The Business Roundtable, a powerful group of 200 CEOs representing some of America's largest companies, announced an updated definition of the purpose of a company that encompassed commitments beyond the traditional shareholder value (Business Roundtable, 2019). The development was described as seismic

Table 4.2 Descriptions, features and benefits of organizational purpose and vision

Area	Description	Desirable features	Key benefits	eg Youth Services Organization
Purpose	– Why do we exist beyond financial gain?	– Emotional appeal – The emphasis shouldn't change over time – Calls for a togetherness – Grabs attention – Memorable – Benefits selected stakeholders (eg employees, customers, society)	– Heart then head appeal – Inspires selflessness – Creates belonging – Catalyst for collaboration – Helps people find meaning – Attracts followers – Creates advocates	– To give hope to vulnerable young people
Vision	– What would success look, feel and sound like?	– Brings purpose to life – Evokes imagery – Takes a long-term view – Increases clarity – Has uniqueness – Presents a challenge – Commercial reference	– Provides an impetus for and inspires action – Creates focus beyond the day-to-day activities – Provides a benchmark to measure progress against	– To become the most respected, innovative and sustainably funded youth services provider in xx countries

and a rebuttal of the Milton Friedman doctrine that elevated shareholder value above everything else (Aziz, 2019). Others, whilst considering the change significant, noted that capitalism had at times in the past embraced a wider perspective and business leaders would need to be held to account (MacLellan, 2019).

Further evidence of the power of purpose was provided during the early stages of the global COVID-19 pandemic in 2020. Hospitals with a purpose 'to save lives' reorganized their services and built new field hospitals in record time. Many businesses with the purpose 'to survive' and others with the purpose 'to help', transformed their business models within days or weeks. Despite the potency of these examples, it should not take a global emergency to harness the power of purpose. We believe organizational purpose will continue to grow in use and the evidence robustly suggests that those companies who sincerely embrace a purpose beyond just profit are more likely to prosper in the long term. So, what does this mean for the idea of team purpose?

Developing a team purpose

Does every team need a team purpose?

If a team wishes to be high performing, it needs a team purpose. Indeed, Katzenbach and Smith (1993) consider a common team purpose essential for a team's long-term survival. In our experience, most teams are not aware of their need for a team purpose and, as reflected on by Hawkins and Smith (2013), few teams can articulate one.

When team coaching, being present as a team agrees their team purpose can be a privilege. The coaching literature discusses the importance of the 'sudden shift or interruption' (De Haan *et al*, 2010: 609) in coaching. With teams, it can be a moment when something settles at a deeper level and they realize why they exist and what they can uniquely offer their organization, each other and society. Paradoxically, the same moment can often feel unsettling, as the team realize the scale of their challenge, in terms of behaviours, performance and accountability. While it is not practical for every team member to experience these moments of shift, we believe it is the responsibility of both the team leader and the team to enthusiastically share with new members the story of their team purpose.

Story: The unloved team who found their purpose
Contributor: Paul

I recall working with a team who, despite a profitable and sizeable turnover, were referred to as the 'non-core' part of the larger organization. They felt unloved.

When discussing team purpose, they realized their team was a key source of talent to the wider organization. They shifted from complaining about their situation to embracing a purpose in which they would support each other, to provide the company with the talent it needed for the future. They had found a powerful and motivating reason for existing beyond just making a profit.

Suddenly, the team realized 'they mattered' and were vital to the organization's success, even if the organization didn't yet recognize it.

What are the benefits of having a team purpose?

A coaching study at a leading UK retailer identified 'alignment on purpose' as one of the main contributing factors towards improvements in team development, effectiveness and performance (Widdowson, 2017). We would agree that a team purpose can:

- identify the collective endeavour the team cannot achieve individually (Hawkins and Smith, 2013);
- make clear the difference a team wishes to make in the world (Hawkins, 2017);
- provide a clear statement about the team's underlying microculture (McKee, 2018);
- encourage the pursuit of team and not individual priorities (Price and Toye, 2017);
- result in aspirations that motivate and cause extra effort (Katzenbach and Smith, 1993a);
- energize, orientate and more fully engage the talents of team members (Hackman, 2011).

The role of leadership in developing a team purpose

When addressing the role of executive leaders in developing a team's purpose, Wageman *et al* (2008) commented that only they 'can establish the purpose. Others can help refine it, but ultimately it is yours' (p. 69). While this may appear a definite statement, they also note that there is not one preferred way and that a highly collaborative approach may be suitable. In contrast, Katzenbach and Smith (1993a) argue that teams must develop their own purpose, with management setting the overall performance challenge. In addition, they warn that while the team leader should be involved, they should exercise caution as their suggestions may be perceived as mandates. Despite a team's need for an overall direction, a team must be allowed enough flexibility to develop their own perspective on what their purpose, specific goals, timing and approach should be (Katzenbach and Smith, 1993b).

The importance of context for team purpose

In deciding how to best arrive at a team purpose, it is important to consider the context. Different situations require different approaches, for example: in times of crisis or rapid change; tightly defined and time-bound projects; particularly sensitive employment sectors, such as the intelligence community (Hackman, 2011); and when teams disband as quickly as they form, in what Edmondson (2012) describes as teaming, there is a rationale for the team leader to articulate a compelling purpose. Hackman (2011) gives a powerful example of a leader in a US government department, whose team was left confused by the sudden change in priorities of a new administration. The leader quickly refocused the team by reminding them that their purpose was 'to serve democracy'.

The case for maximum team involvement in developing team purpose

While context is important, it is essential that every opportunity is found for team members to meaningfully contribute to the team purpose, if not in its creation, at least in how it is kept alive and relevant. Such an approach is supported by the work of Deci and Ryan (1985) who outlined how an autonomy orientation, where employees are given choice, promotes self-determination, as opposed to a control orientation, which can result in compliance and, even worse, rebellion. Importantly, even in situations when it is necessary to tell somebody what to do, autonomy within the person can still be maintained, if they believe they are acting from a place of their own interest and values (Deci and Ryan, 2004). This highlights the importance, particularly for teams with an established purpose, of recruiting not just on capability but also on alignment to a team's purpose, vision and values. Whittington's (2012) assertion that each person 'needs to have an inner sense of their relationship to the purpose of the business and how their role can serve that purpose' (p. 191) is, we believe, equally applicable to an individual's relationship with a team purpose.

What is a great team purpose?

We would suggest that when thinking about team purpose it is important to consider how it is created, what it needs to include and how it is sustained. Referring to available team coaching literature and practitioner texts, Table 4.3 provides a useful checklist of what should ideally be included in a team purpose process and a team purpose. Sustaining team purpose in the long term will be discussed under challenges, in the next section.

Table 4.3 Checklists for the ideal team purpose process and team purpose

The ideal team purpose process should...	The ideal team purpose should...
– energize – inspire – include robust dialogue – demonstrate patience – be emotionally demanding – help reveal discrepancies and conflicts in team members' roles (Wageman *et al*, 2008)	– be clear/give clarity – be challenging – be consequential (Wageman *et al*, 2008; Hackman, 2011)
– take time – take effort – be a joint creation (Katzenbach and Smith, 1993, 1993b)	– provide meaning beyond making money – be aspirational as opposed to preventative and reactive – energize others – encourage collective responsibility – (Edmondson, 2012)
– unearth the motivation and energy of individual members – surface differences of opinion – renew a sense of passion and commitment (Leary-Joyce and Lines, 2018)	– have an element related to winning, being first, revolutionizing or being cutting edge – belong to each individual in the team – belong collectively to the team (Katzenbach and Smith, 1993b)
– involve dialogue with wider system sponsors (Hawkins, 2017)	– orientate a team towards its objective, helping them choose strategies to support their work (Hackman, 2011)

The challenges of team purpose

Purpose beyond words: the importance of collective performance goals

In August of 1963, Martin Luther King, with his 'I have a dream' speech, united millions of people with a common purpose (Carton *et al*, 2014). However, he got specific when he described that in the red hills of Georgia, sons of former slaves and the sons of former slave owners would one day be able to sit down together.

A team purpose must be accompanied by short- to medium-term performance goals, detailing specifically, and ideally in a format that can be measured, what needs to happen for the purpose to become more than words. While purpose should come first (Hackman, 2011), it has been suggested that irrespective of the sequence, 'successful team performance comes from the continuing integration of purpose and performance goals' (Katzenbach and Smith, 1993a: 56). Failing to agree on team performance goals risks the purpose becoming a 'lofty aspiration supported only by good intent' (Hawkins and Smith, 2013: 80) or a 'mere abstraction, perhaps admirable but of little practical importance' (Hackman, 2011: 77). A lack of team performance goals will understandably result in team scepticism regarding the purpose they worked so hard to develop.

Importantly, the team performance goals must be greater than the sum of each team member's individual goals and should only be achievable by the team working together (Hawkins and Smith, 2013). In addition, Katzenbach and Smith (1993a) highlight the need for the team's goals to be different from those of the organization. Team performance goals are about what the team needs to work together on, to fulfil its unique team purpose.

The missed opportunity: the challenge for executive teams in developing a common team purpose

Several reasons have been suggested as to why many executive teams do not develop a common team purpose. These include: teams at the top incorrectly viewing their team purpose and company purpose as the same thing; the expectation that leaders at the top will automatically work collectively as a group on helping each other achieve their individual objectives, but not work collectively on joint endeavours; and top teams avoiding the risk of failure, in moving from working as a group to a team (Katzenbach and Smith, 1993a). Other reasons suggested include an executive leader: prioritizing an individual leader's goals (eg a star performer) over team purpose; wanting to keep a competitive spirit alive; and believing a strong collective leadership could be a threat to their authority (Wageman *et al*, 2008).

Despite the challenges, developing a common team purpose and performance goals is as applicable to executive teams as any other. It has been suggested that if you take five different leadership teams at the top of an organization, they are each likely to have a very different purpose (Price and Toye, 2017). Katzenbach and Smith (1993a) have noted that while talented and committed executives can achieve a lot by sharing insights, best practice and supporting each other, they are unlikely to 'deliver the kind of collective work-products and incremental performance of teams' (p. 234). Another debate is the extent to which a board can be a team, given their need to exercise independence (Clutterbuck, 2020). Our experience has demonstrated that boards can significantly benefit from team coaching to develop as a powerful collective, without losing their independence.

In summary, boards and executive teams need a challenging purpose that reflects collective leadership responsibilities unique to them, that can have a meaningful impact on the organization's performance (Wageman *et al*, 2008). Given the challenges, whether they can do this without the help of a team coach is debatable.

Short-termism, reward structures and the power of the system

The main barriers that get in the way of organizations being purpose-driven have been cited as the pressure for short-term shareholder return, systems and infrastructure that are not aligned to the purpose, and a lack of targets and incentives aligned with the purpose (Harvard Business Review, 2015). Each of these are equally applicable to team purpose.

We would suggest that organization and team purposes have the potential to be an antidote to the pressure of short-termism; however, they face a system that seems intent on maintaining continuity and minimizing radical change. Strong organizational and team leadership will be required if the full benefit of being purpose-led is to be realized.

Tools and techniques for developing team purpose

> ### Using tools and techniques
>
> When applying these tools and techniques, it is essential that the team coach or leader builds connection and psychological safety first. The tools and techniques are offered as a support and guide, which when used should feel natural and in 'flow', with the process and steps behind the tools remaining effectively invisible.

TOOL 1: Developing your 'Why' – why, how and what?

Why use this tool?

There is often confusion about what purpose is and how it is different from a team's vision or mission, as previously discussed in this chapter. This tool can help bring clarity around the difference between the purpose of a team, its reason for existence, 'the why', and what the team actually does. It can help teams to create a clear and compelling purpose.

When to use this tool

- When teams need to establish or re-visit their collective purpose.
- When there are changes to team structure, such as reorganizations or new members joining.

Resources required

- Link to Simon Sinek's YouTube video 'Start with Why'
  See: https://www.youtube.com/watch?v=IPYeCltXpxw
- Flip chart paper and pens, virtual whiteboard/platform.

How to use this tool

Step 1   Show the team the Simon Sinek 'Start with Why' video as an introduction to understanding the 'why' of purpose.

Step 2   Talk through the model using 'Apple' as an example:

The 'why': we believe in everything we do, we believe in challenging the status quo, and we believe in thinking differently.

The 'how': the way we challenge the status quo is by making our products beautifully designed, simple to use and user friendly.

The 'what': we just happen to make great computers.

Step 3 The team explore their 'Team Purpose' focusing on their 'why'. Using the questions below, encourage the team to question and challenge each other in a supportive and positive way:

- Defining what purpose your team ultimately wants to achieve:
  o Why do you exist?
  o What's your purpose as a team?
  o Who ultimately do you serve?
  o Who else?
- Defining the value you add as a team:
  o Specifically what value do you add to those you ultimately serve?
  o What do you do that directly and indirectly helps add this value?
  o What can the team achieve together, in adding this value, that an individual can't?
- Agreeing team commitment to the purpose:
  o How closely are all of the team members aligned to your team purpose?
  o What is it about your purpose that can inspire each team member?

Step 4 Ask the team to capture key themes or words that have emerged from the previous exploration and highlight these using different-coloured paper for different themes. Virtual platforms with their advanced functionality to create collectively (eg ability to use different-coloured virtual Post-it notes) are recommended if working virtually.

Step 5 Using the keywords or themes, the team then craft their purpose statement.

Top tips for team coaches

- Display on the wall some examples of strong team purpose statements or share virtually.

- For larger teams, break into smaller groups with each defining the team purpose. Then ask each group to present back their key thoughts and reflections. This will allow similarities to emerge.
- Many teams find it challenging to craft their purpose statement. It is important to allow flexibility in the time you allocate for this exercise.
- If a team is struggling to come up with the final version, you may suggest that they capture the essence of the purpose statement, reflect on it and then come up with the final version at an agreed time.

Time required

90 minutes plus.

TOOL 2: Memorable Object – connecting to personal purpose

Why use this tool?

Helping team members firstly connect to their own purpose and explore what it means to them can make it easier for the team to work on their collective purpose. This tool also builds trust and connection.

When to use this tool

- At the early stage of a team's development, when it would be helpful for the team to get to know each other better and at a deeper level.
- With teams that need to build trust, rapport and a greater sense of intimacy.
- Before the team works on their collective purpose.

Resources required

Team members will need to bring a memorable object with them or be ready to show or describe it on a virtual platform. For example, the object could be a photo, an autographed football, a piece of jewellery that once belonged to their grandmother or something they picked up on a favourite holiday.

How to use this tool

Step 1   Before the session, you will need to brief the team to find an object that is meaningful to them and that they would be willing to talk about and share with the team. They will need to think about what this object means to them. An object that holds a lot of meaning to them will be easy to talk about. They will need to briefly recall the story (approx five mins) about how they acquired the object, what it means to them and why and how it links to their personal purpose. The team coach(es) will also need to find a memorable object.

Step 2   Gather the team into a circle or on gallery view if working virtually. The team coach should share their object first to role-model openness and honesty, show vulnerability and demonstrate the length of their story. Then ask a member of the team to share next and so on, until all team members have shared.

Step 3   Thank everyone for sharing.

Top tips for team coaches

- In our experience having the team coach share first creates a feeling of safety and sets the tone for sharing more deeply. You may feel that as the team coach is not a team member why would they share – a valid point! Our recommendation is still for the team coach to share, as it can be a catalyst for creating an environment of openness and honesty.

- If working virtually, you could ask the team to take five minutes to ask team members to find an object in their immediate environment. This can work extremely well when team members are working from home, when it is not unusual for a team member to bring a loved one to their screen.

Time required

60 minutes for a team of around 8–10.

TOOL 3: Purposeful Pictures – sharing personal purpose

Why use this tool?

Similarly to 'memorable object', this tool enables team members to first connect to their own purpose and explore what it means to them. In turn, it can then make it easier for the team to work on their collective purpose. This tool also builds trust and connection and therefore can be extremely useful when working on the relatedness characteristic.

When to use this tool

- Towards the start of a team programme.
- Before the team works on their collective purpose.

Resources required

- Visual pictures.
- Picture cards, for example, School of Babel cards or Picture Coaching Cards by Barefoot Coaching.

How to use this tool

Step 1   Lay out visual pictures or picture cards on the floor or a table. If working virtually ask the team to select an image from a prepared montage of the picture cards or search the image library if available as part of the virtual platform being used.

Step 2   Give team members time to select a picture that represents their individual purpose.

Step 3   Invite a member of the team to share, giving a brief description of their picture and how it represents their personal purpose.

Step 4   All team members take it in turns to share their picture and how it represents their personal purpose.

Step 5   Thank the team for sharing.

Top tips for team coaches

- Our suggestion is for the team coach to share first to role-model openness and honesty and show vulnerability.
- Team members may like to take a photo of their picture to remember it.
- Playing background music when team members are selecting their images can help create a reflective atmosphere.

Time required

60 minutes for a team of 8–10 people.

TOOL 4: Word Power – Developing a compelling purpose

Why use this tool?

It is helpful to use this tool or a variation of it, to enable the team to craft their collective purpose statement.

When to use this tool

- Towards the beginning of a team coaching programme.
- For new teams, reorganized teams or any team coming to work together.

Resources required

Flip chart paper and pens, virtual whiteboard/platform.

How to use this tool?

Step 1 Explain top tips on how to write a purpose statement, eg starting with: 'We believe... Together we... As a team we...'

Step 2 Ask the team to brainstorm and capture any keywords that they feel represent their purpose. If the team is large, split into two or three groups. Alternatively to using keywords, ask the team to break out into groups to consider three questions:

- We are best at...
- We are passionate about...
- Our track record allows us to...

Step 3 Capture ideas.

Step 4 The team reviews the keywords or answers to the questions and selects the top words and phrases that they feel are important to include in their team purpose.

Step 5 The team starts to craft their purpose statement.

Step 6 The team reviews and refines their purpose statement.

Top tips for team coaches

- Team coach to share different examples of purpose statements to help the team understand what constitutes a strong purpose statement.
- Many teams find it challenging to craft their purpose statement. It is important to allow flexibility in the time you allocate for this exercise.
- If a team is struggling to come up with the final version, you may suggest that they capture the essence of the purpose statement and may want to reflect on it and come up with the final version at an agreed time.
- Virtual platforms with their advanced functionality to create collectively (eg ability to use different-coloured virtual Post-it notes) are recommended if working virtually.

Time required

90 minutes plus.

TOOL 5: Getting Creative – Developing a compelling team purpose

Why use this tool?

This tool helps team members to work individually and then as a team to develop their team purpose. It can shift the energy in the room as team members are encouraged to leave the room and go outside (even if in a virtual setting), which can often stimulate new ideas and thinking.

When to use this tool

Towards the beginning of a team coaching programme.

Resources required

- Post-it notes, blank card or blank postcards.
- Flip chart paper and pens, virtual whiteboard/platform.
- Ideally, an outside area or a creative indoor space.

How to use this tool

Step 1   Ask each team member to take around 10 minutes' reflection time, preferably outside or in a creative indoor space, to consider what they think the purpose of this team is. Each team member captures their thoughts on Post-it notes, on the card provided or virtually. Ideally the exercise is set up so that team members can walk while they are thinking and capturing their ideas. The movement can create energy that is conducive to creative thinking.

Step 2 Team members place all their Post-it notes or cards on a flip chart or virtual whiteboard/ platform.

Step 3 The team then looks for key themes and groups them together.

Step 4 The team then agrees keywords or phrases that they feel should be part of the purpose statement.

Step 5 Using the keywords or phrases, the team starts to craft a purpose statement. This could either be as a whole team or in subgroups that are then brought together. If using subgroups, when you bring the team together, ask each subgroup to pick the words or phrases they like in the other groups' purpose statements. The objective is to journey with the team as they move towards an agreed team purpose.

Top tips for team coaches

- Encouraging team members to go outside (even if working virtually), get some fresh air and move around, can be very helpful for creating new thinking.
- Many teams find it challenging to craft their purpose statement. It is important to allow flexibility in the time you allocate for this exercise.
- If a team is struggling to come up with the final version, you may suggest that they capture the essence of the purpose statement, reflect on it and then come up with the final version at an agreed time.

Time required

90 minutes plus.

TOOL 6: Team Shield

Why use this tool?

To help the team to develop and capture their compelling purpose, vision, values, strengths and team strapline.

When to use this tool

Towards the beginning of a team coaching programme.

Resources required

Flip chart paper and pens, virtual whiteboard/platform.

How to use this tool?

Step 1   Agree five or six headings for the team to work on, for example:

- Purpose
- Vision
- Goals
- Values
- Strengths
- Qualities
- Agreed behaviours
- Team strapline/motto

Step 2   Split the team into subgroups, depending on the number of headings. Each subgroup takes a flip chart sheet or a virtual whiteboard, with their allocated heading written on the top.

Step 3   Each team works on their part of the team shield for around 30 minutes. Within that time, the subgroups are encouraged to send out scouts to talk with, engage and gain insights from the other subgroups. If working virtually, use breakout rooms.

Step 4   All parts of the team shield are then displayed together.

Step 5   Subgroups are encouraged to ask each other questions.

Step 6   Final thoughts and reflections.

Top tips for team coaches

- Clearly contract that subgroups can send scouts to share and build on each other's ideas. If working virtually, this may mean moving some team members into different breakout rooms throughout the exercise.

- Watch out for subgroups getting strongly attached to the content created under their heading and not being open to feedback or suggested changes from the full team. It is important for the team coach to safely surface what they feel, see and hear to help the team learn about themselves and how they work together.

- More work may be required by the team to craft the exact final working of their team purpose. However, this exercise forms an excellent foundation for future focus on each of the headings.

Time required

90 minutes plus

Tool 6 Example of a shield with headings

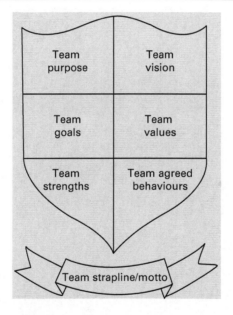

Reflecting on team purpose

- What is your personal purpose?
- How have you explored the individual purpose of each team member?
- What is our team purpose?
- What are our collective team goals?
- Why do we exist as a team?

- Who ultimately do we serve?
- How do we add value as a team?
- What can we only do together that we cannot do apart?
- What is the vision for our team?
- What would success as a team look, feel and sound like?
- How clear is the team strategy?
- How closely are the vision and strategy aligned to the team purpose?
- Beyond commercial targets, what do our key stakeholders require of us?
- What does the future require of us as a team?
- How closely are all our team members aligned to the team purpose?
- What is it about your team purpose that can inspire each team member?

Team identity   05

Why is team identity so important?

Defining identity

Who are you? Despite this not being a question that people tend to reflect on, when posed in a one-to-one coaching session it often brings about a similar type of response. For example, a coachee might state, 'I'm a mother, a successful executive, a spouse, a sibling, I'm French, a Parisian, a child of the 1970s, an MBA graduate and a community activist'. Most people are acutely aware that there are multiple sides to them that form their identity. They know identity is complicated. For some, there is a sense of peace that they have reconciled their many identities. They feel at home in their own skin. Yet for others, home feels far away, as they fight an internal battle between what appear to be irreconcilable parts of themselves.

Identity is how each of us chooses to define who we are. Each of us defines our identity through our personal characteristics, relationships and group memberships. How we choose to identify in any given moment shapes how we behave and interact. However, despite identity being fundamental, identity-related processes tend to be automatic and remain outside of our awareness (Polzer and Elfenbein, 2003).

We agree with the statement that 'Identities are powerful and are impossible to ignore. Wars, alliances, and revolutions frequently have issues of identity at their core' (Balmer, 2008: 882). In organizations, we would suggest that identity is often at the core of conflict between individuals, team and organizational diversity challenges, organization silos, inter-team conflict, innovation blind spots, and failed transformation efforts. In addition, because it mostly operates automatically, outside of our awareness, identity is not given the credit when it helps or the blame when it distracts. This chapter will explore the potency of team identity, both when helpful and unhelpful.

The psychology behind identity

Understanding the self

The notion of 'self' has been an area of debate. Bachkirova (2011) has suggested that there isn't one legitimate notion of 'self'. To further explain, she proposed three stories of what makes up 'self'. Firstly, the sense of a 'prereflective self-consciousness' or what Damasio (2000) calls a 'pre-linguistic consciousness' or 'core consciousness'. Secondly, she describes lots of 'miniselves', mostly unconscious, that she refers to as the 'ego' or 'executive centre'. Four levels of ego are described: unformed ego, formed ego, reformed ego and ego with a soul. She describes the idea of a fully formed ego as the capacity of a person to take ownership of the past, withstand anxieties about the future, and build relationships with others, without losing the sense of who they are. The third and final notion of self is referred to as the narrator, a linguistic function of the conscious mind, commonly referred to as 'self-talk' or 'our inner critic', which is continually presenting stories, some helpful and others unhelpful, about who it is we are.

Another way of considering how to define the self is through the stories we each tell about our self-identity. It has been suggested that these stories, along with the role of unconscious experiences that aren't consciously integrated into our stories, define who we are (Lee, 2003). The link between the idea of self and the stories we tell was highlighted by Davies and Harré (1990) who stated, 'since many stories can be told, even of the same event, then we each have many possible coherent selves' (p. 59). They further noted that to act rationally, we each need to remedy, transcend, resolve or ignore the stories of our many selves. The importance of finding coherence within our identity, or identities, will be a recurring theme throughout this chapter.

It could be argued that each of us is becoming more aware of the importance of identity, as well as the idea of identity choice. This view is supported by Anca and Aragón (2018) who observed that 'individuals now construct identities consciously' (p. 34). They further suggested that as humans we like to play with our multiple identities and use them as we take on different roles.

Group identity, cohesiveness and survival

As humans, we cannot survive alone. We need others both for our physical survival and also, as Bion (1961) has suggested, the fulfilment of our 'mental life' (p. 53). It has been suggested that as humans we approach group behaviour in two stages. Firstly, we need to be in groups for security from threats, to acquire and share resources and information, and to gain competitive advantage. Imagine hunting for food on your own! At these early stages, cohesiveness and shared identity are important, as the group will want to keep its members motivated and working towards the greater good of the group. Strong personal identification with the group (social identity) can help motivate effort and good behaviour. The second stage involves role identification, as group members seek out the advantages and opportunities available within the group. Group members will use these advantages and opportunities to differentiate themselves from others in their group (Baumeister *et al*, 2016).

The dangers of group identity

History is full of stories of how groups can become tribal and mob-like, and at their worst dismissive of others unlike them. The sense of self can become subsumed and lost to the group. Shapiro (2010), when discussing tribal behaviour, describes how members can become so emotionally invested in survival and enhancement of the tribe that they will often put aside self-interest and that of their families to advance the group's causes. Think of this in the context of the executive who puts their company before their family and often their health. At its extreme, to protect the group, members can become blinded to reality and act irrationally. Supporting this view, Brewer (2011) has commented on how the attachment of one's self and self-interest to the group as a whole can mean that 'any perceived threat to the group as a whole is seen as a threat to the self, even if the existence or welfare of the individual self is not directly endangered' (p. 125). Similarly, it has been suggested that within a group, what an individual considers reality will be heavily determined by what is socially acceptable as reality by that group (Lewin, 1945). Given the dangers of group identity, organizations are unlikely to be exempt from destructive group forces.

The importance of identity for organizations

Irrespective of what an organization would like to portray about who it is and what stories it tells, it is individuals, teams and groups who will decide what an organization's identity is. Similarly, Cilliers and Greyvenstein (2012) have suggested that an organization exists in the minds of its people.

Organizations need to attend to the question, 'How can we create an environment where individuals, teams and groups feel positive about their identity?' Dutton *et al* (2010) have proposed that developing a positive work-related identity can socially strengthen employees, with the benefits including 'changing perceptions (eg in-group—out-group boundaries), emotions (eg pride, contentment), and behaviours (eg helping)' (p. 280). Using research into work-related identities, they have suggested that it is important that employees:

- are given the opportunity to express their virtuous qualities (eg compassion, courage, integrity, humanity);
- feel appreciated and good about who they are;
- have opportunities to develop and grow, both through career advancement and other developmental opportunities (eg projects, cross-team working);
- are provided with opportunities to express themselves.

Identity is becoming more important both at an individual and organizational level. Organizations used to provide certainty, with their hierarchical structures, lifetime careers and the familiarity of local faces. Within today's organizations that are less hierarchical, with global, virtual and more diverse teams, there is need more than ever to proactively develop team and organizational identities. Teams in their very essence are highly social entities, where individuals can hopefully find and be themselves. The following sections will explore the opportunities and challenges of developing a team identity.

Developing team identity

Story: When a board discovers a new and empowering team identity

Contributor: Lucy

I was working with a UK board of a large well-known global manufacturing business. The team consisted of high-performing individuals who were doing fantastic jobs at leading their own functions, but were working in silos rather than as a powerful collective. Not uncommon in many organizations we work with.

In exploring their strategy and objectives, the language of the team focused on how they would implement global strategy, rather than influence it. Interestingly, as the team worked on deepening their relationships, exploring interdependencies and getting clearer on their strategic direction, their conversations started to change.

Their team identity shifted from talking about being an implementing market to working together and being a driving and influencing market.

The UK was due to host a global sporting event and the team decided that they would pull together a proposal to sponsor the event. I started to hear real belief that they could achieve this, as well as convince their global head office. That belief paid off as the team successfully secured the opportunity to sponsor the whole event. A major collective achievement and a lesson that if you develop your team identity by cohesively working together and have the belief you can do it, then often you can!

Understanding team identity

In organizations today, it would appear discussions on identity are mostly reserved for matters relating to inclusion and diversity. However, as evidenced in this chapter so far, identity is at the heart of everything we think and do. In our earliest years, we assume elements of our identity from areas such as family, ethnicity and faith. Eventually, a person may cast aside areas of their assumed identity and adopt new elements. Either through choice or subconsciously we are open to continually constructing who we are, and how much of ourselves we wish to invest in other vehicles of identity. These other vehicles include how much of ourselves we wish to invest in the teams, groups and organizations in our workplace.

It is our view that thoroughly understanding the opportunities and complexities of team identity is essential for teams and team coaches. A team may have a compelling team purpose, but it is likely to be unnecessarily derailed if matters of identity are not attended to. Litchfield *et al* (2018) have described team identification as 'a strong form of attachment where individuals partially derive their self-definition from the team' (p. 350). They further point out that team identity 'unifies team members into a socially identifiable whole and encourages members to favour activities that benefit the group's interests' (p. 353). Unfortunately, acting in the team's interest may not always be in the best interests of other teams and the organization. These issues and how to moderate them will be discussed further as the chapter continues. Despite its challenges, there is agreement on the benefits of developing team identity. This is evidenced by the findings by Lee *et al* (2011) from their study of 71 cross-national project teams, which has linked the strengthening of group identification with a heightened sense of general team belief, referred to as team potency, that results in improved group performance.

The importance to team identity of finding and being yourself

To be our authentic self among others, we need to find who it is we are in the context of the other people. Just like in our families, we may not get to choose who is in our team. However, unlike in a family, it can be more difficult to be ourselves when we are with colleagues. When we cannot be our authentic selves, behaviours such as withdrawing, avoidance, stress and conflict are not uncommon. An identity negotiation is required, where a team member aligns self-perceptions with the perceptions of team members. Reaching a place of alignment is described as congruence, which is viewed as essential if team members wish to express themselves and not compartmentalize parts of who they are. The role of the team leader is central in creating the psychological safety that allows for a genuine exchange of identity-relevant information (Polzer and Elfenbein, 2003). We will outline several tools and techniques later in this chapter that can help individuals explore their identity in the context of their team.

Team coaching has three crucial contributions to make in this area. Firstly, it can help move this often-forgotten area onto the agenda of teams and organizations. Secondly, a team coach can help team members discover how to safely find and be themselves within their team. Thirdly, a team coach can proactively help a team to develop an identity that they wish to become known for.

The importance of common goals towards developing team identity

The importance of collective team goals as the crucial element in bringing alive a team's purpose has been clearly stated in Chapter 4. However, team goals also act as a unifying force towards developing team identity. From their study of teams, Lee *et al* (2011) have confirmed that 'fostering the acceptance of group goals that are interdependent was important for increasing group identification' (p. 1147). When team members are agreed on what work they need to achieve together, they can start to interpret their individual contribution to the team goal, as well as how they and the team collectively need to interact with each other (norms, values, behaviours). This processing is a necessary part of the team identification process. While some high-level goals may be given to the team, team coaching would encourage the team to jointly interpret these high-level goals and also to co-create as many of their own team goals as possible.

It is also imperative that individual team member goals do not work against the spirit of the team goals. This is particularly relevant when team membership is drawn from different departments, functions or customer client sectors. We have experienced these identity challenges when team members have individual goals, sometimes with financial rewards attached to them, that are contrary to the team effort. For organizations to take the work of their teams seriously, it is important that reward structures are aligned or, at a minimum, their impact is openly discussed and managed.

How team member differences strengthen team identity

We have already outlined the core benefit of being our authentic selves within a team. An important way to be yourself is to ensure you bring your unique skill set to the team. Research by Baumeister *et al* (2016) has highlighted the importance of the unique contributions and the skill sets of each team member being valued. It has been suggested that when individuals submerge into a group, with their voice effectively disappearing, it can result in situations where team members are not held accountable or responsible. It is also deemed unhelpful when there is no sense of competition, no distinctiveness of role, and little public identification or reward. Importantly, the same research has also highlighted that people will contribute more to the team effort when their input can be individually identified.

Similarly, it has been demonstrated that it is not enough to just feel included in a team; feeling valued counts the most. When a person feels valued, not only do they identify with the team, they are more willing to invest in the team effort (Ellemers *et al*, 2013). Another benefit of valuing each team member's uniqueness and contribution is a decrease in status differences. Research by Mitchell *et al* (2015) among medical professionals concluded that valuing everyone's professional contribution decreased perceived status differences between team members, which improved shared team identity and interprofessional team performance.

Creating your team story

It has been suggested that one of the central objectives of coaching is to help coachees develop their stories, both current and new (Stelter, 2009). The coaching literature highlights the useful role of *narrative coaching* when considering a person's identity. Law (2007: 179) has suggested that a key element of Narrative coaching is uncovering a coachee's 'landscapes of consciousness' which 'are composed of the storyteller's own identity'. Lee (2003: 29) has commented on how when coaching individuals, 'self-identities become the objects of scrutiny'.

The benefits of narrative coaching should not just belong to working with individuals. The team coach can help a team reveal, discuss, reconcile and align their current identity story. Getting feedback from other stakeholders can play a useful role in this process. It is also vital that a team coach helps a team consider how their identity may need to change, for them to deliver on what the future requires of them. This can result in the writing of a new identity narrative that keeps the best of the old, while embracing the future. A team coach can help hold the team accountable as they start to live out their new revised identity.

The challenges of team identity

How team identity can accentuate destructive inter-group conflict

A real risk of stronger team identities is a destructive conflict between teams (though we support the view that the right type of conflict in a safe environment is considered a generative force for teams – see Chapter 8 on team relatedness).

Once in a conflict, the invisible forces of group dynamics can take over. It has been stated that during a conflict, 'groups tend to view themselves in a one-sided way involving self-glorification and self-praise, ignoring any information that might shed any negative light on the group' (Rosoux, 2009: 550). In addition, parties to a conflict will make what has been referred to as 'denial statements', rejecting the other parties' need for identity recognition, whilst simultaneously highlighting the validity of their own identity. Hills (2016) has highlighted that when people feel threatened, the effect of in-group identification becomes more intense. When in conflict, the link between a team not being able to see past their own position and the strength of a team's identity, is likely to be positively correlated.

Writing extensively about conflict resolution, Kelman (2004) has outlined how it is necessary for each party to revise its own identity enough to accommodate the identity of the other. This, he argues, is not about necessarily fully agreeing with the other's narrative; it is about recognizing the legitimacy of others to hold what they consider their own truth. The process of reconciliation, it is suggested, requires a certain level of negotiation of identity. He states, 'the primary feature of the identity change constituting reconciliation is the removal of the negation of the other as a central component of one's own identity' (Kelman, 2004: 119).

For a team to consider adjusting its own identity to help resolve a conflict, it must develop its field of perception. Taking inspiration from Personal Construct Psychology and the work of Burr *et al* (2014), it can be useful for the team to reflect on the following questions:

- How do we perceive ourselves as a team?
- How do we perceive the other team?
- How do we think the other team perceives us?
- How do we think the other team perceives themselves?

Writing about conflict resolution and issues relating to identity, Barbour and Bourne (2020) have highlighted the usefulness of adapting the same questions to reflect on the future relationship. For example:

- How do we need to perceive ourselves as a team?
- How do we need to perceive the other team?
- How do we need the other team to perceive us?
- How do we need the other team to perceive themselves?

If the team coach is working with both of the teams in a conflict, it can be useful for each team to answer the questions separately and then for a team coach to bring the teams together to share their findings with each other. The same approach can also be used when working on a conflict between individuals.

Even by just increasing awareness of what is really going on, a team coach can play an important role in helping a team or teams change enough of their identity to embrace different truths.

How strong team identity can harm innovative behaviour

Innovation, the ability to do things differently, is central to the future of all organizations. It is unlikely that innovation can be executed by one team on its own. A team will need to work with other teams.

It has been found that team identity can harm innovative behaviour if it is not developed in the right way. Litchfield *et al* (2018) concluded from their research that cross-team innovative behaviour works best when strong team identity is accompanied with reflective practice.

Importantly, reflective practice is about more than just thinking, it is about learning and then doing something different. Finlay (2008), commenting on the work of Donald Schön, to whom reflective practice is attributed, noted his main contribution was to identify two types of reflection: reflection-on-action (after-the-event thinking) and reflection-in-action (thinking while doing).

Learning to become a reflective practitioner of reflexivity is a central pillar of being a coach. Team coaches are well placed to help teams develop their expertise in reflexivity.

The perils of ignoring team history and the wider system

A team identity that does not take account of its history, perceived as either good or bad, is likely to struggle from invisible forces they cannot explain. Whittington (2016), when writing about the power of the system, has commented that 'whatever you try to exclude will always hold a powerful energy that will distract until it is re-included' (p. 14). For example, a new team leader trying to forge a new team identity who fails to recognize the allegiances of some team members to the previous leader.

Team history is more important than it is normally given credit for. Clutterbuck (2014) has suggested that teams who have been together for more than a short period will have a history that will include history imported by team members, from both inside and outside the organization. He noted there is likely to be low awareness within the team about the current impact of these separate histories. In research carried out in academic medical libraries, previous history or tradition was identified as the 'single most common barrier' to team effectiveness by some of the groups under study (Martin, 2006: 276). We have both witnessed how, when teams do not respect the history of those who came before, it can quite quickly and unknowingly derail a team. Discussing these issues, Clutterbuck (2014) has suggested that 'psychodynamic conversations can help the team recognize, accept or challenge, and manage these histories' (p, 280).

It is not just history that a team's identity needs to take account of. The team need to become aware of what is happening in its wider environment. In our experience as team coaches, as supported in research (Cilliers and Greyvenstein, 2012), teams operating in silos create one of the most common challenges we come across, with identity issues being a key part of the problem. As outlined in other parts of this book, it is no longer enough to just talk about a singular team. Organizations and team coaches need to consider how different teams are collaborating both within and across organizations: a 'team of teams' approach is required.

When considering team identity, the team coach has a key role to help a team discover which parts of its history and its present need to be brought into awareness, reconciled and included or consciously discarded. This needs to include consideration of all the other teams a team relies on to fulfil its purpose.

The role of team identity in overcoming diversity challenges

We believe that teams can play a key role in helping organizations benefit from greater diversity. Jones *et al* (2013) in their book, *The Psychology of Diversity: Beyond prejudice and racism*, have highlighted the benefits of rising above our biases to embrace diversity. Besides a strong moral argument regarding fairness and legal aspects, there are also performance benefits of developing team diversity. For example, there is a positive correlation between higher levels of group collective intelligence and a greater number of females in a group (Bender *et al*, 2012; Kim *et al*, 2017), an area that will be explored more fully in Chapter 8.

However, the evidence would suggest that it is not as simple as just creating diverse teams and hoping for the best, as Mannix and Neale (2005) highlighted from their review of almost 50 years of social science research on diversity. They have stated that 'to implement policies and practices that increase the diversity of the workforce without understanding how diverse individuals can come together to form effective teams is irresponsible' (p. 32). From their review of the literature, they have recommended the benefits of focusing the team's effort on complex tasks that require exploration and dialogue, building team bridges by focusing on what the team have in common (eg their common identity) and ensuring minority voices are heard. Similarly, Eckel and Grossman (2005) have noted that while aspects of our identity like age, race, sex, or ethnicity are fixed, social identity theory proposes that our *social identity* can be manufactured. Their research demonstrated that actions taken to enhance team identification contributed to improved levels of team cooperation. They also noted that just being identified with a team is not enough for individuals to overcome their self-interest. Efforts to develop team identity are therefore essential.

Another risk to team diversity relates to what Lau and Murnighan (1998) have referred to as group faultlines or subgroups. These have been defined as 'hypothetical dividing lines that split a group into relatively homogeneous sub-groups' (Kaczmarek *et al*, 2012: 5). Team faultlines can form based on attributes such as gender, experience, education, professional discipline, and so on. For example, Molleman (2005) discovered that demographic (gender, age, race etc) faultlines negatively influenced the functioning of a team and resulted in decreased cohesion and increased intra-team conflict. Importantly, Lau and Murnighan (1998) have discovered that faultlines are most likely to occur where there are moderate levels of diversity. Consequently, they have recommended recruiting group members who have different and/or unique attributes.

In summary, team diversity is good for business, but an effort is required to realize these benefits. Key among these efforts is developing a common team identity. It is also clear from the evidence that just being moderately diverse is not enough. As in our experience of team coaching, team identity is not an area that teams spend much time working on; however, we believe that focusing on developing common team identities can not only help teams perform better, it can also contribute to supporting the development of diversity.

The challenges with board identity

Kaczmarek *et al* (2012) identified several task-related board faultlines that had a strong negative effect on organization performance. These included:

- faultlines created by overly long-tenured CEOs;
- non-executive directors with multiple board seats and therefore split loyalties and identities;
- reward structures that do not support the overall board effort.

While recognizing the difficulty of changing such board characteristics, we have summarized the following potential actions from their research:

- leadership that prioritizes board cohesiveness and accentuates the overall board effort;
- selection of non-executive directors who identify strongly with the company;
- reward structures that support the overall work of the board.

In summary, identity and team identity, while complex, has a significant role to play in the effectiveness of teams at all levels within organizations. This little-discussed area of team effectiveness should be on the agenda of team coaches. The following section will outline the tools and techniques that we have successfully used when helping teams to explore their team identity.

Tools and techniques for developing team identity

Using tools and techniques

When applying these tools and techniques, it is essential that the team coach or leader builds connection and psychological safety first. The tools and techniques are offered as a support and guide, that when used should feel natural and in 'flow', with the process and steps behind the tools remaining effectively invisible.

TOOL 1: Logical Levels – exploring your team's identity

Why use this tool?

Teams can be unclear about who they are as a team, why they do what they do and how they do it. This tool helps teams gain clarity about what their identity needs to be to achieve their purpose. It also enables teams to identify how they can become more aligned, coherent and congruent in why they do what they do, who they are, and what they do.

When to use this tool

- Once the purpose of the team is clear and the team now needs to think about who they are as a collective unit.
- With teams who are attempting to merge, align, transform or gain clarity about who they are as a team and what they want to be.
- With boards or teams where there might be conflicting identities and who therefore need to develop and agree on their common identity.

Resources required

- Flip chart paper and pens, virtual whiteboard/platform.
- A3 cards with the six logical levels (Dilts, 1990) headings printed on them as below (you can also use flip charts or display virtually):
  1. Purpose
  2. Identity
  3. Values and Beliefs
  4. Skills and Capabilities
  5. Behaviours
  6. Environment

How to use this tool

There are many different ways to use this tool. It can be used as an aspirational team activity, helping the team to think about what they want their identity to be and how they want to be known in the future. Alternatively, the team can explore their logical levels concerning where they are now and then where they want to be. Exploring where they want to be is described below:

Step 1 Explain the logical levels ladder. For example, based on the work of Gregory Bateson, Dilts (1990) has outlined a model of human behaviour called Logical Levels. It assumes that human processes can be described along a ladder of categories that influence each other. The lowest level is the environment, followed by behaviour, skills and capabilities, values and beliefs, identity and purpose.

Step 2   Place six A3 cards or flip charts with purpose, identity, values and beliefs, skills and capabilities, behaviours and environment in a ladder formation on the floor or display virtually.

Step 3   Move to each of the logical level steps (physically if working in person) and explore the following questions. After you have explored each logical level step, capture key thoughts:

- Purpose
  o What is their team purpose?
- Identity
  o What does their identity need to be to achieve the mission and purpose?
  o How do they want to be known and described as a team?
- Values and beliefs
  o What is it they need to value and believe to achieve their purpose?
- Skills and capabilities
  o What skills and capabilities do they need as a team to achieve their purpose?
- Behaviours
  o How do they need to behave as a team to achieve their purpose?
- Environment
  o What environment do they need to create to achieve their purpose?

Step 4   Now ask the team to review all the outputs and for each aspect of the ladder prioritize the top three themes or thoughts.

Step 5   Ask the team to consider what their next steps will be and how they will use this information.

Step 6   Team to confirm their next steps – what they will do and when.

Top tips for team coaches

- The team coach should explain the logical levels ladder model first – more details about the model can be found in Chapter 6.

- Another way to use this model is to first explore where the team is now. This would involve the team physically walking up the ladder (or moving along each step virtually) capturing how their environment is now, what behaviours they see displayed in this team etc. Capture their outputs at each stage. The team would then move to where they want to be and follow the ladder using the steps mentioned earlier. This helps the team to see and explore the difference between where they are now and where they want to be.

- If working virtually, encourage team members to physically move by placing A4 sheets on their floor, if possible, with each sheet representing one of the six logical levels.

Time required

60 – 90 minutes. (If the team explores where they are now and then where they want to be, this can take around 90 minutes.)

TOOL 2: Picture this! Exploring identity

Why use this tool?

Having a strong sense of who you are as a team and how you want to be described can help the team, their stakeholders and colleagues identify with the team as a collective rather than a group of individuals.

When to use this tool

At any stage, if the team is not clear on what their identity is and how they want to be known as a team.

Resources required

- Picture cards, eg School of Babel or Barefoot.
- Flip chart paper and pens, virtual whiteboard/platform.

How to use this tool

Step 1   Place the picture cards (or similar) on the floor or a surface and ask the team members to choose a picture that they feel represents this team's identity. If working virtually ask the team to select an image from a prepared montage of the picture cards or search the image library, if available, as part of the virtual collaboration platform being used.

Step 2   Ask team members to each share with the team why they chose the cards.

Step 3   The chosen cards are then placed together. Ask team members to choose just one card that they feel represents their team identity – who they are and how they want to be described.

Step 4   Ask the team to agree why they chose that card, what it represents.

Step 5   Ask the team to consider – how will this be helpful to them as a team?

Step 6   Ask the team to consider – how will they bring their identity to life back in the workplace? Capture the specific actions.

Top tips for team coaches

Spend some time helping the team to understand what identity is and what it means to them before working on the team identity. For some, the idea of identity can feel quite conceptual or abstract and therefore more difficult to grasp.

Time required

30–45 minutes.

TOOL 3: Newspaper Headlines – creating your identity

Why use this tool?

Helping teams to explore, develop and agree their team identity in a creative way can bring energy and build connection within the team.

When to use this tool

At any stage, if the team is not clear on what their identity is and who they are as a team.

Resources required

- Variety of newspapers, magazines or visuals, printed-out words.
- Scissors, glue or tape etc.
- Flip chart paper and pens, virtual whiteboard/platform.

How to use this tool

Step 1   Place all the newspapers, magazines, visuals etc on a table or virtually. Ask the team to search for words or any visuals that represent their identity as a team.

Step 2   Team members now collate all the words and visuals and categorize them into key themes.

Step 3   Ask team members to agree on what the top one to three themes are from the key themes.

Step 4   Finally, from the themes, ask the team to choose the visual and words that create their newspaper headline, symbolizing their team identity.

Step 5   Ask the team to consider – how will they bring their headline to life back in the workplace? Capture the specific actions.

Top tips for team coaches

Before exploring team identity help the team explore what identity is and what it means to them.

Time required

45 minutes.

TOOL 4: *Personal Identity Timeline – exploring who I am*

Why use this tool?

Creating an opportunity for team members to develop and share their own personal identity will help the team to understand each other better, build rapport and connection, and make it easier for them to work on their collective team identity.

When to use this tool

Explore personal identity at an early stage of team coaching, to help the team members to build their relationships and deepen their connection.

Resources required

- Flip chart paper and pens, virtual whiteboard/platform.
- A3 cards with the following questions written on them:
  o Now – how am I described now?
  o Future – how do I want to be described?
- The team will be working in pairs, so you will need one set of A3 cards per pair.
- If working virtually, create a timeline that can be annotated on by team members.

How to use this tool

Step 1   Ask the team to split into pairs with each pair taking the A3 cards or the questions written on a flip chart. If working virtually use the prepared timeline and place pairs into breakout rooms.

Step 2   Place one card at each end of a timeline a metre or two apart. Working with their partner the pairs should take it in turns to explore their identity and then:

- Partner 1 – first stand on the 'Now' card – partner 1 to explore and share – How I am described now?
- Partner 1 to then move to the 'Future' card – partner 1 to explore and share – How do I want to be described?
- Partner 1 to then stand back and look at the 'Now' card and consider what actions do I want to take to move to my future self?

Step 3   Pairs to then swap and partner 2 to explore in the same way. If working virtually, ask each partner to annotate the timeline when they are exploring each question, using drawings, other images or text.

Step 4   Debrief – what was the learning from the exercise?

Top tips for team coaches

- It may be helpful for the team coach to demonstrate how the timeline exercise will work with one of the team members and show how you will move along the timeline.

- Explain that the timeline isn't about finding a new identity, it is about exploring and celebrating who you are now and who you want to be.

Time required

45 minutes.

TOOL 5: Personal Identity Wheel – understanding my identity

Why use this tool?

This tool can enable team members to be clear about who they are and what is important to them. Through sharing their thoughts with other team members it can help to deepen their connection and enable them to understand the importance of having both individual and team identities.

When to use this tool

Early in the team coaching programme to help strengthen relationships and the team members understanding of each other's identities.

Resources required

- Personal wheel templates.
- Flip chart paper and pens, virtual whiteboard/ platform.

How to use this tool

Step 1   Introduce the personal wheel template or suggest team members draw the wheel on a flip chart. Example questions in the template on p105.

Step 2   Ask team members to write their name in the circle. At the ends of the arrows, team members capture their answers to the questions. Allow around 20 minutes for completing the wheel. If working virtually, ask team members to turn off their video and sound when preparing their answers.

Step 3   Team members then share their wheel with the rest of the team, taking it in turns. Use screen share if working virtually.

Step 4   Thank each team member for sharing.

Tool 5   Personal wheel template

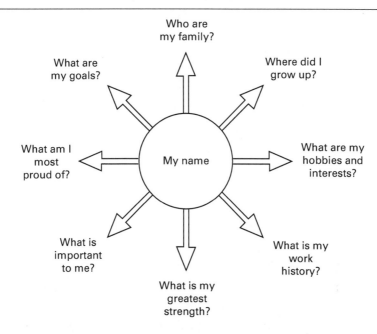

Top tips for team coaches

- It is important to build psychological safety and contract clearly around confidentiality before this exercise.

- Some team members may be less comfortable with sharing personal information about their identity. Explain that team members can choose how much they share.

- Questions or areas to share can be changed. For example, instead you may want to ask them to share what their strengths are or three things that have had the greatest influence on who they are.

- For larger teams, you may want to split the team into smaller subgroups (use breakout rooms if working virtually), although ideally for team connection we would recommend everyone to share with the team together.

Time required

60 minutes depending on the number of team members.

TOOL 6: What's your story? Sharing personal identity

Why use this tool?

To help team members to develop their own story and be able to share this with the team. This can help them develop a coherent narrative about their identity and can also help the team think about their collective narrative.

When to use this tool

Towards the start of the team development, to help the team connect and create ideas for developing the team's common identity.

Resources required

Flip chart paper and pens, virtual whiteboard/platform.

How to use this tool

Step 1   Ask team members to take some flip chart paper and create their story. The story can be in the form of the journey they have been through in life, eg where they lived, went to school, work, family through to where they are now. Ask them to think about how the different parts of their journey formed their identity. This should be done for approximately 20 minutes. If working virtually ask team members to create their story on a virtual whiteboard.

Step 2   Once the journeys are complete, team members should share their journeys with the rest of the team.

Step 3   Thank each team member for sharing.

Top tips for team coaches

- As with Tool 5, it is important to build psychological safety and contract clearly around confidentiality before this exercise.
- Some team members may be less comfortable with sharing personal information about their identity. Explain that team members can choose how much they share.
- For larger teams, you may want to split the team into smaller subgroups, although ideally for team connection we would recommend everyone to share with the full team.

Time required

60 minutes depending on the number of team members.

Reflecting on team identity

- How would you describe your team?
- How do you want to be described?
- What would help you achieve this?
- Who are you as a team?
- What do you want your team's story to be?
- How diverse is your team?
- How can you leverage your team's diversity?
- What is your identity?
- Who are you as a leader?
- How would you describe your organization's identity and culture?
- How would you want it to be described?
- What would you need to change to achieve this?

Team values and beliefs

Why are team values and beliefs so important?

Defining values and beliefs

If you had to rank the following three questions in terms of how easy or difficult they are to answer, what would you say?

1 What is your purpose in life?

2 Who are you?

3 What are your values and beliefs?

From our experience when coaching, the first two questions tend to pose coachees the greatest challenge. As humans, trying to place words on something so profound as our purpose can be difficult. Trying to put into words our multiple and changing identities can also prove daunting. However, when it comes to stating what our values and beliefs are, we seem to find these easier.

What is also revealing, both during one-to-one and team coaching, is the level of commonality on each individual's values that we hear expressed. Caring for others usually ranks highly, as do respect, honesty and fairness. For people, values are those things they hold most precious to the nature of who they are. They are the visible reflection of their identity, that mostly act subconsciously in guiding their decisions.

Another area operating largely subconsciously is our beliefs. Most coaches would agree that working with coachees on a mindset or belief that is holding them back is a relatively common occurrence. A belief may be considered as 'something that is accepted, considered to be true, or held as an opinion' or 'a state or habit of mind in which trust or confidence is placed' (Merriam-Webster.com). Our beliefs could be described as a less visible reflection of our identity that nonetheless are important in how we choose to live our lives. As humans, whether individually or in groups, what we believe can either drive us forward, cause stagnation or drag us backwards.

Values and beliefs are closely linked. Indeed it is common for values to be described as deeply held beliefs (Boniwell, 2012; Renshaw, 2018). However, we are clear that each is distinct enough to merit discussion in the context of coaching teams.

The psychology behind values and beliefs

How the human experience shapes our values and beliefs

It has been suggested that values 'are deeply held beliefs that we usually internalize during our upbringing or decide on as we grow older' (Boniwell, 2012: 63). We would suggest that our values are likely to be shaped somewhere in between, on what we would describe as a continuum of 'spoken' and 'lived' values. As we grow up, we hear statements that instil in us what our values should be. For example, 'treat people the way you would like to be treated yourself', 'remember your manners', 'you get what you work for', 'you shouldn't talk behind people's backs', 'a smile goes a long way' and so on. When we get to the workplace, company value statements may adorn the walls. Importantly, though, we also experience 'lived' values, through what we see, hear and feel. For example, the parent who says, 'you shouldn't talk behind people's backs', and then proceeds to continually gossip. Or a company that says, 'we believe that our people make the best decisions', but only involve a few people in its decision making. Somewhere in between our experience of 'spoken' and 'lived' values, we make up our minds on what we consider to be important. Humans can hold values at an individual, group and organizational level, and in any of these situations, acting against our values can create significant discomfort.

Beliefs can become embedded like unquestionable facts because 'we build beliefs by generalizing from our experience of the world and other people' (O'Connor and Seymour, 1990: 83). Many parents and other important adults, knowingly or unknowingly, instil beliefs into their children. Some of our earliest held beliefs may drive us to do great things while others can prove very limiting. Encouraging a child to think through their issues, to be trusted on their decisions and to ask for support when needed could instil beliefs such as, 'I can make good decisions for myself' and 'It's ok to ask for help'. Alternatively, constantly comparing the child to the accomplishments of other siblings or classmates could result in a child believing, 'No matter what I do, I will never be good enough' or 'I'm stupid'. It is important to note that each of these experiences could have been interpreted positively or negatively by the child. As adults, we start to exercise greater discernment on what we choose to believe, irrespective of what others, including family, governments, faith communities and our employers, may wish us to believe.

Changing our values and beliefs

The link between our values and beliefs and how we choose to behave in any given moment is clear. Nevertheless, at times in our life, it may serve our greater purpose and who we want to become to strengthen or develop some new values or beliefs. Agreeing that values can be changed, Boniwell (2012) has commented that 'few people can maintain absolutely identical values throughout their lifetimes' (p. 63). Similarly, it has been stated that 'beliefs can be a matter of choice' and that we can drop beliefs that limit us and establish new beliefs that help us to be more successful (O'Connor and Seymour, 1990: 85).

Values can be changed by placing our emphasis in a selected direction, and through exposing ourselves to chosen people and situations (Hardingham *et al*, 2004). For example, if you wanted to become more caring, it could be useful to volunteer at a local community project. Life experiences such as birth, death, marriage, career progression, divorce, illness, redundancy and retirement are also likely to influence what we consider important and valuable.

Beliefs can also be changed by reversing the process by which they were created. Hall and Belnap (2004) have noted how our experiences give way to thoughts. These thoughts, if confirmed and validated in our mind, can become beliefs that drop out of our awareness. We perceive the world through the beliefs that we hold and subconsciously look for information to confirm what we already believe. Doubt arises in the space between certainty and questioning. To change a belief, we need to become aware of our thinking, invalidate an old pattern of thinking, validate a new one, and retain a new level of awareness.

Values and beliefs in context

A useful model for discussing values and beliefs in context is the Gregory Bateson-inspired Logical Levels Model. Proposed by Dilts (1990), the model suggests that change at the higher level of the hierarchy (eg purpose) will necessitate change at the lower levels (eg identity), in order to support the higher-level change. The six levels consist of:

1 Purpose

2 Identity

3 Values and Beliefs

4 Skills and Capabilities

5 Behaviours

6 Environment

For example, a person who starts to believe that they can advance their career (values and beliefs level) will need to ensure that the supporting change has taken place at the lower levels of capabilities and behaviours. Similarly, an organization wishing to instil new company values (values and beliefs level) should ensure that they provide employees with the right developmental support (capabilities), encourage behaviours that reflect the new values, and create the right organizational environment. Dilts (1990) suggested that changing something at the lower levels could, but will not necessarily, lead to change at the higher level. We have found the model very useful when coaching individuals and teams, to create awareness of each aspect, how they interlink, and to help teams then identify at what level(s) they need to consider making changes.

The importance of values and beliefs for organizations

Exploring organizational values and beliefs

Interestingly, little has been written specifically about beliefs in the context of entire organizations, though beliefs at a team level have drawn the attention of researchers, as we will discuss later. It is as if organizations expect employees whose wages they pay to automatically believe in the collective effort.

Values, however, have been extensively explored. Senge (2006) has suggested that it is difficult to imagine any organization that has sustained some level of greatness not having deeply shared values. We like to think of organizational values as windows into an organization's culture. They can help employees to prioritize, make decisions, and form the basis of how people aspire to communicate and treat each other. In recent years, we have witnessed an increasing number of organizations attempting to bring their values to life. Some examples we have come across include:

- **Values in Action (VIA) programmes.** Where employees who demonstrate the organization's values to an exemplary level are selected by their colleagues or manager, their work is profiled, and some form of reward is provided.

- **Values 360 diagnostics.** Where each employee is assessed, by a selected number of other employees, on each organizational value.

- **Value champions.** Where selected personnel from different departments lead initiatives to bring organizational values to life.

- **Values from descriptions to actions.** For example, from 'respect' to 'we will listen deeply and seek to understand each other'.

- **Value recruitment and progression policies.** Where employees are recruited based on their 'values fit' and where progression is only possible if an employee is considered a 'values fit'. This might also mean that people who are not a 'values fit' may choose to leave a company.

The challenge of 'spoken' versus 'lived' values

We consider an organization's culture to be the sum of its individual, team and group behaviours – behaviours that should be driven by the organization's values. However, as discussed earlier there is a difference between 'spoken' and 'lived' values. These differences can occur irrespective of the efforts made by the organization to embed their values. Imagine a new employee, who during their induction is proudly introduced to the organization's values. During their first break, a new colleague starts to share stories about 'how things really get done around here'. The new employee may already feel a disconnect between the 'spoken' and 'lived' values.

A key challenge for employees is that when there is a disconnect between spoken and lived values, they don't feel safe enough to talk about their concerns. Argyris (1980) discussed how stating the truth can feel threatening and result in individuals and teams distorting the truth to protect themselves. More recently, the same disconnect has been described as being responsible for 'what can and cannot be discussed' (Leahy and Mia, 2019: 177).

Another key challenge is when values are developed and spoken about, but it is incorrectly assumed they are lived. This point has been illustrated by Schein (2013) who discussed how some organizational values, by consensus, may be taken for granted and fall out of consciousness. He argues that 'tacit assumptions' (p. 53) are what really drive an organization's culture. Talking about US corporate culture and teams in particular, he has stated, 'we claim to value teamwork and talk about it all the time, but the artefacts – our promotional systems and reward systems – are entirely individualistic' (p. 53).

Developing team values and beliefs

Does having team values matter?

Based on the challenges explained in the previous section, surely the last thing a team needs is more values! However, the fact that the evidence shows that organizations struggle to embed values is even more reason for the team to have a robust discussion on the role and importance of values. Schein's (2013) perspective that when organizational values fall away, they are replaced with 'tacit assumptions' (p. 53), we would suggest is equally applicable to teams. That is, in the absence of agreed team values, unwritten collective values will be established. Therefore, if a team wants to be a top-performing team, they should agree on team values. I as importantly, the team should commit to 'lived' values and not just a set of words. It has been suggested that team values represent an internal code of behaviour (Sandahl and Philips, 2019). Team values are about how we want to behave as a team, when we are together and apart.

In our experience, sometimes teams question the need for separate team values; however, we are very clear that they are essential. The importance of unique team values is supported in research. In answer to the question 'is sharing values with the overall organization or the group to which a person belongs more important?' Adkins and Caldwell (2004: 977) answered that both are important. Their results also suggest that when subcultures are created, improving the fit between individuals and the culture of the group can increase employee satisfaction. In addition, their observation that group cultures are easier to change could support a hypothesis that developing team values and culture can support organizational culture change.

Developing team values

From our experience, team values should be:

- **Unique to the team.** As shown in Table 6.1, team values should be specific to the team. They are not necessarily for public display or sharing unless the team decide otherwise.

- **Decided on together.** The team must decide on their team values together, as this forms the basis for holding each other accountable.

When helping a team to develop their team values, some important factors for the team coach to consider include:

- the effectiveness of getting the team to first reflect on and share their personal values, in order to help bring alive the importance of values;
- reviewing the team's commitment individually and collectively to the organization's core values;
- ensuring the team values underpin the team purpose (including team goals) and team identity;
- the importance of expressing the team values as calls to action;
- assessing how the team are currently positioned, in terms of living the new team values (present-day benchmarking);
- helping the team to reflect on the values they display when together and when apart;
- agreeing on action plans to bring the new team values to life;
- discussing and agreeing what helpful (good day) and unhelpful (bad day) behaviours are;
- discussing openly how the team will support and hold each other accountable.

Table 6.1 Descriptions, features, benefits, and examples of organization and team values

Description of values	Desirable features of values	Key benefits of values
– What is important to us? – What does this mean for how we behave?	– Ideally expressed as a call to action – Are clear on helpful 'good day' and unhelpful 'bad day' behaviours – Provide culture cues – Underpins purpose and identity – Reflective of what the future requires of us	– Drives ideal behaviours – Helps 'course correct' behaviours through accountability measures – Acts as a cultural compass – Supports recruitment and progression efforts – Builds subtle links with individuals' values

(*continued*)

Table 6.1 (Continued)

Organizational values eg Youth Services Organization (YSO)	As an organization...... – We stand up for those who struggle to stand up for themselves – We are careful with other people's money – We will always act with honesty and integrity – We do our best to have fun while doing serious work
Team values eg Senior Management Team (SMT)	As a leadership team...... – We can disagree when together but are united when apart – We will model to our teams what it means to show gratitude and care for staff – We will talk about the future and dream big – We will develop plans that inspire our stakeholders, confidence

VALUES TEST – change each value into a question, eg how well are we showing gratitude and care for staff?

What is so important about team belief?

> For a moment, try to recall a time when you were part of a top-performing team where anything felt possible. Try to reimagine the conversations and meetings. What can you recall seeing and hearing? How did it feel to be a part of this team? How was the team different from other teams? How did others describe the team? What did the team believe about itself and its work? How did team belief contribute to the team's performance?

We have asked you to reflect on this because, although belief may not be the most common word in the organizational vocabulary, our own experience as team members, leading teams and team coaching, has shown that reflecting on team beliefs is essential. Interestingly, the well-known quote attributed to Henry Ford, 'whether you think you can, or you think you can't, you're right', when it first appeared a few months after Henry Ford's death in 1947, actually read, 'whether you believe you can do a thing or not, you are right' (*Reader's Digest*, 1947: 64).

Whereas team values have been likened to representing an internal code of behaviour, team beliefs have been discussed as a mindset that tends to be more externally focused on circumstances and how the team chooses to respond (Sandahl and Philips, 2019). Gully *et al* (2002), in their meta-analysis of 67 empirical studies, confirmed that 'at the team level, both team efficacy and potency had positive relationships with performance' (p. 819). They refer to team efficacy as a team's belief that it can successfully perform a specific task, and team potency as the generalized belief of the team in its capabilities, no matter what the task. Similarly, Collins and Parker (2010) have confirmed from their research that 'teams that have positive beliefs about their capability tend to perform more effectively' (p. 1003). They outlined that such teams set higher goals, develop strategies to achieve their goals and are more persistent in the face of setbacks.

Another interesting perspective is the role of leaders. Fransen *et al* (2015) discovered from their research with athletes that when leaders expressed high team confidence, team members' performance increased. In comparison, when leaders expressed low team confidence, team members' performance decreased. It is clear, therefore, that a leader's belief in their team is key for achieving results.

Story: The team member who believed differently
Contributors: Lucy and Paul

We were commissioned by the team leader to carry out a team coaching programme for a senior team. We found that the team was divided into sub-teams who were working well together. With the need for business growth and a changing marketplace in the future, the team identified that they needed to work together more effectively as a unit.

The team did some fantastic work on developing their purpose and agreeing on how they wanted to be known as a team. Whilst exploring their values and beliefs, we sensed that some of the team appeared to see the value of working together as a whole team more than others. As a result, we decided to explore this further.

We asked the question… How important was it for this team to be a team? The team was asked to stand along a continuum ranging from 1 (it wasn't important for the team to be a team) to 10 (it was very important). All team members stood at 9 or 10 except for one who stood at 3. To the team's surprise and our own, the team member standing on the 3 was the team leader.

At this point, we encouraged the team and team leader to explore their different beliefs. The team identified and discussed with the team leader several areas where they believed they could do more as a collective than they could do apart. It was brilliant to observe the openness and honesty in the discussion that followed. In exploring the difference in beliefs and opinions, the team and the team leader became united in their belief that to achieve their growth and performance objectives, they needed to work together as one.

Developing team belief

A team coach is perfectly placed to listen to the team's stories of victory, joy, defeat, uncertainty, friction, frustration and chaos. In these stories will lie clues that uncover patterns of belief, that are either propelling the team forward or holding them back. The stories a team tells will range between truth and myth and the role of the team coach is to safely bring to the team's awareness patterns of team belief. Once awareness has been created, the team coach can either help strengthen useful beliefs, discard limiting beliefs, or develop new ones.

A useful model for getting to the root of an issue is Hawkins and Smith's (2013) four levels of engagement model. Mostly discussed in the context of one-to-one coaching, we believe it is particularly useful for working with teams at the deeper level of beliefs. Hawkins and Turner (2019: 89) have described the four levels as:

- **Level 1:** data and narrative.
- **Level 2:** patterns of behaviour.
- **Level 3:** emotional patterns and triggers.
- **Level 4:** mindset, assumptions, beliefs – the stories we live within.

We would agree that level 4 is 'the most transformational level of engagement' that 'leads to the longest-lasting change' (Hawkins and Turner, 2019, p. 92). Writing about the same model, Hawkins and Smith (2013) have suggested that when coaching at a transformational level, 'the coach uses these four levels to work directly 'in the room' with the issues and immediately rehearse the shifts and changes that have been explored' (p. 41). In our view, this ability to successfully work at a deeper transformational level 'in the room' is further evidence to support the importance of the 'being, doing and knowing' of a team coach discussed in Chapter 2. Especially the 'being' element.

So, what can a team coach do once a team is aware of a belief that they agree to work on? Neenan (2016), in his discussion on cognitive behavioural coaching (CBC), derived from cognitive behavioural therapy (CBT), has highlighted three helpful insights. First, 'you largely feel the way you think'; second, 'no matter how you acquired your unhelpful beliefs, you still choose to subscribe to them today'; and third, 'the way you get rid of or weaken these beliefs is to continually act against them by adopting a more helpful viewpoint' (p. 141). We would suggest that with post-awareness raising, a team coach can help a team to change how they think about a past or future experience. The team can then support each other to maintain their new thinking and mindset. The final section of this chapter details some useful tools for working with team beliefs.

The challenges of team values and beliefs

When individual and team values don't align

A team should only agree on team values if they are serious about the associated behaviour that will be required. If there is an agreement to proceed, a team coach should then ensure appropriate time is spent discussing and agreeing on the team values. If it is rushed or approached like a tick-box exercise, it will do more harm than good. As some of the team may already be sceptical about the seriousness of the organization's values, taking time to robustly discuss and agree on team values is an exercise in commitment itself. The team and not the leader should become the guardians of the team values. During any future discussion on behaviours, any team member should be able to reflect and say, 'we all discussed and agreed on the importance of xx value and the resulting behaviours', which will carry with it the weight of accountability. Nevertheless, despite everyone's best efforts, disagreements on values will occur. Pisarski *et al* (2008) have demonstrated that in teams that have a consistent approach to team values, intra-team conflicts decrease. However, unlike disagreements with an organization's values, in a team, there is nowhere to hide.

Disagreements on values may manifest themselves subtly or more acutely. Few would describe such differences in values as a conflict, but given that conflict has been described as 'when two or more parties perceive that their values or needs are incompatible' (Tillet and French, 1991:7), it technically is. Disagreement on team values requires a similar approach to any conflict resolution. The team coach can play a key role in helping the necessary dialogue take place, safely and respectfully. Creating psychological safety is paramount because as stated by McCann (2012), 'we are much less likely to compromise when our values are under threat' (p. 98). Resolving value disagreements can be an excellent opportunity for the team to learn and develop. Nevertheless, despite everyone's best efforts, conflict resolution will not always be possible. Ultimately a team member may decide to leave, or start a journey that results in the same outcome.

It is very important for the integrity of the team coaching work that a team values exercise is not used cynically to isolate a team member who is perceived to be problematic, nor should it be used to cover up for a lack of leadership on a matter. From the discussion in this section, the importance of recruiting new team members who are aligned to the team values should be evident. In addition, it is also clear from the research presented in Chapter 4 that the more an individual's work is aligned to their values, the greater their motivation, effort, goal attainment and well-being (Deci and Ryan, 2000; McGregor and Doshi, 2015; Linley *et al*, 2010; Sheldon *et al*, 2004).

Can a team have too much belief?

Most people will admit to not easily warming to individuals who display overconfidence. The same is likely to be true of a team who overly believe in their own greatness. The same type of vulnerable confidence discussed for team coaches in Chapter 2, could also benefit teams.

Too much team belief can be a particular issue in the setting of stretch goals. In their research, Porter *et al* (2011), while noting the common practice of setting stretch goals, found that the failure experience of not achieving especially high goals can be extremely demotivating. The demotivation was stronger for low-efficacy teams (teams with a low belief that they can successfully perform a specific task). As a result of their findings, they suggested that the self-setting of goals should be reserved for high-efficacy teams (teams with a high belief that they can successfully perform a specific task). They also suggested that high-efficacy teams should be warned of the dangers of setting especially high goals, given that experiences of failure can demotivate.

In summary, while team values and team beliefs are both essential for top-performing teams, neither are an easy path. We trust this chapter and the tools and techniques to follow can assist team coaches to help teams on this necessary but often overlooked area.

Tools and techniques for developing team values and beliefs

Using tools and techniques

When applying these tools and techniques, it is essential that the team coach or leader builds connection and psychological safety first. The tools and techniques are offered as a support and guide, that when used should feel natural and in 'flow', with the process and steps behind the tools remaining effectively invisible.

TOOL 1: Values Cards – Exploring your team's values

Why use this tool?

Many organizations have developed their spoken and sometimes lived values; however, often teams still have work to do in agreeing on the values that are important for the individuals in the team and the team as a whole.

When to use this tool

At any stage if the team is not clear on what their values are and if there is a lack of alignment of team values.

Resources required

- Values cards, eg The Values Cards.
- Flip chart paper and pens, virtual whiteboard/platform.

How to use this tool

Step 1   Using values cards (or similar), place the cards on the floor or a surface (if using a virtual platform share a pre-prepared montage of the values cards) and ask the team members to choose up to 10 cards that they feel represent the team's values.

Step 2   Ask team members to agree on their 3–5th core values.

Step 3   Ask the team to split into subgroups (if working virtually use break-out rooms). Each subgroup takes a core value and works on developing the value stated as an action. For example, respect could be stated as, 'We will listen deeply and seek to understand each other'.

Step 4   Ask the subgroups to share their values, stated as an action, with the full team. Discuss and agree as a team.

Step 5   Ask the team to consider how they will bring these values to life, in the workplace. Team to agree their next steps. Capture actions.

Top tips for team coaches

- Before starting step 1, spend some time helping the team to understand what values are, including the challenge of 'spoken' versus 'lived' values.

- You may choose to make your own values cards, eg values printed out on card or A5/A4 pieces of card. If using a virtual platform you could create a collage of values cards.

- You can use a similar approach to help team members explore their own values. Exploring personal values can be a powerful way to introduce the subject of values.

Time required

45 minutes.

TOOL 2: Fly on the Wall – Observing our team values and beliefs

Why use this tool?

Ensuring that the team values and beliefs are aligned will enable the team to work together as a collective rather than a group of individuals. Agreeing on the team values and beliefs will bind the team together and forge a deeper connection.

When to use this tool

- At a stage of development when the team is ready and able to review and reflect on its own performance rather than having an external person share their observations.

- If new members join the team, it is helpful to check the alignment of values and beliefs.

- At a point in the team coaching programme when the team have been working together for at least half a day or more.

Resources required

- Post-it notes or similar.
- Flip chart paper and pens, virtual whiteboard/platform.

How to use this tool

Step 1   Discuss what values and beliefs are with the team.

Step 2   Ask the team to imagine they were a 'fly on the wall' observing the team in action and think about what they would notice about which values and beliefs were present. Ask the team members to individually reflect on their observations, and then capture what values and beliefs they see present in the team on Post-it notes or capture on the virtual platform (one Post-it note per value or belief).

Step 3   Have two flip charts on the wall or floor (or virtual whiteboards), one for values and one for beliefs. Team members place their Post-it notes on each of the flip charts, as appropriate. If working virtually, use options such as an annotate or the more advanced functionality available on some virtual platforms (eg virtual Post-it notes).

Step 4   Ask the team to look for key themes and cluster similar values and beliefs together. Discuss and agree on key values and beliefs (if working virtually, using the more advanced functionality available on some virtual platforms, eg grouping of virtual Post-it notes is recommended).

Step 5   Ask the team to consider what values and beliefs they will need to achieve their purpose. Discuss with each other.

Step 6   Ask the team to consider which values and beliefs are still relevant and what is missing.

Step 7   Capture any values and beliefs that are missing.

Step 8   Ask the team to agree on which 3–5 values and 3–5 beliefs will be most important to this team and record them.

Step 9   Ask the team to consider and capture the key actions that will ensure they bring these values and beliefs to life in their interactions and work together.

Top tips for team coaches

- It may be helpful to explain what values and beliefs are at the start of the exercise.

- Alternatively, you can ask team members to stand up and step back from where they were sitting and then imagine they are the 'fly on the wall' with the team sitting in front of them and ask them to think about what they notice.

- This exercise can also be used with a team when completing an actual business activity, either held in the normal environment of the team or at another neutral setting. Allow the team to run a usual meeting, so that team coaches can observe values and beliefs and feed back if their observations are different from the team's. At the end of the meeting or at an appropriate time, ask the team to reflect on the values and beliefs that were present.

Time required

45– 60 minutes.

TOOL 3: Living Your Values – Understanding good and bad day behaviours

Why use this tool?

To help the team to reflect on their values and consider how these link to team behaviours. To enable the team to identify how they demonstrate their values in their daily interactions and to help them know how to ensure they adopt helpful behaviours to improve team performance.

When to use this tool

- At any stage of development when the team is ready and able to review and reflect on its own performance.

- If new members join the team, it is helpful to check the alignment of values and beliefs.

Resources required

- Values template as illustrated.
- Flip chart paper and pens, virtual whiteboard/platform.
- Flip chart paper with values template headings detailed (question 1 written on flip chart sheet 1, and so on) or share template virtually.

Tool 3 Example of values template

Question 1	Question 2	Question 3	Question 4	Question 5
Values stated as an action	Good day behaviours	Bad day behaviours	Where do we want to get to?	How can they measure?
- What are your values stated as actions?	- What would good look, feel and sound like?	- What would bad look, feel and sound like?	- How can they shift bad day behaviours into good day behaviours?	- How will they know if they are good or bad day behaviours?

How to use this tool?

Step 1   Place five flip charts up in the room or use the values template illustrated.

Step 2   Ask the team to first consider question 1. What are your values stated as actions? Eg value of respect, 'We can disagree when together but are united when apart'.

Capture and agree.

Step 3   Ask the team now to consider question 2. For each value identified, what would good look, feel and sound like? (good day behaviours).

Capture and agree.

Step 4   Ask the team now to consider question 3. For each value identified, what would bad look, feel and sound like? (bad day behaviours).

Capture and agree.

Step 5   Ask the team now to consider question 4. How can they shift bad day behaviours into good day behaviours?

Capture what actions they will take.

Step 6 Ask the team now to consider question 5. How can they measure these values going forward? How will they know if they are good or bad day behaviours? How will they know when a shift in behaviour has taken place?

Capture key insights and actions.

Top tips for team coaches

It would be useful for the team to understand what their team values are before embarking on this exercise and to have ideally explored the difference between 'spoken' and 'lived' values.

Time required

30–45 minutes.

TOOL 4: Growth Mindset – Understanding how our beliefs affect our mindset

Why use this tool?

To help teams understand how their beliefs impact the mindset they adopt and consequently how this impacts the team's performance. This tool helps the team to understand that mindset and beliefs can be changed.

When to use this tool

- At an early stage of the team coaching programme to help the team identify their helpful and unhelpful beliefs and mindsets.
- To reconnect the team members with their beliefs or when new members join the team.

Resources required

- Flip chart paper and pens, virtual whiteboard/platforms.
- Masking tape.
- Two flip charts with the fixed mindset diagram illustrated on one and the growth mindset diagram on the other, or posters could be printed of each (alternatively display both illustrations on a virtual platform).

How to use this tool

Step 1 Place flip charts or posters of fixed and growth mindsets at different ends of the room and join them together with a line on the floor of masking tape (alternatively, mark out on a virtual whiteboard/platform).

Step 2   Briefly explain the work of Carol Dweck (2012), regarding growth and fixed mindset:

- In a fixed mindset, people believe their basic abilities, their intelligence, their talents, are just fixed traits. They have a certain amount and that doesn't change. Success becomes about proving you are either smart or talented. In contrast, people with a growth mindset understand that their talents and abilities can be developed through effort and persistence. They believe everyone can get smarter if they decide to work at it (Dweck, 2012). In our experience, the same principles can be applied to teams and organizations (see Chapter 10 for a more detailed explanation).

Step 3   First, ask the team to work in pairs and think about a time when they had a limiting belief that prevented them from learning a new skill, but they are now able to perform the skill well.

Step 4   Ask the pairs to explore and discuss what they did to change this belief and their fixed mindset to a growth mindset.

Step 5   Discuss as a team some examples from the pairs. Focus on what they did to shift their belief and mindset. Capture the learning points.

Tool 4   Illustration of a fixed and a growth mindset

Fixed Mindset	Growth Mindset
• We are only good at certain things • We give up when it gets too hard • We hate challenges • We take feedback and criticism personally • We don't like doing what is new to us	• We can be good at anything • We try until we get the result we want • We embrace challenges • We welcome feedback and criticism • We like exploring things that are new to us

SOURCE Adapted from Dweck (2012)

Step 6   Ask the group to now stand up by the fixed and growth mindset continuum. Ask the team members to stand on the line where they feel this team is now concerning a fixed and growth mindset (if working virtually, ask each member to annotate where they are on the continuum).

Step 7   Ask who would like to share what made them decide to stand where they are. Explore with the team members what could they do as a team to help them adopt more of a growth mindset and challenge fixed beliefs.
Capture key themes.

Step 8   Split the team into subgroups and ask each subgroup to think about areas of mindset and belief that are fixed and discuss actions to help make positive shifts (if working virtually use breakout rooms).

Step 9   Ask the subgroups to share their insights. Place all the actions captured together and ask team members to vote on the top three actions they feel are important for the team to take forward.

Step 10   Review the votes and agree on the top three actions.

Top tips for team coaches

Time permitting, you could ask the team to stand (or place themselves virtually) on the continuum for each aspect of fixed and growth mindset, eg where do you think the team is in terms of embracing challenges or avoiding challenges and so on.

Time required

90 minutes.

Tool 5: Immunity to Change – Exploring our negative beliefs

Why use this tool?

Often team members and teams come up with many actions and objectives to improve their effectiveness and performance; however, they don't always achieve them. Helping teams identify what is stopping them or getting in the way of achieving their objectives can be very helpful.

When to use this tool

At any stage of the team coaching programme. It can be particularly helpful to use this tool again at the end, to review commitment to actions.

Resources required

- Immunity to change template or similar. Adapted from the work of Kegan *et al* (2009).

- Virtual whiteboard/platform if working virtually.

How to use this tool

Step 1   Ask team members to think about any ideas they have for an improvement goal that they want to achieve and capture in column 1.

Step 2   In column 2, ask team members to state their goal and one to three reasons why they want to achieve it.

Step 3   Next, ask team members to think about what they are doing or not doing, instead of focusing on the goal and capture in column 3.

Step 4   Ask team members to capture in column 4 what hidden commitments are stopping them from focusing on the goal, eg fears.

Step 5   Ask team members to then consider and capture in column 5 what is the belief or big assumption that is leading to this competing commitment, eg I assume that if I did... then... would happen.

Step 6   Ask team members to think about what they will do to overcome the limiting assumption and then consider an experiment to test out whether they still hold the assumption. Capture in column 6.

Top tips for team coaches

- This exercise can be used individually with team members and as a collective team.

- It may be helpful to use it individually first with team members so they are familiar with how it works before working as a whole team.

Time required

30 minutes approximately for using individually, 45 minutes for working as a team.

Tool 5 Immunity to Change template and example

1. Ideas for improvement	2. Commitment (improvement goal)	3. Doing/not doing	4. Hidden competing commitment	5. Big assumption	6. Actions & assumption test
Improve my organizational skills	I am committed to introducing a daily, weekly and monthly planner and calendar to schedule my deadlines and key milestones for projects to be more organized and have more time at home **Reasons** 1. This will enable me to set realistic project timescales 2. I will have clear sight of forthcoming deadlines and workload 3. I will have more time to spend with my family	**Doing** Agreeing to take on additional tasks I work late in the evening I get distracted by constantly checking my e-mail and phone for messages **Not Doing** Setting realistic dates Creating quality time with my family	I am committed to… Not wanting to upset people by saying no to work Not leaving on time in case it leaves a bad impression Not taking time for myself	I assume that if I say no to work that people will think I am less committed to the job I assume that if I leave on time then people will think I am lazy	1. Implement my new planner and calendar starting from tomorrow 2. Review my planner and calendar before agreeing to take on new work 3. Leave on time two nights a week **Test** Request feedback about the impact of my actions above with my Line manager

SOURCE Adapted from Kegan *et al* (2009)

TOOL 6: *Different Truths – Challenging our team beliefs*

Why use this tool?

Helping a team to become aware of their team beliefs will enable them to strengthen their useful beliefs, challenge or discard limiting ones, and/or develop new, helpful beliefs.

When to use this tool

At any time during the team coaching programme when it will be helpful to explore the team's beliefs.

Resources required

Flip chart paper and pens, virtual whiteboard/platform.

How to use this tool

Step 1　Discuss what beliefs are and examples of their team beliefs. Capture these.

Step 2　Ask the team to think about a challenging work situation they are currently experiencing.

Step 3　Explore with the team what their beliefs are regarding the situation. Capture these.

Step 4　Divide a flip chart or virtual whiteboard into two columns. In column 1 capture the consequences of holding this belief and in column 2 capture the benefits.

Step 5　Ask the team to explore different stakeholder perspectives or potential 'different truths' on the situation, ie what would others say (other individuals, teams and stakeholders)?

Step 6　Explore what might be limiting the team's thinking, by asking the team to reflect on what the future requires of them as a team and what advice they would give themselves from that future place.

Step 7 Hypothesize and imagine what could happen if the team changed its thinking on the matter and adopted different beliefs. Capture the team's thoughts.

Step 8 What could these beliefs be? What would the team hear, see and feel if these new beliefs were in place? What would others experience (other individuals, teams and stakeholders)?

Step 9 Agree as a team to either retain the old belief or select a new belief.

Step 10 If agreed, select a new belief that would be most helpful for the team in this situation. Explore the consequences and benefits of adopting this new belief, both for the team and others. What would be helpful to retain from the old belief?

Step 11 Discuss and agree on how the new thinking will be evidenced, who will do what with whom and when. Highlight any mitigation measures for identified risks and how the team will keep a check on their progress.

Step 12 Agree on learnings from the team dialogue and capture key actions.

Top tips for team coaches

- It is important to build psychological safety and contract clearly around confidentiality before this exercise.
- This exercise can be used in different ways, for example using flip charts to capture outputs and actions, or by posting flip charts or the questions on sheets around the room, with the team moving around answering each question. Alternatively, the exercise can be adapted for use on a virtual platform.
- The questions can be used working with the full team or with the team split into subgroups. It can be useful for the subgroups to explore their view of the team's beliefs and then share their outputs with the full team at the end of the exercise (if working with subgroups virtually, use breakout rooms).

Time required

45 minutes.

Reflecting on team values and beliefs

- What do you value most about working in this team?
- What does the team need to value or believe, in order to achieve their purpose?
- What values are important to this team?
- What values are important to you as a member of this team?
- What do you believe about yourself?
- Why is this important to you?
- What do you believe about the people in your team?

Team awareness 07

Why is it important to develop awareness both within and beyond a team?

Defining awareness

How aware are you? How aware are you of your own thinking? How aware are you of the relationship between your own thinking, your feelings and ultimately your behaviours? How aware are you of what you see, hear, smell, taste and touch? How aware are you of other people's thoughts, feelings and behaviours? In our experience, most people will answer these questions by stating they are not aware enough. They will often say they would like to be more aware, more in tune with the connection between their thoughts, feelings and actions, more in touch with their senses and ultimately more attuned to other people and the world around them. Reasons for not being more aware usually include the busyness of life, imprisonment to routine, and a lack of awareness about the benefits of becoming more awake.

What if the cost of not being aware is too high? De Mello (1990), in his book entitled *Awareness*, has suggested that 'most people, even though they don't know it, are asleep. They're born asleep, they live asleep, they marry in their sleep, they breed children in their sleep, they die in their sleep without ever waking up. They never understand the loveliness and beauty of this thing we call human existence' (p. 5). We will argue in this chapter that for individuals, teams and organizations, awareness is not just a useful thing to do, it is a necessity. Without awareness, we are trapped in a cycle of sameness. Without awareness, we are blind to the choices before us. Without awareness, change flounders.

'The quality or state of being aware', while similar, is not mindfulness, which is 'the practice of maintaining a non-judgmental state of heightened or complete awareness of one's thoughts, emotions, or experiences on a moment-to-moment basis' (Merriam-Webster.com). When we are aware, we make judgements, we make decisions, we give ourselves a platform for considering making change.

This chapter will explore the benefits of team coach awareness, team awareness of group dynamics, team systemic awareness, and team individual and collective self-awareness.

The psychology behind awareness

What humans pay attention to

Without self-awareness, we could not 'take the perspectives of others, exercise self-control, produce creative accomplishments, or experience pride and high self-esteem' (Silvia and O'Brien, 2004: 475). However, if being self-aware is so important to the human experience, why is it so difficult?

To explain, imagine sharing an office with seven colleagues. Using the estimate that we each speak on average 16,000 words per day (David and Congleton, 2019), this means in our office environment we could be exposed to 112,000 words in a day. Now count the words you speak and the words that only ever appear as thoughts. Now consider everything else you hear, see, smell, taste and touch. The reality is our brains could not cope. Thankfully we are 'blessed with a mechanism that continually seeks to lower our awareness to the level of just enough to get by' (Whitmore, 2009: 36). As humans, our subconscious automatically deletes, distorts and generalizes whole portions of what we really experience (Bandler and Grinder, 1975) and for good reason.

Awareness as a catalyst of change

It is difficult to change what we are not aware of. Lee (2003) has suggested that 'without awareness, we are controlled, like a robot, by programmed patterns of stimulus and response' (p. 57). Furthermore, awareness creates choice, as it allows us to examine our biases and question if they are appropriate or useful. Whitmore (2009), when discussing change, has highlighted that after we become aware, we need to take responsibility for our own change journey. Similarly, Goleman (2006) in his influential book *Emotional Intelligence* has explained that after self-awareness comes self-regulation.

However, it is not just a matter of becoming aware and then deciding what to change. Awareness is an ongoing part of how we change. Stober's

(2006) Awareness-Choice-Execution (ACE) Cycle of Change model highlights how learnings from execution must be fed back into the person's awareness, completing the cycle of change.

Surely it would be much easier if other people could just tell us what we need to be aware of? The truth is, that is not how humans are made. Few people like being told what they should think, feel or do. Along with the psychological need to love and be loved (relatedness), we also have a desire to make our own choices in alignment to our values (autonomy), as well as to each fulfil our own innate potential (competence) (Deci and Ryan, 2000). As humans, we are born to create, to think and to make choices for ourselves. Therefore, the more a person experiences their own moments of awareness, the more likely they are to consider changing. Whitmore (2009) has described self-generated awareness as 'infinitely richer, more immediate, more real' (p. 36).

Developing awareness of what happens when we communicate

When you communicate directly with another person, how aware are you of what is going on beyond the words you speak? To help us become more aware when communicating, Kantor (2012) has proposed four levels of communication:

- **Level 1: The four action stances.** They include: move (initiate a communication); follow (support another's communication); oppose (challenge a communication); and bystand (reflect without agreeing or disagreeing). The importance of pitch, rhythm and tone is highlighted. People with a high level of communicative competency take one of four stances as the need arises (see Figure 7.1)

- **Level 2: Domains of communication.** Viewed as the orientation through which we make our communication. These include making communication with: affect (your own and others' feelings); power (getting things done); and means (what it all means). Which domain we choose to communicate in can represent what matters to us at a deeper level. A balance of using all three over time is recommended for maximum functioning.

- **Level 3: Systems in control of speech.** It proposes that our speech takes place in the context of operating systems, that each provide a set of implicit rules. Three operating systems are highlighted, including: open (work gets dome through deliberation and exploration of each other's

Figure 7.1   The four action stances

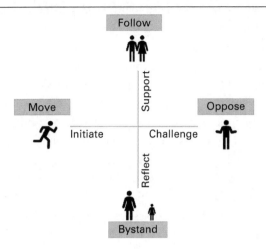

SOURCE Adapted from Kantor (2012)

needs); closed (the backbone of most organizations with an emphasis on leadership, tradition and process adherence); and random (associated with start-ups, with an emphasis on making new rules and infinite possibilities). While we are likely to prefer a certain system, we can make shifts if the situation requires. Each operating system has values and limitations.

- **Level 4: Identity and personal stories.** In level four we answer the identity question of 'who am I?' through the stories we tell ourselves and others. While levels one to three describe communication behaviours, level four represents some of the sources for how we choose to communicate.

If we reflect on communication at these four levels, we can start to become aware of things that were previously invisible. We can start to develop awareness by listening beyond the words.

Developing awareness of our implicit bias

The Implicit Association Test (2011), also known as the IAT, was authored and is used for research by academics from the University of Washington, University of Virginia, Harvard University, and Yale University. To date, they claim that some 25 million people have visited the site and contributed to their scientific research on implicit bias (our conscious and unconscious preferences).

The test results often reveal that most people have an automatic preference for: light skin relative to dark skin; thin people relative to fat people; straight people relative to gay people; and young people over older people. In addition, the test results also often reveal a relative link between liberal arts and females and between science and males (Project Implicit, 2019). Thankfully, having an implicit bias does not mean a person will act upon it. When we make ourselves aware of our unconscious preferences, it gives us an opportunity to regulate our own thinking against potential bias. Interestingly, they warn on their website, 'If you are unprepared to encounter interpretations that you might find objectionable, please do not proceed further' (Project Implicit, 2019).

Developing awareness of group dynamics

In Chapter 2, group dynamics was referred to as 'all the invisible and emotional forces and communications between individuals in a group' (Hardingham *et al*, 2004: 168). Becoming aware of such forces could seem like an impossible task. Usefully, Thornton (2016), based on the work of S H Foulkes, has outlined nine of the most significant group dynamic processes (see Table 7.1).

Table 7.1   Group dynamic processes

Group dynamic process	Description of group dynamic process
The Group Matrix	Consists of: the 'dynamic matrix', the totality of our communication and history, both past and present; and the 'foundation matrix', our broader biological and cultural heritage.
Communication	Viewed as anything we can attach a meaning to.
Translation	The process of putting into words, communication that has been made in some other way.
Mirroring	How we non-consciously compare current experiences with previous experiences, to help us make sense of them.
Exchange	Experience of the new, different or the previously unknown.
Resonance	When we resonate with another or others.

(*continued*)

Table.7.1   (Continued)

Group dynamic process	Description of group dynamic process
Condenser phenomena	Describes shifts in the group, that take place when previously unconscious or hidden material is shared.
Location	Is the concept that every event, even if it appears to be only confined to one or two individuals, in some way involves the whole group.
The Reflection Process	The Reflection Process describes when a group member tells a story or recalls a conversation. The other group members pick up and feel the emotions attached to the story.

SOURCE Adapted from Thornton (2016)

Developing systemic awareness

We each exist in one overall system. Each person's system consists of many parts, for example, our family, community, workplace, profession, politics, environment and nation-state. The dictionary has defined a system as 'a regularly interacting or interdependent group of items forming a unified whole' (Merriam-Webster.com). We cannot find a dictionary definition of a system that specifically includes people, therefore we would propose that a system can be described as 'the interactions and connections, both conscious and unconscious, between people and things that make them part of a unified whole'.

To better understand what is meant by a system, it may be helpful to reflect on the following questions:

- How would you describe the system you are part of?
- What parts of the system can you clearly identify?
- How aware are you of the interactions and interdependencies of the various parts of your system?
- How much do these interactions and interdependencies influence your life?
- Which parts of your system need attention?

Reaching agreement on the idea of a unified whole is slightly more challenging. The idea of oneness and connectedness of everything can result in conversations on religious faith, non-religion-based spirituality, quantum physics, and our connectedness through nature.

While our individual views may differ concerning each of these, many people will agree:

- we are all connected in some way;
- our actions can have consequences we may never become aware of;
- despite our best efforts, we can't control everything;
- there is a liberation in knowing that we cannot control everything;
- sometimes we have to put our trust in something bigger than ourselves without fully understanding it.

The idea of being unified as part of one system became very clear during the COVID-19 2020 pandemic. With the virus spreading across the globe, it highlighted our connection both at a physical and also a deeper human and emotional level.

It has been suggested that thinking about this wider system – systemic thinking – is a relatively new scientific paradigm. We have existed under a worldview that utilizes a mostly mechanistic and reductionist approach, which is dominated by linear thinking and looks to blame an individual (Cavanagh, 2006; Senge, 2006). As an example, at the time of the 1995 collapse of Barings Bank, the name 'Nick Leeson' became synonymous with the event, despite well-discussed systemic issues. In contrast, systemic thinking describes systems that: are complex; exist in the past, present and future; are full of hidden dynamics; and will 'sacrifice members in order to achieve coherence and completeness' (Whittington, 2016: 12).

Becoming systemically aware implies recognizing connections both visible and invisible. It is about bringing into our consciousness that which we may usually ignore. Asking questions we may not like the answer to.

Considerations for awareness in organizations

The impact of not being aware of the system

It has been suggested that for an organization to be healthy, it must think about the entire system in which it exists. Ignoring the system can result in an organization losing its competitive advantage or suffering from inertia. In addition, it is proposed that an organization needs to embrace 'systems thinking', as a way of doing business (Whittington, 2016). Therefore, it is not enough to be systemically aware – an organization needs to think and act systemically.

Systemic awareness and thinking demands that organizations ask tough questions of themselves and others. It requires decisions to be made in service of the overall system. An example of the difficulty of moving from systemic awareness to action is evident in the perceived slowness, in the eyes of environmental campaigners, of organizational responses to climate change. On climate change there is an awareness and broad agreement that radical change is required; nevertheless, the journey from awareness to action is littered with challenges, as different parts of the system compete for attention.

The system has a power that needs to be respected and understood. We have both witnessed during our corporate and coaching careers that complex systems sacrifice individuals, teams, organization initiatives and indeed entire organizations. In addition, we regularly hear individuals and teams talk about the existence of harmful organizational silos, of the organization being too internally focused or of examples where there is a perceived lack of action on issues everyone appears to be openly aware of.

It is our view that team coaching can help individuals, teams and organizations safely reveal and examine what is not being said. Team coaching, at its heart, is about developing systemic awareness in a way that encourages purposeful action.

Developing team awareness

Team awareness

This section will explore the importance of developing: team coach awareness; team awareness of group dynamics; team systemic awareness; and team individual and collective self-awareness (see Figure 7.2). Our suggested areas of focus are not significantly different from the findings of Hastings and Pennington (2019), who highlighted from their study of experienced team coaches that one of the main reasons team coaches use a range of methods, tools and approaches is to act as a catalyst to help develop team self-awareness and insight. They further noted that 'all participants aligned in describing their methods as providing insight through data and assessment, educating and developing self-awareness, and challenging or pointing

Figure 7.2 The key elements of developing team awareness

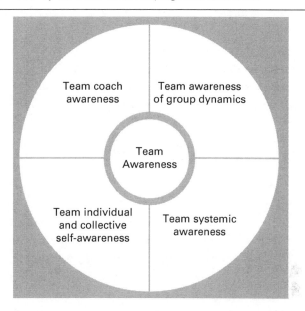

things out in the moment' (p. 181). Without team awareness, change cannot take place. Without change, a team is unlikely to survive.

Developing team coach awareness

For the team coach to help the team develop its awareness, it is our experience that the team coach should become a vehicle of awareness, in service to the team and its wider system. From the first moment the team coach is engaged by a team, they are on a journey of awareness. Each conversation, correspondence, meeting and visit to the team's working space can provide the team coach with valuable information. Discussions around contracting, as well as the various forms of diagnostic methods, each offer an excellent opportunity for the team coach to develop their awareness of the team. In addition, working with another team coach, always our preference when possible, is an excellent source for developing team coach awareness. What one team coach misses, another may become aware of. By becoming aware of things that others rarely see or comment on, not only is the team coach able to increase the quality of their work with the team, they are also able to role-model what it means to be more fully aware.

Chapter 2 discussed how team coaches, by using how they are feeling 'in the moment', are themselves instruments for creating awareness. However, having feelings is not enough. The team coach needs to have the confidence, courage, connection and experience to know when to use what they are feeling in the service of the team.

In addition, it is important for the team to be aware of the boundaries in the role of a team coach. Given the complexities of team coaching and the ease with which an intervention can be derailed, it is essential, as highlighted in Chapter 3, that the team coach continually contracts with the team.

Team awareness of group dynamics

There are two key elements to team awareness of group dynamics: firstly, educating the team in group dynamics. It is our experience that individuals and teams benefit greatly from the insight and team self-awareness generated by what has been described as 'providing psycho-education' (Hastings and Pennington, 2019: 184) or, in other words, education on the psychology of the human mind. By making the invisible visible, teams can reflect on new ways of relating, thinking and working. In our work, we have detected a desire and fascination, both with individuals and teams, for learning about how humans work and don't work, concerning each other. Therefore it is important that the team coach is self-aware of providing psycho-education that serves the team coaching intervention, in contrast to their own interests or the curiosity of the team.

Secondly, the team coach needs to use what they themselves are witnessing and feeling, both when with the team and apart, to help the team develop an awareness of the group dynamic. Making psycho-education live, relevant and experiential can act as an antidote to spending too much time effectively in a teaching role. Jones *et al* (2019) note how by 'considering the multiple perspectives of team members simultaneously and observing and interpreting dynamic interactions' (p. 74), a team coach can develop a team's awareness. We believe that one of team coaching's strongest assets is its ability to help teams develop their own awareness on what is not being said. However, when a team struggles to do this, it can be helpful for the team coach to call out specific examples and ask the team to reflect.

Some illustrative examples of the kind of things we would say as team coaches include:

- I've noticed in the last 10 minutes some tension (or joy) in the room and I'm curious about what others have felt and what that might be telling us.

- There is something I've noticed that I would like to share. When listening to your discussion in the last 45 minutes, most of the team appear to stop engaging at the first sign of conflict. It's as if there is a fear of saying what needs to be said. This could lead to important information not being discussed. How would you describe how the team manages conflict?

- I've noticed a change in energy and tone when you talk about xx leader (or stakeholder) compared to when you talk about xx leader (or stakeholder). I'm curious about this and wonder how you would describe your relationship with these leaders?

- I have observed that since we have worked together, each time you agree on deadlines, when they are reviewed, on many occasions they are not completed. I'm wondering how representative this is of how you work as a team.

Team systemic awareness and constellations

To be as clear as possible, our definition of team coaching intentionally uses the phrase 'together, with others and within the wider environment', instead of the word system. However, our choice of words does not make our approach any less systemic. We stated in Chapter 1 that 'a team will only fully succeed if it is aware of, understands, acknowledges, interacts and ultimately serves the stakeholders in its wider environment'. Whittington (2016) has described systemic coaching as coaching that 'acknowledges, illuminates and releases the system dynamics' (p. 37) so that each part of the system can function with ease. O'Connor and Cavanagh (2016) have highlighted that it is the 'system's insight' (p. 488) that makes team coaching possible.

Examples of stakeholders that we believe are important for a team to consider, in the past, present and future, include:

- other team members;
- direct reports of the team members;
- other teams within the organization;
- the staff within the organization;
- the board and company shareholders;
- client teams and partner organizations;
- suppliers;
- end consumers;

- communities, wider society and our eco-system;
- government bodies and other influencing bodies.

In our experience, constellations are extremely powerful for illuminating the invisible and unspoken dynamics of relationships within the system. A constellation has been described as 'a three-dimensional spatial model, sometimes described as a living map' that can be used to 'illuminate new information and liberate fresh resources' (Whittington, 2016: 36). We regularly use drawings, wooden models of people or empty chairs to create a 'living map' that helps illuminate the real dynamics behind multiple stakeholders. Elements relating to the past, present and future need to be recognized, acknowledged and given their place, in order for the system to come to a place of ease. An example we have come across several times is team members who have loyalty to something in the past (an old boss who was pushed out of the organization, a part of the business that has been sold off, a change the team did not agree with, and so on). Often the memory of what has happened is forgotten, not appreciated or disrespected by the current organization, creating harmful forces whose source may remain outside the consciousness of all those concerned. Constellations can help illuminate that which has remained hidden.

Story: Creating team awareness by using constellations
Contributor: Lucy

Working with a senior retail team we decided to physically explore their connections and relationships within their organizational system using a constellations exercise. One team member stood in the middle of the room to represent their team. Other team members, each representing a stakeholder, stood at different places around the room. The distance each stakeholder representative stood away from their own team indicated the strength of the relationship with the team.

This simple exercise helped the team to become aware that the stakeholder that they needed the strongest connection with was actually their weakest relationship. As a result, they decided to embark on a team of teams approach to team coaching, with both teams embarking on a team coaching journey together.

Team individual and collective self-awareness

It is vital that during the team coaching intervention, each individual team member develops self-awareness and understands what this means for how they relate to themselves, each other, the team as a whole and the team's stakeholders. However, this is not enough. The team as a whole needs to know how it relates to its own team members and each of the key stakeholders. Chapter 8 on relatedness will discuss the benefits of understanding team and individual personality traits, as well as developing team emotional intelligence.

Hastings and Pennington (2019), when discussing how team coaches create awareness, in addition to the already mentioned challenging team dynamics 'in the moment' and providing psycho-education, have also drawn attention to team coaches' use of team assessment or diagnostic tools. Examples of team assessments include the Team Connect 360 diagnostic (Hawkins, 2017), the Team Diagnostic Survey (Wageman *et al*, 2008) and our own 'Creating Team Edge Profile' (CTEP) diagnostic instrument (2015). The Creating Team Edge Profile consists of 42 questions – six for each characteristic. Typically, respondees include the team members themselves, other internal teams or groups, client teams or groups and senior organizational stakeholders. To provide anonymity, responses are reported by each key grouping, at an aggregated level. As outlined in Table 3.3, our preference is to conduct one-to-one interviews with each team member and then follow this up, by issuing a team 360 diagnostic for the team and the selected stakeholders. Tool 1 later in this chapter will illustrate one question from each of the seven characteristics, in what we refer to as the 'Creating the team edge – team mini questionnaire'.

While individual psychometric tools are useful, as discussed in Chapter 3 and 8, they should not be prioritized before one-to-one interviews and the use of a 360 team diagnostic. Nevertheless, we are both qualified in various psychometric tools, including the Myers-Briggs Type Indicator® (MBTI®) (Lucy) and the Lumina Learning® suite of psychometric tools, including their signature product Lumina Spark® (Paul). A recent addition to the Lumina Spark® model includes the Team Viewer application which allows coachees to visually explore their team's dynamics. This includes an aggregate of the team's personality profile that can then be compared to other teams' aggregated personality profiles. This online feature is highly interactive and can create powerful team insights.

The challenges of team awareness

Can developing greater team awareness ever do more harm than good?

If feedback is provided, even if delivered professionally and with the purest of intent, it may still not develop awareness. Hardingham *et al* (2004) have argued that while feedback can lead to increased self-awareness, this often isn't the case. Jones *et al* (2016), while discussing feedback in one-to-one coaching, discovered that coaching without multi-source feedback 'had a significantly stronger positive impact on outcomes' (p. 31). These findings are consistent with the research of Kluger and DeNisi (1996), who discovered only a moderate impact between feedback and performance. In addition, they also found that one-third of feedback actually resulted in lower performance (see Chapter 8 for further discussion on the challenges of giving feedback).

The general aversion to receiving even well-intentioned feedback can be explained by our neurological disposition for moving away from a threat and towards a reward. Rock's (2008) SCARF (status, certainty, autonomy, relatedness and fairness) model is useful in explaining what may be happening. We may perceive the feedback to be an attack on our status, our level of certainty, our autonomy, the status of our relationships, or we may just perceive what has been said to be unfair.

So what can a team coach do to ensure feedback actually creates useful awareness? We would suggest:

- Contract clearly on the importance of feedback when team coaching.
- Develop a strong knowledge of the team context.
- Ensure that comments used from one-to-one interviews are non-attributable.
- Ensure that team 360 diagnostic reports are aggregated, so that individuals are not identifiable. Exercise caution and judgement if there is only one respondent in any feedback group.
- Maximize the use of 'in the moment' feedback, based on your own observations of the team in action.
- Ask the team to set their own criteria and give themselves feedback.
- Ensure feedback focuses on the impact of the behaviour, not only the behaviour itself.

The challenges of using personality psychometrics when developing team awareness

Despite our position that when team coaching, one-to-one interviews and team 360 diagnostics should be prioritized before using psychometrics, there are some procurers of team coaching who have a strong loyalty to the use of personality psychometrics. It is important to explain that while personality psychometrics are extremely useful in generating insights quickly and in creating a shared vocabulary (Rogers, 2016), in the context of team coaching, learning about the team as a collective, within the context of its stakeholders, needs to take priority.

If personality psychometrics are used as part of the team coaching intervention, it is important to:

- ensure you are using a tool that is strongly validated;
- allow enough time to professionally debrief the profile (it can take up to a day to do this properly);
- avoid labels and putting people into boxes, and instead talk about personality preferences and traits;
- use a tool that best compliments the team coaching effort.

Tools and techniques for developing team awareness

Using tools and techniques

When applying these tools and techniques, it is essential that the team coach or leader builds connection and psychological safety first. The tools and techniques are offered as a support and guide, that when used should feel natural and in 'flow', with the process and steps behind the tools remaining effectively invisible.

TOOL 1: Systemic Awareness – Understanding team strengths and areas of development

Why use this tool?

Helping teams to understand how they measure up against the seven characteristics of the 'Creating the Team Edge' framework (purpose, identity, values and beliefs, awareness, relatedness, ways of working, transformation) will enable them to become clearer on their strengths and areas of development. Asking their stakeholders' views of where the team is can provide valuable insights. This can help them to then focus on what strengths they can leverage and areas that they may want to pay attention to.

When to use this tool

At the contracting and discovery stage of a team's development journey.

Resources required

Questions to explore with stakeholders.

How to use this tool

Step 1   Agree with the team which stakeholders or customers they want to obtain feedback from.

Step 2   Arrange one-to-one interviews to explore the seven characteristics of ' Creating the Team Edge'.

Step 3   Suggested questions you may want to explore with the stakeholders or customers:

- View of the effectiveness of the team – how effectively do they think the team works together?
- What is the view of the team's leadership? What helps the team to be high performing and what gets in the way?
- What do they think is the purpose of the team?
- How is the team described or known within the organization?
- What do they think are key values and beliefs of this team?
- What do they believe are the strengths and areas of development for this team?
- How well do they get on as a team? How do they deal with conflict?

- How effective are their meetings? How good are they at decision making?
- How does the team innovate and continue to grow?
- What do you need from this team?
- How would you describe your relationship with this team?
- What works well?
- What could be improved?

Step 4   Collate a summary of the responses to be able to feed back to the team.

Top tips for team coaches

- To ensure anonymity, it is important to have more than two stakeholders or customer interview responses to feed back.
- We would encourage you to explore and probe further with these questions.

Time required

45 minutes.

TOOL 2: Support and Challenge – Getting the balance between team support and challenge

Why use this tool?

High-performing teams establish a balance of support and challenge within the team. Teams that operate with too much challenge may leave some members feeling stressed. Equally, too little challenge can cause apathy. If a team understands what is required of them within their organizational context, they are more likely to be successful and achieve high performance.

When to use this tool

- At the beginning of the team coaching programme to help set the tone and contract for how the team will work together.
- For teams that are not challenging each other as effectively or as often as they could.
- For teams that need to establish a climate of support.

Resources required

- Support and challenge model (adapted from Sanford, 2017) on posters, A3 cards, flip charts or share on a virtual whiteboard/platform.
  - The support and challenge model has two axes: the vertical axis represents the level of support and the horizontal axis the level of challenge. Both axes are labelled from low to high.
  - There are four quadrants in the model:
    1 Low support and low challenge represent 'apathy'.
    2 Low support and high challenge represent 'anxiety'.
    3 Low challenge and high support represent 'comfort'.
    4 High challenge and high support represent 'growth'.
- Flip chart paper and pens, virtual whiteboard/platform.
- Floor space to experientially and physically explore the model.

How to use this tool?

Step 1　Clear a large space within the room and place the model on the floor using posters or A3 cards (or adapt for use virtually).

Step 2　Explain the Support and Challenge model to the team and the four different quadrants.

Step 3　Ask the team what behaviours or conditions would they see in each quadrant? For example:

Apathy – lack of action and proactivity, inertia, disinterest, lack of follow-through on actions and objectives.
Anxiety – high level of stress, fear of speaking up, lack of ideas sharing, tension, blame culture, lack of trust.
Comfort – implementing actions rather than driving actions, strong working relationships, low challenge between team members.
Growth – strong connection between team members, a healthy challenge in the team, an innovative culture where team members share ideas, team members giving and receiving feedback.

Step 4　Ask team members to think about their organization and their perception of where the organization is in relation to support and challenge. Emphasize that there is no wrong or right answer. Team members then stand on where they feel the culture is.

Step 5   Invite team members to share why they stood where they did.

Step 6   Ask team members to stand where they think the level of support and challenge is within the team itself.

Step 7   Invite team members once again to share why they stood where they did and encourage them to ask further exploring questions of each other. Ask each team member to share to ensure everyone's voice is heard. Explore the following with the team:

- What does support look like within this team?
- What does challenge look like within this team?

Step 8   Having explored where they think the team is now, ask: where does the team want to be? Discuss and then ask the team to explore some of the following:

- What would help them to get to where they want to be?
- What do they want the level of support to look like in the team?
- What do they want the level of challenge to look like in the team?
- What do they need to do more of/less of to create the right level of support in this team?
- What do they need to do more of/less of to create the most appropriate level of challenge in this team?
- When they have the right level of support and challenge, what behaviours would they see?
- How can they hold each member of the team accountable for maintaining the most appropriate level of support and challenge?
- How could they achieve this?

Step 9   Team to capture thoughts and ideas.

Top tips for team coaches

- Where possible, ask each member of the team to ensure everyone's voice is heard.
- This tool could also be used to ask team members to individually think about their leadership style and the level of support and challenge within their own teams.

Time required

Approximately 30 minutes.

TOOL 3: *Stepping into another person's shoes – Developing individual and team awareness*

Why use this tool?

Understanding other team members' and stakeholders' perspectives can be invaluable in helping to improve communication and resolve conflicts. Perceptual positions (explained further in the steps below) enable you to view a situation from three different viewpoints: your own, the other person's and an objective outsider.

When to use this tool

- During team or one-to-one coaching.
- When conflicts arise between team members or stakeholders.
- When communication and understanding need to improve between team members or stakeholders.

Resources required

- Space to establish three different positions.
- This tool can be adapted and used virtually.

How to use this tool?

Step 1   Explain that the Perceptual Positions exercise is taken from Neuro-Linguistic Programming (NLP). Its goal is to show you, in a structured way, how to see other people's points of view. The Perceptual Positions exercise allows you to look at a situation from three different viewpoints.

- your own (person A);
- the other person (person B);
- an objective outsider (person C).

Step 2   Ask team members to identify a relationship that they would like to improve or one where they have a challenge influencing another team member or stakeholder.

Working with a coach one-to-one or with a partner, the team member first explores their own position regarding this relationship or situation.

Step 3 Set up a space where you can have three different positions as shown in the diagram below.

Tool 3 Diagram showing positions

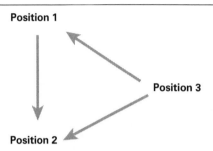

Position 1

Position 3

Position 2

The team member first gives a brief description of the challenge or relationship they would like to improve.

The team member (person A) stands at position 1. They imagine that person B (state their name if they are happy to) is standing at position 2 in front of them. (If working virtually you can ask the team members to change their physical position if space allows or they could use different objects to represent different positions.)

The team member's partner asks them some questions, for example:

- Imagine you had resolved this issue. What would a good outcome be?
- What do you currently think or feel about this outcome?
- What will it achieve?
- What is getting in the way?
- Think about your interaction with person B. How do they make you feel?
- What do you say to yourself when you are with person B?
- What are you assuming about them?
- What is it about you that might be getting in the way?
- What else do you want to explore?

Step 4 Team member (person A) now moves away from position 1. Every time they switch positions, take a quick break and do something entirely different to free their mind of that role. For example, they could drink some water, read a paragraph from a book or go for a quick walk around the room.

Step 5   The team member now moves to position 2 and becomes person B. Ask the team member to imagine that they are standing there looking in front of them at person A (ie themself).

Ask them to be person B, standing as they would, use similar facial expressions and then think as they would.

The team member's partner then asks them some questions to explore this position, for example:

- As person B, what is the outcome you want from this relationship?
- What do you currently think or feel about this outcome?
- How do you feel about person A?
- What do you say to yourself when you are with person A?
- What are you assuming about them?
- What do you need from person A?
- What could improve this relationship or situation?

Step 6   The team member takes a quick break and then moves to position 3.

Now looking from the observer position, the team member's partner asks some further questions, for example:

- What do you see happening in this relationship?
- What behaviours do you observe?
- What can you see that gets in the way of achieving the outcome?
- What can both parties learn from this situation?
- What advice could you give them?
- How could person A improve this relationship?
- What actions can they take?
- When can they take this action?
- What else can they do?

Step 7   Take a few minutes to write down and analyse what you have learned from the exercise.

What did you learn about yourself? What did you learn about the other person? How do you want to move forward from here?

Step 8 The team member says thank you to their partner.

Top tips for team coaches

- The exercise can also be used with chairs to represent the different positions.
- If the exercise is used either one-to-one or with the team, then contracting around confidentiality is key.
- You can use this with only one pair or continue with further pairs.
- You may want to explain that the majority of people find this a positive experience; however, it can sometimes be emotional to review your own behaviour objectively and this is normal.

Time required

45 minutes for both pairs to explore.

TOOL 4: Johari Window – Developing deeper awareness

Why use this tool?

Teams that lack awareness tend to fail, fast. Failing to notice a lack of progress, or the current state of individuals on the team or how its stakeholders view the team, is a recipe for disaster. Being tuned in to what is happening within and beyond the team enables high-performing teams to act decisively and in an informed way.

When to use this tool

- With teams to increase self-awareness of themselves and others.
- With teams to develop deeper relationships, to support working together in new ways.

Resources required

- Johari window model.
- Johari window template.

How to use this tool

Step 1 Briefly explain the Johari Window model, adapted from Ingham and Luft (1955). A four-paned 'window' divides personal awareness into four types: open, hidden, blind, and unknown.

1 Open – things we know about ourselves and others know about us.

2 Hidden – things we know about ourselves and others don't know.

3 Blind – things we don't know about ourselves but others do.

4 Unknown – things we don't know and others don't know either.

The lines dividing these four panes are like window shades – they can move as an interaction progresses. We build trust by opening our personal shades to others so that we become an open window. The team coach should share a story with the team of a time when they were given feedback that they weren't aware of and how that increased their self-awareness.

Step 2 Ask the team member to list personal characteristics about themselves that fall into the first two window panes. Allow 10 minutes:

- Open (quadrant 1). Examples include, I get energy from sharing ideas with others, I like structure in a meeting.

- Hidden (quadrant 2). Examples include, belief in religion, political leanings, fears, dreams. When we open this window to share something about ourselves, we invite others in. Disclosure builds trust.

Step 3 Working in pairs, the team members share what they have captured in the first two window panes. Allow 15 minutes.

Step 4 In the same pairs, the team members then give and receive feedback to help open up their blind pane. Allow 15 minutes:

- Blind (quadrant 3). Examples include: you have a real gift for making people feel comfortable or it would be good to hear more of your ideas at meetings. When you let someone open this window on you, you will create trust between yourself and that person. You decide when, where, how, and how often you want to receive this feedback. Opening this window requires compassion and kindness.

You can then ask others to give some feedback to help open up the 'blind' windowpane further:

- What are their strengths as a member of this team?
- What can get in the way?

Step 5 Explain that window 4 will often open up during interactions:

- Unknown (quadrant 4). This is the area of mutual discovery, collaboration, and surprise. The future is in this window. This is what we will discover in one another and ourselves by interacting and building relationships.

Working with their partner, each team member is to think about:

- How can they open up this pane?
- Where would it be helpful to explore?

Top tips for team coaches

This exercise can be used solely in pairs within the team or by asking each team member to think about feedback for two other team members, or the full team.

Time required

Approximately 50 minutes.

TOOL 5: Constellations – Creating systemic awareness

Why use this tool?

Using constellations can help teams to identify the strength of the relationships within their system. They can also be helpful in illuminating where relationships are now, versus where they need to be.

When to use this tool

- At any stage of team development.
- When the team is working in a silo or is unclear about their relationships with stakeholders.

Resources required

Floor space or virtual whiteboard/platform.

How to use this tool

Step 1 Clear a large space within the room and ask one team member to stand in the middle. Explain that this person represents the team. (If using a virtual whiteboard mark the team member in the middle of the screen and use the annotation features for the rest of the exercise.)

Step 2 Now ask the team to think of their stakeholders and where they would be positioned in relation to the team. For example, if a relationship with a stakeholder is strong, the team member representing the stakeholder would stand near to the centre. If further away then the relationship needs more work.

Step 3 Once the team's constellation is in place, some suggested questions you may want to explore are:

- What do they notice about the constellation?
- What surprised them?
- What pleased them?
- Where relationships are strong, what does the team do to make this a strong relationship?
- Where relationships need more work, what could the team do to improve the relationship?
- Who should be in the constellation that isn't already?
- What else could they learn from this?

Step 4 Ask the team to:

- capture key learnings;
- discuss what actions they need to take.

Top tips for team coaches

- As an alternative to asking team members to stand where stakeholders are, you could use props. For example, chairs to represent stakeholders.
- Instead of using the physical space you could use a flip chart or virtual whiteboard and ask the team to draw where stakeholders are within their system.

Time required

60 minutes.

TOOL 6: The Power of Thoughts – Ways to reframe our thinking

Why use this tool?

Helping teams to identify their thoughts and assumptions and then to be able to reframe them can be very powerful. Reframing is a way to change the meaning/content of behaviour or a situation.

When to use this tool

- At any stage of team development.
- When a team is stuck in a pattern of unhelpful behaviour, thinking or assumptions.

Resources required

Flip chart paper and pens, virtual whiteboard/platform.

How to use this tool?

Step 1 Ask team members to think about the unhelpful behaviours, assumptions and thoughts they might be adopting regarding their relationships with stakeholders, customers and external partners. Write these down.

Step 2 Team members now review the outputs with a partner and consider: 'What else could this mean?'

For example, a stakeholder might be giving little feedback and praise about how the relationship is working.

To reframe this they could say: 'The stakeholder trusts our relationship and doesn't need to give praise.'

Step 3 Each partner is to think about their top three unhelpful behaviours and note down their reframe for each one.

Step 4 All team members are then asked to share one on a flip chart or virtual whiteboard.

Step 5   The team reviews the assumptions and reframes and considers if there are any themes.

Step 6   The team members now consider and discuss what unhelpful behaviours and assumptions they are holding as a team.

Step 7   Next, the team identifies their top three assumptions and works on reframing these.

Step 8   Debrief with the team:

- What have they learnt?
- What can they do differently?
- How will this be useful for them?

Step 9   Capture final actions.

Top tips for team coaches

It can be helpful to share personal examples of reframing behaviours or assumptions to help provide clarity on how to reframe.

Time required

Approximately 30 minutes.

Reflecting on team awareness

- How aware are you of the interdependencies within your organizational system?
- How could you become clearer about the interdependencies?
- How can you create more awareness at an organizational and team level?
- What are the helpful group dynamics within the team?
- What are the unhelpful group dynamics within the team?
- What are the strengths within your team?
- How can the team leverage their strengths more?
- What are the areas for development?
- How is feedback currently handled within the team? How could this be improved?

Team relatedness

Why is building trust and connection so important?

Defining relatedness

The *Oxford Dictionary* defines relatedness as 'the state or fact of being related or connected'. While humans can form connections to anything in their world (people or things), this chapter is concerned about the relatedness of 'feeling connected to others, to caring for and being cared for by those others, to having a sense of belongingness' (Deci and Ryan, 2004, p.7). Based on our experience and the significant body of research on human relations, we would suggest that without relatedness, work will still be completed; however, individuals, teams and organizations will not be as purposeful, productive, profitable, creative, innovative and will suffer more from unhelpful forms of anxiousness and stress.

Our views are in line with the work of Hagerty *et al* (1993), who when proposing a Theory of Relatedness suggested that for a person to feel connected (the highest level of relatedness) with another person, object, group or environment, they must both feel involved; however, the involvement must promote a 'sense of comfort, well-being and anxiety reduction' (p. 293). Figure 8.1 proposes our adaptation of Hagerty's states of relatedness. This chapter will explore the psychology and practicalities of true connection and creating teams, where each person's unique capabilities and involvement are celebrated, in a setting where mental and physical well-being matter.

Figure 8.1   States of relatedness

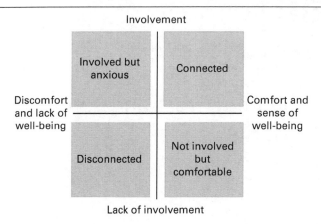

Involvement

| Involved but anxious | Connected |

Discomfort and lack of well-being ——————————— Comfort and sense of well-being

| Disconnected | Not involved but comfortable |

Lack of involvement

SOURCE Adapted from Hagerty *et al* (1993: 293)

Story: Creating a deeper team connection through our vulnerability

Contributor: Lucy

I was jointly running a team coaching session for a large team. The team had been working together for about six months, but due to their geographical locations they had only met as a whole team via video conference.

One of the objectives for the team coaching intervention was to help them get to know each other better. We decided to use the 'Making Connections' exercise described at the end of this chapter (tool 6). The team stood in a circle and each chose a card at random and then shared their response. The team leader chose to go first and answered the question, 'Imagine you wake up tomorrow and a miracle has occurred... describe your day from the moment you open your eyes.' The team leader created a beautiful visual picture of a life very different from their own. It included a large family with lots of children. They currently had one child. In telling the story they showed such vulnerability and emotion that ultimately there weren't many dry eyes in the room.

The bravery of this team leader to show their emotions and express their regrets was a catalyst for the rest of the team. The team continued to open up and share their beliefs, values, assumptions and emotions. It was evident at the end of the exercise that the team had deepened their connection and had created a safe space to open up.

The psychology behind relatedness

The link between relatedness and human survival

Much has been written about the innate needs of human beings. Sandold (2013: 28), commenting on Spitz's work in the 1930s and 1940s on the impact of babies who were denied handling, has stated that the 'clear implication of Spitz's research is that basic needs for physical affection, love and affirmation of self-worth are present at birth' and are required for the 'survival and further development of humans in general'. Continuing the theme of understanding human needs, Berne (1964), writing in his popular book, *Games People Play: The psychology of human relationships*, described how for survival, humans require the following needs to be met: stimulus (intimacy), especially after birth; recognition, with the level required differing per individual; and structure, how humans fill the void called time. While it may not be popular to talk about it in the context of organizations, we all need to be loved. Indeed, it has been powerfully stated that 'the self cannot survive without love. The self starved of love dies' (Gilligan, 1996: 47).

We would propose that the Self-Determination Theory (SDT) is particularly useful when considering innate human needs, especially in the context of organizational life. The SDT identifies three innate needs: relatedness, existing in safe communion with others; autonomy, perceiving to be the source of one's own behaviour; and competence, feeling effective in a social environment and experiencing opportunities to express your potential (Deci and Ryan, 2004). In our experience, discussing this theory can help re-awaken in people what it means to be human at work.

The impact of 'the early years' on how we relate to one another

Our earliest experiences and perceptions of how we were loved as a baby, while maybe lost to our conscious memory, are not lost to how we choose to relate to other adults both at home and in work. Indeed it has been commented that 'scientists often treat love and work as two separate realms, but being deeply social creatures, humans cannot easily separate the two' (Hazan and Shaver, 1990: 279).

An influential study of how secure babies feel to explore their world (Bowlby, 1958) was further developed by Ainsworth *et al* (1978). Commonly known as attachment theory, their research identified three infant attachment styles: secure, anxious/ambivalent and avoidant. Relating attachment theory to adults in the workplace, Hazan and Shaver (1990) demonstrated that securely attached adults tend to value relationships, enjoy work activity, have greater overall well-being and are relatively unburdened by the fear of failure. Anxious ambivalent respondents frequently feared rejection for poor performance, with a key motivation of work being their desire to gain respect and admiration. In addition, anxious ambivalent respondents had the lowest average income of the three groups. The last group, avoidant respondents, used work to actively avoid social interaction. While they reported an average income in line with the secure group, they were less satisfied in their jobs.

Harms (2011: 289) has commented that 'trust in the workplace, in both leaders and co-workers, is almost by definition an outcome of attachment styles' and their research has suggested that approximately 60 per cent of adults consider themselves to be generally in the securely attached group. Commenting on this, Harms (2011) noted that it is surprising that there is almost no research on how to developmentally support those who would consider themselves less securely attached. Harms (2011) cites one study by Hardy and Barkham (1994) which they state demonstrates the 'potential of attachment-focused interventions as a means of preventing managerial derailment' (p. 291). We would suggest that, in many cases, executive coaching is helping to address management derailments that likely result from deeper attachment issues. We will discuss how team coaching can assist later in this chapter.

In-groups, out-groups and empathy bias

To survive, not only do humans need love from a caregiver and recognition from others, they also need to be part of groups. While we may not choose our family or initial community grouping, we do spend much of our lives identifying with those we feel an affinity towards, referred to as in-groups, while viewing others as out-groups. We use gender, age, ethnicity, profession, religion, country of birth, politics, sports teams, education, appearance, personality, among other things to categorize people. To fully consider relatedness, in the context of in-groups and out-groups, it is essential to discuss our abilities as humans to empathize.

Empathy has been defined as our 'ability to appreciate the emotions and feelings of others with a minimal distinction between self and other' (Decety,

2011: 93). The neuroscience of empathy is considered to consist of affective (emotional sharing), cognitive (perspective taking) and regulatory (our emotional response) components (Xu *et al*, 2009; Decety, 2011; Molenberghs, 2013). When we are empathetic, it is similar to showing others that we feel their pain. This comment is a lot more literal than many might think, as the part of the brain that is activated when we feel pain is also activated when we see others in pain (Molenberghs, 2013). Not only do we feel with others, we also have a natural desire to help others (Warneken and Tomasello, 2006). Despite our inherent ability to feel others' pain and a desire to help, we do not encounter each other's pain equally. Research has demonstrated that 'empathic responses to perception of others in pain decreased remarkably when participants viewed faces of racial in-group members relative to racial out-group members' (Xu *et al*, 2009: 8528).

Research has indicated that the initial bias reaction in our amygdala, the emotional centre of the brain, can be instantly regulated and nullified by activity in the prefrontal cortex areas of the brain, its executive centre. While culture and how we are brought up can have a negative impact on our ability to regulate against in-group biases, it is equally true that our brain's ability to build new neural pathways means it is possible to develop healthier regulation patterns (Molenberghs, 2013). Interestingly, studies have found that the more empathy a person shows towards members of their own group, the more empathetic they are towards members of other groups (Xu *et al*, 2009)

Therefore, if we want to improve relatedness both individually and as a collective, building our ability to empathize is essential. Helpfully, empathy can be developed, as evidenced by the work of Riess *et al* (2012), who through a brief training intervention were able to increase empathy among medical and surgical trainees. We believe that developing empathy is essential for both developing team relatedness and reducing out-group prejudice.

Moving towards reward and away from threat

It has been suggested that our primary emotions can be categorized and linked to potential behaviours as follows: fear, anger, disgust, shame and sadness are linked to escape/avoidance/survival behaviours; surprise/startle to either escape/avoidance/survival or attachment behaviours; and excitement/joy, love/trust to attachment behaviours. Given the number of emotions geared towards our survival, it is not surprising that it is much easier to develop the motivation to stay away from things that cause us concern. The emotions of survival ensure energy goes inwards to protect the individual, compared to the emotions of attachment where energy goes outwards towards nurturing and creating (Brown *et al*, 2009). When considering what activates rewards and threats in our brain, the SCARF model (status, certainty, autonomy, relatedness and fairness) introduced by Rock (2008) is extremely useful, with each of the elements discussed in the context of how we behave in social situations.

In an age of increased virtual connection, homeworking and loneliness, we need to remain mindful that social connection is vital to our survival. Indeed, research from 148 studies, that included 308,849 participants (Holt-Lunstad *et al*, 2010) found a '50 per cent increased likelihood of survival for participants with stronger social relationships' (p. 1) when compared to those with weaker social relationships. Put simply, strong social relationships are life-giving and organizations need to play their part in helping employees develop them.

A theory of relatedness

Hagerty *et al* (1993), when proposing a theory of relatedness, put forward four relatedness competencies:

1 **Sense of belonging.** Where a person feels an integral part of a system or environment.

2 **Reciprocity.** Defined as an 'individual's perception of an equitable, alternating interchange with another person, object, group or environment that is accompanied by a sense of complementarity' (p. 294).

3 **Mutuality.** A shared vision, goals and sentiments including shared acceptance of differences.

4 **Synchrony.** Defined as 'a person's experience of congruence with his or her internal rhythms and external interaction with persons, objects, groups or environments' (p. 294).

It has been suggested that a person will experience connectedness, with respect to a particular relationship, when they experience greater levels of sense of belonging, reciprocity, mutuality and synchrony.

The importance of relatedness in organizations

How we relate to other people in work matters

Berne (2016) has placed the same survival value on the human requirement to fill time and avoid boredom as on infants' need for stimulus (intimacy). So how do we fill our time? Using multiple sources and based on an average 79-year life span, Campbell (2017) has detailed how the average person allocates their time (see Table 8.1).

Given the earlier discussed life-giving power of deeper social relationships (Holt-Lunstad *et al*, 2010) and the number of years we spend in work, it may be less surprising that it has been discovered that the risk of mortality is 'significantly lower for those reporting high levels of peer social support' (Shirom *et al*, 2011: 268). Indeed, it could be suggested that the opposite of high levels of peer social support is relatedness issues that trigger a harmful

Table 8.1 How humans spend their time

Activity	Average years spent doing	Other information
Bed	26 years sleeping and 7 years trying to sleep	• The average worker spends 24 per cent of their time working during a typical 50-year period of employment
Working	13 years 2 months + 1 year 2 months doing unpaid overtime	
Screen time	11 years 4 months	
Eating	4 years 6 months	
Holidays	3 years 1 month 3 weeks	• 66 per cent of workers eat at their desk and take on average a 28-minute lunch break
Exercise	1 year 4 months	
Romance	1 year 30 days	
Socializing	1 year 3 days	• On average we spend 12 times more time working than socializing
School	334 days	

SOURCE Adapted from Campbell (2017)

stress response. In a study into the factors that can trigger the emergence of stress, Wardhana (2018) reported several relating to workload and pressure triggers, but also a number that can be linked to relatedness. Among these were inter-personal relationships, including disputes with colleagues, disagreements among the leadership, lack of appreciation from superiors, and a lack of help from colleagues and superiors.

Despite the evidence that relatedness in the workplace matters, all is not well in the modern workplace. The well-known Gallup survey of 195,600 US employees has reported that: only 33 per cent of employees are engaged at work and enthused about what they do; 16 per cent are actively disengaged, feeling both unhappy and resentful; and 51 per cent are not engaged, and are described as 'psychologically unattached' (Gallup, 2017). Their survey asked employees 12 questions on their basic, individual, team and personal growth needs. From our review of these questions, we would suggest that at a minimum, five of them are directly linked to relatedness. Writing in the foreword to the 2017 report, Jim Clifton (Chairman and CEO of Gallup) suggested six steps to transform your workplace culture:

1 Executive agreement to move from a command-and-control culture to one of ongoing development through coaching conversations.
2 Not to fear mistakes and failures in the journey.
3 Change from a culture of 'employee satisfaction' focused on perks and benefits to a 'coaching culture'.
4 Change from a culture of 'paycheck' to a culture of 'purpose'.
5 Work on transforming managers and leaders at all levels of the organization.
6 Develop a leadership philosophy based on developing strengths versus fixing weaknesses (Gallup, 2017).

While we agree with each of the points on this list and particularly welcome the emphasis on coaching and purpose, we believe that coaching in the context of individuals and teams would be an important addition.

Developing team relatedness

A model for team relatedness

From our experience as leaders and team coaches, we believe that five key elements are core for teams to develop team relatedness (see Figure 8.2).

Figure 8.2   The key elements of team relatedness

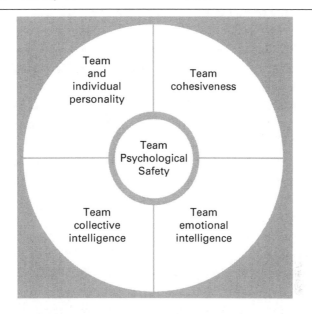

The importance of team psychological safety and how this is created

In our view, at the heart of team relatedness is team psychological safety. Psychological safety has been defined by Kahn (1990) as 'feeling able to show and employ one's self without fear of negative consequences to self-image, status, or career' (p. 708). From our experience of working with teams, we have observed that when team members feel safe, they are more open and honest, willing to give each other feedback, likely to show vulnerability, comfortable to make mistakes, and ultimately produce better work.

Upon a review of the evidence from empirical studies, Edmondson and Lei (2014) have highlighted three key insights regarding psychological safety. Firstly, it has consistently been shown to play a role in enabling performance, especially when there is uncertainty and a need for either creativity or collaboration. Secondly, it is an enabler for people to learn as they are more able to admit mistakes, suggest ideas, ask for assistance and provide feedback if they perceive it is safe to do so. Thirdly, it is an enabler for people to speak up at work, allowing for the status quo to be challenged, and problems as well as opportunities identified.

In the context of teams, psychological safety has been defined as 'a shared belief that the team is safe for interpersonal risk-taking' and goes beyond just interpersonal trust in a 'team climate characterized by interpersonal trust and mutual respect in which people are comfortable being themselves' (Edmondson, 1999: 354). Well known for his work on teams, Lencioni (2002) has highlighted the importance of trust among team members in allowing for vulnerability in front of each other, supporting openness about mistakes and weaknesses.

Discussing trust within a team, Hawkins and Smith (2013: 79) commented that 'absolute trust between human beings is an unrealizable goal, particularly in work teams. A more useful goal is the team trusting each other enough to disclose their mistrust'. This sentiment is aligned to what we have both witnessed, that when teams feel psychologically safe, the right type of conflict can be productive. Our experience is supported by the findings of Bradley *et al* (2012) who from their research with 117 project teams discovered that 'a climate of psychological safety allows task conflict to improve team performance' (p. 155). This evidence points to the need for teams to exercise caution regarding task conflict, if there is not a climate of psychological safety. Indeed, task conflict in the absence of psychological safety is likely to lead to relationship conflict that will be detrimental to both team performance and team members' well-being. How to deal with unproductive conflict will be discussed later in this chapter.

Example: The secret to team performance at Google

An example of an organization that has discovered the power of team psychological safety is Google. In 2012, Google embarked on Project Aristotle. They concluded that psychological safety, above everything else, was key to a team's performance (Duhigg, 2016). Delizonna (2017) quotes Paul Santagata, Head of Industry at Google, who stated: 'In Google's fast-paced, highly demanding environment, our success hinges on the ability to take risks and be vulnerable in front of peers' (p. 3). Delizonna (2017) proposes that six lessons can be learned about team psychological safety from replicating Santagata's work at Google:

1. Embrace conflict as a collaborator, replacing fight-or-flight reactions with a win-win approach.

2. Speak human to human, appreciating each other's deeper needs such as respect, status, competence and autonomy.

3 Anticipate reactions and plan countermoves, by thinking through how your intended audience will respond to your messaging.

4 Replace blame with curiosity, by adopting a learning mindset.

5 Ask for feedback on the messages you deliver.

6 Measure psychological safety by surveying the team or asking questions such as 'what could increase your feelings of safety?'

Building team cohesion and its relationship with inclusion

Group cohesion, discussed in Chapter 2, 'implies the highest level of interdependence among group members' (Rom and Mikulincer, 2003: 1231). Bradley *et al* (2012) define cohesion as 'team member commitment to the team's task and to each other' (p. 152) and have noted that it has a different role from psychological safety, which they highlight facilitates constructive disagreements, whereas team cohesiveness is about togetherness. While we agree on the pre-eminence of team psychological safety, it should not be at the exclusion of other crucial areas. Research by Mwangi (2019) has confirmed the importance of group cohesion in team performance.

Another important consideration, in relation to team cohesion, is group attachment theory. It is based on the typology put forward by Brennan *et al* (1998) who have proposed two basic attachment dimensions: anxiety and avoidance. Smith *et al* (1999) have found that group attachment anxiety is characterized by feelings of unworthiness or worries about being accepted within the group, whereas group attachment avoidance is characterized by a person viewing closeness to the group as unnecessary, with a tendency to avoid dependence on groups. Research by Rom and Mikulincer (2003) has found that 'group cohesion significantly attenuated the development of group attachment insecurity, either anxious or avoidant' (p. 1233). Importantly, they found that high group cohesion helped reduce group attachment anxiety. Despite the benefits of group cohesion, they also found that for those with an attachment avoidance style, developing group cohesion can add to their distress.

It is our view that, just as executive coaching is helping to improve management derailments resulting from attachment issues, team coaching is helping to build a more inclusive workplace, where employees who feel anxiously or avoidantly attached towards groups and other individuals, can find their place within a team and thus the organization. It is also clear that in the most sensitive of cases, a team coach's competency will be tested, particularly in relation to their ability to create a safe psychological space of non-judgement and compassion, where even the least securely attached can make significant progress in how they relate to others.

Developing team emotional intelligence (TEI)

Discussions on emotional intelligence are commonplace in leadership development, but we would argue that it is equally important for teams. This is supported by Druskat and Wolff (2001) who commented that 'just like individuals, the most effective teams are emotionally intelligent ones' (p. 90). It has also been suggested that scholars have largely overlooked TEI as a cognitive skill to be developed and harnessed (Dunaway, 2013). A team coach needs to help teams safely become aware, surface, understand, process and respond to their individual and collective emotions.

To build TEI, it is essential to establish norms that encourage the constructive use of emotions. Druskat and Wolff (2001) have stated that the most successful teams have 'established norms that strengthen their ability to respond effectively to the kind of emotional challenges a group confronts on a daily basis' (p. 85). These norms (agreed behaviours), they suggest, should create resources such as a common vocabulary for working with emotions, foster an affirmative environment, and encourage a proactive approach to problem solving.

Group collective intelligence and gender diversity

The saying that 'two heads are better than one' reflects our own experience of being in teams, team coaching and indeed, writing this book. Woolley *et al* (2010) have demonstrated that collective intelligence, 'the general ability of the group to perform a wide variety of tasks' (p. 687) exists within groups. They demonstrated that in groups of between two and five people working on collective tasks, the group (or team) collective intelligence is a better predictor of group performance than the average or maximum individual intelligence.

Their finding that collective intelligence is a factor of not just the composition of the group (eg average member intelligence) but also factors to do with how the group members interact is of particular interest to us regarding team relatedness. They found that the following factors significantly positively correlated with collective intelligence: greater levels of social sensitivity of group members, defined as 'the personal ability to perceive and understand the mind and mood of others' (Bender *et al*, 2012: 403); higher levels of conversational turn-taking between group members; and a greater number of females in the groups. In addition, they reported (in line with other research) that females score higher on social sensitivity than men. Similarly, Kim *et al* (2017) noted that groups composed of individuals who can better perceive subtle emotional and interpersonal cues are better equipped to develop higher collective intelligence. They commented that 'women score higher on tests of such abilities, on average, explaining in part why having more women in a group raises collective intelligence' (p. 2317).

While a team coach may not be able to change the gender composition of a team, they can make organizational stakeholders and the team itself aware of the links between gender diversity and how a team relate. Furthermore, increasing the levels of social sensitivity of team members, particularly in male-dominated teams, is likely to improve team relatedness. Developing the ability of team members to empathize, as discussed earlier in this chapter, should be beneficial in developing the social sensitivity of team members. In addition, when a team is developing team emotional intelligence norms, it should include norms around conversational turn-taking and listening.

Considering individual and team personality traits

Despite our own use of psychometric tools in our work, we are of the view that using such tools without a wider team coaching programme can have a more limited impact. Nevertheless, studies into the relationship between personality and team performance have highlighted some interesting findings, including that:

- high levels of extraversion and emotional stability contributed positively to social cohesion within teams (Van Vianen and De Dreu, 2001);
- agreeableness was positively related to task cohesion and extraversion to social cohesion (Aeron and Pathak, 2012);
- personality diversity becomes more relevant when team autonomy is high and intense cooperation is required (Molleman, 2005);
- personality can be useful when selecting 'potential team members for efficient combination' (Aeron and Pathak, 2017: 49).

While much of the focus tends to be on individual personality, it is also important to consider the overall personality of the team (see Chapter 7). This can be especially useful when reflecting on how different teams interact and perceive each other. In summary, while more research would be helpful on individual and team personality, we believe that there is enough evidence to suggest that an awareness and appreciation of personality diversity can help improve team relatedness, both within and between teams.

The challenges of team relatedness

Unresolved intra-team conflict

Du Nann Winter (2006: 171), writing about conflict, has described how 'anger, hostility, and certainty about the rightness of one's own views' can keep us away from the vulnerability required to consider an opposite position. Research that Paul has conducted on conflict resolution in the context of Northern Ireland has led us to discuss the idea of exploring and accepting 'different truths' (Barbour and Bourne, 2020). This idea bears similarity to what Price and Toye (2017) describe as embracing the paradox. They describe four levels of thinking from level 1, where problems are viewed in binary terms, to level 4, thinking that 'finds ways of making two objectives – apparently at odds – not only mutually compatible but also mutually reinforcing' (p. 252). When considering how to resolve conflict, Kelman (2004) has suggested that there is merit in identifying if the conflict exists at the level of interest (eg different objectives), relationships (eg different personality traits) or identity (eg gender). Another helpful contribution is the stages of conflict proposed by Bercovitch (2009), which include prevention, management, resolution and transformation.

Unresolved conflict at board level is particularly challenging due to the likely negative effect on colleagues and functional teams, the potential negative impact on organizational performance, and the risk attached to the well-being of the adversaries involved and those caught in the crossfire. The Conflicts in the Boardroom Survey (2014), conducted by International Finance Corporation, found among other things that:

- 29.6 per cent of respondents had experienced a boardroom dispute affecting the survival of an organization;
- 42.8 per cent of respondents reported that conflict had decreased trust among board members;
- 67.2 per cent reported that they had encountered unresolved issues;

- after competing factions on the board, the most frequent complicating factor was cited as handling the emotions of those involved;
- disputes on organizational matters are closely followed by personal disputes (behaviour and attitude of directors);
- 74.8 per cent of those surveyed described training that helped them deal with different personalities as very useful.

Team coaching, through its approach and the direct influence of the team coach, can play a significant role in creating the right environment and safety for team members to surface and work on conflict.

Managing the dark side of personality

Normally referred to as the dark side of personality, or the dark triad, Machiavellianism, narcissism, and psychopathy (Spain *et al*, 2013) are features of the modern workplace that have and are likely to continue to slip past the net of even the most diligent recruiters. It is important to note that 'dark personality characteristics are not simply extreme variants of normal personality traits' (Harms and Spain, 2015: 17). While there may be some benefits to a little of each of these in our personality, they are not considered desirable, as exemplified in the book *Snakes in Suits: When psychopaths go to work* (Babiak and Hare, 2006). So what can team coaches do when confronted with team members or leaders who demonstrate Machiavellian, narcissistic, or psychopathic tendencies?

There are differences of opinion on whether dark personality characteristics and their associated behaviours can be changed, with Burke (2006) highlighting concern and Hogan *et al* (1994) suggesting possibility. Spain *et al* (2013) suggested that interventions that focus on reducing the negative impact of dark personality traits can be more effective than trying to change the personality itself. As referred to in Chapter 3, one-to-one coaching will often be used in parallel with team coaching. In such cases, it would be useful for the one-to-one coaching to safely surface and focus on the consequences of such personality traits.

The feedback conundrum

Despite nearly every leadership and management programme advocating a feedback model, it is not uncommon to find both appreciative and developmental feedback largely missing. In terms of appreciative feedback, we need positive recognition. Fredrickson (2004) discovered that a ratio of three positives to one negative resulted in individuals, marriages and business teams flourishing. While we need developmental feedback, most people find it difficult to give and receive. Indeed, only 23 per cent of employees strongly agree that their manager provides meaningful feedback to them (Gallup, 2017). The difficulty of giving developmental feedback can be partly explained, as outlined earlier in this chapter, by our human nature to want to help other people (Warneken and Tomasello, 2006) and the finding that we physically feel others' pain (Molenberghs, 2013). When we hurt someone's feelings, even unintentionally, we also get hurt. The difficulty of receiving developmental feedback may be in part explained by what happens in our brain when we feel rejected. Eisenberger *et al* (2003) discovered that social exclusion uses some of the same neural machinery as with physical pain. Getting feedback, even if it is well-intentioned and professionally delivered, may literally feel like getting physically attacked.

This may explain the findings of Kluger and DeNisi (1996), who, when reviewing some 600 studies from over 100 years of research on feedback interventions, discovered only a moderate link between feedback and performance and that in one-third of observations, feedback interventions decreased performance. Despite the challenges of feedback, we believe it is an essential element to any great team. While models, tools and techniques can be useful, what is more important when giving feedback is the purity of our intention towards the other human in front of us. Also of importance is embedding a coaching culture where the focus is placed on asking a colleague to reflect on their own performance, rather than being provided with another's perspective. How we receive feedback will be determined not only by the intention of the person delivering and the approach used, but also by our own attitude to learning and development. Developing each of the elements discussed in the team relatedness model (see Figure 8.2), especially psychological safety, is the essential foundation for building a feedback culture that works.

Beyond gender diversity: the neurodiversity blind spot

The benefits of gender diversity for team relatedness have already been clearly outlined; however, there is another diversity opportunity that if not approached with the right mindset will be a significant challenge to the idea of team relatedness. Neurodiversity is a relatively recent concept that is growing in importance. Fenton and Krahn (2007), in their article entitled 'Autism, neurodiversity and equality beyond the normal', have suggested neurodiversity includes autism, as well as neurological or neurodevelopmental disorders such as attention deficit-hyperactivity disorder, bipolar disorder, developmental dyspraxia, dyslexia, epilepsy, and Tourette's syndrome.

We would argue there is a moral and legal imperative, as well as an economic benefit, to a neurodivergent workforce. While accepting that some people can be restricted in their ability to work, there remains a large section of the population that is working but struggling in silence (73 per cent of dyslexic people hide their dyslexia from employers (Made by Dyslexia, 2017)) or finding it difficult to get into work or hold down a job (only 16 per cent of autistic adults are in full-time paid work (British Association of Social Workers, 2016)).

From a team relatedness perspective, imagine an autistic colleague (this example is for illustrative purposes only and does not intend to generalize the uniqueness of each individual) who is above average ability at their core role, always speaks the truth in a given situation and can take useful perspectives that others miss. An organization and a team that truly believes in the benefits of diversity would attract, embrace and accommodate those who think and act differently. The role of neurodiversity in transformational teams will be discussed in Chapter 10.

In summary, it is clear that there are multiple aspects to understanding and developing team relatedness. Despite its challenges, our experience and the research highlights the importance of developing team relatedness at the outset and throughout the team coaching journey.

Tools and techniques for developing team relatedness

Using tools and techniques

When applying these tools and techniques, it is essential that the team coach or leader builds connection and psychological safety first. The tools and techniques are offered as a support and guide, that when used should feel natural and in 'flow', with the process and steps behind the tools remaining effectively invisible.

TOOL 1: Stakeholder Mapping – Understanding the strength of team relationships

Why use this tool?

Teams do not operate within a vacuum; they have key stakeholder relationships to develop and maintain within their organizational system. This tool helps teams to identify who are their key stakeholders, the strength of the relationships, and enables them to start to think about how they can create a plan for effective stakeholder engagement.

When to use this tool

- Following changes to organizational or team structures.
- When teams have to consider who they need to build relationships with or influence.

Resources required

- Flip chart paper and pens, virtual whiteboard/platforms.
- Stakeholder map on a flip chart or displayed virtually.

How to use this tool

Step 1   Brainstorm who the key stakeholders are that the team work with and capture on a flip chart or virtual platform.

Step 2   Using the stakeholder grid (see figure on p179), place them according to their current level of engagement and their level of influence and power. For example, a team may consider the Chief Financial Officer (CFO) to be a key stakeholder as they currently have a high level of power and influence over the work of the team; however, the team feels that the stakeholder's level of engagement with the team is low. In this example, the stakeholder would be placed in the top left-hand box.

Stakeholders may be individuals, teams or groups of people.

Step 3   Now place the stakeholder on the grid where you would like the relationship to be. In this example, the team wanted the CFO to be in the high level of power and influence box and the high level of engagement box, top right. It is not necessary to have all stakeholders fully engaged and motivated, but key influencers need to be engaged.

Step 4   Once all key stakeholders are entered onto the grid, the team brain-storms ideas about how to move stakeholders from their current position to the desired position. The team may want to consider what action they need to take with different stakeholders depending on where they are positioned:

- **High Power, High Engagement.** Manage these stakeholders closely to maintain their engagement.

- **High Power, Low Engagement.** Establish what the block might be, create common ground and seek to re-engage.

- **Low Power, Low Engagement.** Decide how important these stakeholders are to the success of the team; if there are few or no consequences as a result of low engagement, monitor it but put in minimum effort. If there are consequences, then they probably have more power than you first thought (if not through rank).

- **Low Power, High Engagement.** Keep these stakeholders informed to maintain their engagement.

Tool 1   Example of a stakeholder map

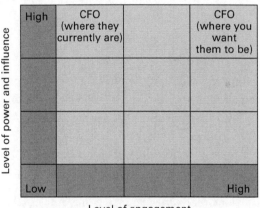

Top tips for team coaches

Once the team have brainstormed key stakeholders it may be helpful to ask them to consider which relationships are the most important. Select the top 5 or 10 and start by placing those on the grid.

Time required

60–90 minutes depending on the size of the team and number of stakeholders.

TOOL 2: Feedback Goldfish Bowl – Developing open and honest conversations

Why use this tool?

Teams often shy away from having 'real' open and honest conversations. However, it is essential for teams and team members to have robust conversations, to work more closely together, build strong relationships and ultimately improve their individual and team performance.

When to use this tool?

With any team once a feeling of psychological safety has been developed.

Resources required

- Flip chart paper and pens, virtual whiteboard/platforms.
- Team members to have a device or notepad to capture feedback.

How to use this tool

Step 1   Discuss with the team important aspects of giving and receiving feedback: for example, feedback should be given with positive intention, feedback is received with the mindset of 'feedback is a gift' and feedback should be specific and where possible explain the impact of the behaviour.

Step 2   Brief the exercise. Everyone in the team will consider each team member and answer the following questions:

- In what ways does the team member contribute to this being a high-performing team?
- In what ways does the team member hinder this being a high-performing team?

Step 3   Give everyone around 15 minutes to consider and capture their feedback for each team member.

Step 4   All the team then come together in a circle, either sitting, standing or on a virtual platform.

Step 5   Each team member takes it in turn to receive feedback from every team member.

Step 6   For each team member receiving feedback, another team member volunteers to capture the feedback in writing for their colleague, to allow the person receiving the feedback to be able to listen. It is important to rotate this scribing responsibility.

Step 7   The team member receiving the feedback doesn't enter into dialogue around the feedback but just says 'thank you'.

Step 8   The team member who has captured the feedback gives or sends the written notes to the team member who has just received the feedback.

Step 9   Once all the feedback has been offered and received, it can be helpful to leave some time for personal reflection and for team members to note down any actions.

Step 10   After the exercise, it is important to ask the team to consider how they will continue to give and receive feedback on an ongoing basis.

Top tips for team coaches

- In most cases, this proves to be an extremely powerful, insightful and in many instances a transforming exercise for team members. It can also be very challenging if team members haven't previously provided feedback for each other. It is therefore important to help the team build connection and rapport with each other beforehand and also for the team coach to create a feeling of psychological safety and trust. The team coach may need to make a judgement call on the readiness or otherwise of the team members to give each other feedback, using this technique.
- It is also vital that the team coach takes time at the start of the exercise to contract clearly with team members regarding how the technique works and the spirit in which the feedback should be given.

Time required

Approximately 90 minutes, depending on team size.

TOOL 3: Tell Me – Giving and receiving feedback

Why use this tool?

Team dynamics can be complex within teams, with varying levels of understanding between team members. This exercise can help teams to improve levels of openness and understanding with each other.

When to use this tool

Once a team has developed a high level of psychological safety with each other. This is likely to be an established team rather than a newly formed team.

Resources required

'Tell Me' questions printed out for team members or shared virtually (please note that this exercise has been shared among team coaches and team development facilitators over many years and it is not, to our knowledge, attributable to an original source).

How to use this tool

Step 1   Form pairs based on your assessment (often informed by the team leader's view) of which relationships, if they were strengthened, would have the greatest positive impact on the effectiveness of the team.

Step 2   Explain that the pairs will be given a series of questions to ask each other. They have around 10 minutes initially to consider their answers to the questions.

Step 3   Explain the ground rules:

- Partners to listen, respect each other's views, not to challenge feedback and respect the importance of confidentiality.
- Stick with the structure and complete ALL 8 sections in the order 1 to 8.
- Each pair to decide who will go first.
- Avoid debate. Ask the question, listen, say 'thank you' and move on to the next question.
- Don't miss out the 'thank yous'!
- When both partners have completed the exercise, take a couple of minutes each to reflect on the answers. Then take three minutes each to share what you've learned and what, if anything, you are going to do as a result.
- There is no compulsion to do anything as a result.

Step 4 Before asking the pairs to start, reinforce timings for a 'change-over' point, so that both partners receive a fair allocation of time. It is often helpful to get the pairs to complete the exercise while walking outside. If working virtually use breakout rooms.

Step 5 Ask for insights and learnings when the full team come back together.

Step 6 Optional – form additional pairings and run the exercise again.

The questions

Question set one
Tell me something you like about me.
Thank you.
Tell me something you think we agree on.
Thank you.
Tell me something about yourself you think I should know.
Thank you.

Question set two
Tell me a goal you have for life.
Thank you.
Tell me a goal you have for our relationship.
Thank you.

Question set three
Tell me something you've done to me that you think you shouldn't have done.
Thank you.
Tell me something you failed to do for me that you think you should have done.
Thank you.

Question set four
Tell me how I've disappointed you over the last couple of years/months.
Thank you.
Tell me how you think you might have disappointed me over the last couple of years/months.
Thank you.

Question set five

Tell me about a contribution that I make that you value.
Thank you.
Tell me how you think I don't contribute.
Thank you.

Question set six

Tell me a way I could help you.
Thank you.
Tell me a way you could help me.
Thank you.

Question set seven

Tell me a problem you are having in life.
Thank you.
Tell me what I need to know in order to understand your problem.
Thank you.

Question set eight

Tell me an outstanding ability of yours.
Thank you.

Top tips for team coaches

- Be very clear on contracting and setting up the rules. It is important for the pairs to ask and answer all the questions.
- Team members may choose to continue to agree on additional pairings and conduct the exercise again in between team coaching interventions.

Time required

60 minutes.

TOOL 4: Swimming Pool – Discovering your place in the team

Why use this tool?

Helping teams to consider how they relate to each other and explore how connected they feel as a team can help improve team relationships. This exercise can help teams to express the 'unsaid' or 'elephants in the room', providing a catalyst for having open and honest conversations.

When to use this tool

Once psychological safety and rapport are built within the team.

Resources required

- Room with no tables and a good amount of space. (Please note that this exercise has been shared among team coaches and team development facilitators over many years and it is not, to our knowledge, attributable to an original source.)
- This exercise can also take place using a virtual whiteboard/platform.

How to use this tool

Step 1 Clear a large space within the room or draw a room on a virtual platform.

Step 2 Ask the team to then imagine that in the space is a swimming pool. There is a shallow end, deep end, diving board, spectator's gallery and changing room – show where each area is in the room (draw each area if working virtually).

Step 3 Ask the team to position themselves where they feel they are in relation to the team. For example, if they are new to the team they might be in the changing room etc (use annotation feature if working virtually or an image of the team member if using a more advanced virtual platform).

Step 4 Ask who would like to share why they are in that particular position. Team Coach to ask probing questions: What makes them feel like that? Where do they want to be? What can the team do to help them get into the pool for example?

Step 5 Encourage the team to start asking each other questions too – supporting and challenging each other.

Step 6 Debrief with the team – what did they learn? What new insights did they gain from the exercise?

Step 7 How will these insights be helpful to the team on an ongoing basis? What are their next steps?

Top tips for team coaches

- Contract clearly around confidentiality.
- Consider when is appropriate to use this exercise. The team will need to have built rapport and psychological safety.
- Allow time and space for team members to explore and help the team to start to ask questions of each other at an early stage of the exercise, rather than the team coach asking all the questions.

Time required

90 minutes with a willingness to flex.

TOOL 5: Professional Gossiping – Appreciating the strengths of team members

Why use this tool?

Showing appreciation and giving feedback on the strengths of team members can help the team to get to know each other better and increase the understanding of what each team member uniquely brings to the team.

When to use this tool

At any stage of team development.

Resources required

Chairs for team members or the use of a virtual platform.

How to use this tool

Step 1   Ask every team member to consider what they appreciate about each team member and the strengths of that team member. Allow 10 minutes.

Step 2   Team members to sit in a circle (not relevant if working virtually).

Step 3   Team members take it in turns to turn their back to the group (team member to switch off their video feed if working virtually) and the team then discuss among themselves what they appreciate about the team member and their strengths. Allow approximately five minutes per team member. The team member receiving the comments does not respond, only listens and makes notes if they choose to.

Step 4 Debrief the exercise. How did they feel receiving the feedback? How did the rest of the team feel about discussing the team member without them facing/seeing them?

Step 5 Team to consider: How can they leverage the different strengths within the team? What actions can they take?

Top tips for team coaches

- Teams who have not experienced this exercise before may be resistant to one member turning their back; however, assure the team that this can lead to a free-flowing discussion.

- This type of exercise can also be used for problem-solving and action learning exercises.

- To help manage time the team coach may want to contract with the team that they will put a timer on when the appreciation and feedback are being discussed. This will help focus the team on the key points they want to offer and avoid lengthy discussions.

Time required

45–60 minutes depending on the size of the team.

TOOL 6: Making Connections – Getting to know each other better

Why use this tool?

Sharing personal information in an open and honest way can help the team to forge deeper connections and rapport. This exercise can create a space for showing openness, honesty and vulnerability through personal disclosure.

When to use this tool

At any stage of team development.

Resources required

- Coaching cards.
- If working virtually create a series of random questions inspired by a set of coaching cards. Give each question a corresponding number.

How to use this tool

Step 1   Ask the team to stand in a circle (not relevant if working virtually – use gallery view instead).

Step 2   Each team member chooses a card randomly without revealing the question (if working virtually, ask team members to pick a random number). If working virtually, only reveal the numbered questions once each team member has selected a number.

Step 3   Team members read the question and think for a few minutes about their answer.

Step 4   Invite someone in the team to share their response first.

Step 5   Each team member then shares their answer.

Step 6   Thank the team for sharing.

Top tips for team coaches

- Use Barefoot 'Coaching Cards for Everyday Use' or similar.
- Contracting with the team leader about showing openness and vulnerability in their answer can help create an environment of openness and honesty and may encourage others to share more.

Time required

30 mins.

Reflecting on team relatedness

- How well do you really know other members of the team, ie what is important to them?
- How well do the team demonstrate an awareness and appreciation of personality diversity?
- When there are challenges in the team, how well do team members support one another?

- When conflict occurs, how is it managed in this team?
- What is the level of trust like in this team?
- How would you rate the level of trust out of 10, 10 being high and 1 being low? If it's less than 10 what could you do to improve the level of trust?
- How willing are team members to disclose personal information and show their vulnerability?
- How safe does it feel to have open and honest conversations?
- How do team members have tough conversations in this team?
- How regularly do team members give each other honest feedback?
- What team norms (behaviours) have been agreed to maximize the team's emotional intelligence?
- To maximize their collective intelligence, what have the team done to develop norms around conversational turn-taking and listening?
- How well do team members take accountability in this team?

Team ways of working 09

How can teams keep reinventing how they work together?

Defining ways of working

Put simply, ways of working is about how teams work, including team decision making, team internal and external processes, team meetings, and team communication processes. The importance of ways of working has been highlighted in a study by Lawrence and Whyte (2017) into what team coaching practitioners do. They noted that most of the team coaches in their study agreed on the importance of 'ensuring that individual's roles and responsibilities are clear, and that processes such as team meetings and decision making are attended to' (p. 106).

The psychology behind ways of working

To discuss the psychology behind ways of working, we believe it is helpful to consider the two areas of our psychological needs and how these relate to how we work and how we make decisions.

The link between our psychological needs and our work

Chapter 4 highlighted the work of McGregor and Doshi (2015), who, by developing the research of Deci and Ryan, outlined the six main reasons why people work, the most important of these being the intrinsic causes of increased motivation and performance, play, purpose and potential. The same research also identified and prioritized several company processes that contribute to employee motivation and a high-performance culture. Table 9.1

outlines the main company processes identified and the psychological needs each of these processes help to meet.

It is evident from Table 9.1 that humans are most fulfilled and productive when they do work that is interesting (play), has meaning (purpose), provides opportunities for growth and development (potential), creates belonging (community), provides process, tools and resources (workforce and resource planning), gives hope and direction (leadership), and rewards fairly (compensation).

Table 9.1 Company processes linked to employee motivation ranked in order of importance and supporting research

Company processes linked to employee motivation (ranked in order of importance)	Supporting research and further reading
Role design	• Our need to play - linked to our curiosity and need to create and explore (McGregor and Doshi, 2015) • Our need for autonomy and competence (Deci and Ryan, 2004) • The need to fill time with structure, of which work is identified as central (Berne, 2016)
Organizational identity	• Our need for purpose – work that identifies at a level of values and identity (McGregor and Doshi, 2015) • Acting in line with our own interests and values (Deci and Ryan, 2004; Linley *et al*, 2010)
Career ladders	• Our need to maximize our potential (McGregor and Doshi, 2015) • Our need for competence (Deci and Ryan, 2004)
Community	• Our need for relatedness (Deci and Ryan, 2004) • Our need for inclusion - to connect, belong and feel significant and openness - previously referred to as affection (Childs, 2012)

(*continued*)

Table 9.1   (Continued)

Company processes linked to employee motivation (ranked in order of importance)	Supporting research and further reading
Workforce and resource planning	• Our need for certainty (Rock, 2008) • Our need for control (Childs, 2012)
Leadership	• Being led in a way that helps to meet our needs of relatedness, autonomy and competence (Deci and Ryan, 2004) • Our need for hope and some certainty about the future (Rock, 2008)
Compensation	• Our need for status, certainty and fairness (Rock, 2008) • Our need for recognition (Berne, 2016)

SOURCE Adapted from McGregor and Doshi, 2015

The psychology of decision making

The most powerful reality for any person is that they can change their future with their next decision. However, decision making is a complex activity for the brain. For each decision, our brain must create options, attach values to each option, make a choice or choices based on the likely benefit to be gained, execute the choices made and then review. Our brain makes these evaluations by accessing previous experience and calculating the likelihood of an outcome. Cohen *et al* (2007) have outlined how the brain needs to estimate the uncertainty (risk/cost) and the utility (benefit) of each decision we make. However, not all decisions are the same, with some being simple and others uncertain, complex or ambiguous. In addition, people have different levels of aversion to risk (Bossons *et al*, 2015).

In his popular book *Thinking, Fast and Slow,* Kahneman (2011) has outlined two models of thinking, which he refers to as system one and system two. System one operates automatically and quickly, whereas system two allocates attention and concentration to the task at hand. It is suggested that system one is constantly generating suggestions (impressions, intuitions, feelings etc) for system two. On most occasions, system two acts on these suggestions; however, when difficult decisions arise, system two takes over as we place our attention and concentration on trying to decide on the best option. System one contains biases that help us make decisions quicker. Some of these biases can result in poorer decisions; for example, confirmation bias, where we seek out information that supports our position, or the halo effect, where we give extra weighting to first impressions.

As human beings, we move towards those things that we perceive as rewarding and away from those things that we consider a threat. In most cases, this constant scanning and reacting to our environment keeps us safe and helps us make decisions. However, the problem arises when we try to attribute a reward or a threat to something that is not immediate. Goleman (2013) gives examples of how difficult it is to get people to consider the impact of their current decisions on long-term issues such as health, retirement savings or climate change. For example, on climate change, it is difficult to get people to change their behaviours on issues that they may perceive as not immediate. In contrast, the COVID-19 pandemic in 2020 demonstrated the ability of humans to take immediate actions when a threat is considered imminent.

The importance of ways of working for organizations

How we go about our work is changing. It has been commented that 'offices without walls, teams without clear role descriptions, conflicting expectations and a flattened hierarchy can be perceived as modern and efficient, but also as a great source of anxiety for many in our organizations' (Wilke and Thornton, 2019: 225). It should never be about change for change's sake, but rather asking ourselves, how do we need to work as an organization at an individual, team and collective level, in order to serve our purpose? There are two key themes we would like to draw attention to. Firstly, the opportunity for designing our ways of working around the psychological needs of employees (see Table 9.1) and secondly, the necessity for an organization to adapt a team of teams approach, something we believe is strongly underpinned by an agile mindset.

Designing ways of working based on the psychological needs of employees

As previously outlined, research is clear on what organizational processes motivate employees and the psychological needs behind each of these processes. Inspired by this research, Table 9.2 presents a series of questions that organizations could consider, in order to build work processes and practices that tap into each of our deepest human needs.

Table 9.2   Questions for organizations to consider regarding their company processes that affect how motivated employees feel towards their work

Company processes linked to employee motivation (ranked in order of importance)	Questions for organizations to consider regarding company processes that affect how motivated employees feel towards their work
Role design	How can we make the actual work itself more enjoyable? How can employees contribute to making improvements in role design? How can we help employees access their innate creativity?
Organizational identity	How can we develop links between the values, beliefs and purpose of the individual and the work itself? How can employees be encouraged to bring more of themselves into their role?
Career ladders	How can we help every individual best fulfil their unique potential both through career progression and/or growth opportunities (eg learning opportunities, projects, secondments).
Community	How can we best build community within the workplace?
Workforce and resource planning	Are the right structures, processes, tools, resources and skills development plans in place? Is each employee clear on what value they add to the organization and are they clear on how they can best add this value?
Leadership	Are leaders communicating a clear and compelling strategy in which employees can believe? Are leaders visible, connecting authentically and showing care towards their employees (relatedness)? Are leaders trusting of their employees (autonomy)? Are leaders providing opportunities for each employee to fulfil their unique potential (competence)?
Compensation	Are employees compensated in a way that demonstrates they are valued? Are dealings regarding compensation dealt with in as fair and transparent a way as possible?

SOURCE Adapted from McGregor and Doshi, 2015

Figure 9.1   Illustration of traditional siloed organizations and team of teams agile mindset organizations

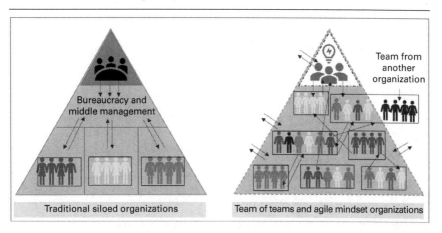

Becoming a team of teams

In their book *Team of Teams* (2015), McChrystal *et al* describe the change from Taylorism, developed in the 1880s with its emphasis on reductionism and replicable efficiency, to today's world where technology supports unparalleled connectivity and networks, whose power exists in their emergent and non-linear behaviours. The same authors detail that when fighting al-Qaeda in Iraq, the allied forces had to discard a century of conventional wisdom and create a 'team of teams' which combined extremely transparent and decentralized communication. The same organizational developments that took place in the plains of Nineveh are evident in the organizations we work in today. While there is little consistency on both the trajectory and speed of the journey, organizations are changing. Figure 9.1 illustrates the change we are increasingly seeing as organizations journey from traditionally siloed organizations to team of teams and agile mindset organizations. In truth, most organizations exist somewhere in between.

Traditional organizations are evidenced by:

- non-diverse, hierarchical leadership and management structures;
- command and control decision making with limited team autonomy;
- tightly controlled top-down and long-term planning cycles;
- a narrow view of stakeholder return (eg primarily shareholders);
- inside-out focus, with customers viewed as clients and stakeholders viewed as entities to be managed;

- rigid and bureaucratic processes;
- reliance on annual personal development plans/reviews;
- talent development focus placed on selected individuals;
- slow adoption to and adaption of technological advances;
- functional teams operating largely in silos;
- focus on the individual (eg bonus structures, development programmes);
- information protection and sharing on a 'need to know' basis.

Team of teams and agile mindset organizations are evidenced by:

- diverse, open and available leadership and management structures;
- strong team autonomy with strategic intent clear and resources provided;
- bottom-up and top-down medium-term planning cycles, open to iterative changes;
- purpose, vision and values-driven with a broad view of stakeholder return;
- outside-in focus, with key customers and stakeholders viewed as partners;
- rigid and flexible processes with an emphasis on achieving a process rhythm;
- daily appreciative and developmental feedback, supported by annual appraisals;
- talent development and growth opportunities made available to all employees;
- technology viewed as an enabler;
- functional teams, cross-functional teams, and cross-organizational teams (teams with leaders, self-led and hybrid);
- individual and team development focus;
- transparent communication and information sharing, with emphasis on the generation of local insight.

Developing an 'agile way of being'

An interesting area, when discussing ways of working, is the development of 'agile' within the software industries and increasingly other industries. The Agile Manifesto (Beck *et al*, 2001) highlighted Twelve Principles of Agile Software and four areas they valued in this new way of working:

1 individuals and interactions over processes and tools;

2 working software over comprehensive documentation;

3 customer collaboration over contract negotiation;

4 responding to change over following a plan.

If you substitute the word software with 'product' in value number two, the four values are equally applicable to the future type of organization we have described in Figure 9.1. Rico and Sayani (2009) have suggested that scholars are starting to understand that 'agile values' are more important than any one of the many agile methodologies. In her article entitled 'How Agile helps non-technical teams get things done', Thong (2018) has described agile as a way of organizing teams to work in an iterative, incremental, and highly collaborative manner. She describes two of the best-known agile methodologies as Kanban (a lightweight framework that places a focus on visualized tasks on boards, both physical and digital) and Scrum (a more prescriptive and complex method, with specific roles, meetings and time-boxed sprints).

In our work as team coaches, we have increasingly incorporated methods inspired by the agile movement. However, while these methods have proved extremely useful, it is the agile values, or the mindset, that we believe has so much to offer with regard to how teams go about their work. Supporting this perspective, Kroll and Shea (2018), when discussing agile coaches, proposed that teams who performed better were 'being agile' rather than just 'doing agile'. They further note that at the core of 'being agile' is the ability to communicate ideas and interact through relationships with others, the first agile value. It is our view that team coaching is strongly placed to help embed an 'agile way of being' into teams and organizations. At the same time, team coaching can benefit from learning more about the 'agile way of doing' in order to help teams to explore improved ways of working.

Developing team ways of working

When discussing a team's ways of working, we have found it useful to look at the areas outlined in Figure 9.2.

Team decision making

A team coach can help a team think more deeply about the types of decisions they need to make, as well as how the team makes these decisions. Earlier in this chapter, we referred to the key types of decisions that range

Figure 9.2   The key elements of team ways of working

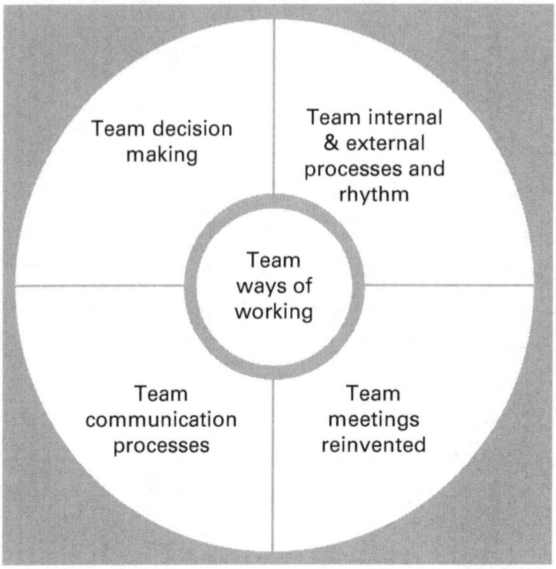

from simple to uncertain, complex and ambiguous (Bossons *et al*, 2015) or indeed, a mixture of each. Table 9.3 highlights our thoughts on the challenges of each decision type and suggests questions that a team coach can use to help a team to reflect on how they approach different types of decisions.

It is also important to consider how teams make decisions. When teams make decisions, they are doing much more than deciding which option to move forward with. Making decisions at a team level is complicated. Clutterbuck (2007) has referred to the need for multiple inner dialogues to become a single open one. In developing this, there exists the risk of a few team members dominating the dialogue, the team leader having too much influence, 'group think', or the team submitting to various types of unconscious bias. Research has demonstrated that allowing team members to contribute their autonomous thoughts, even if it leads to dissent, can help avoid 'group think' and result in better judgements and decisions (Baumeister *et al*, 2016).

When we team coach, we regularly ask the team to reflect on a decision individually first, write down their thoughts and then share their independent thinking before moving to a wider discussion. When options have been narrowed down, we would repeat the same exercise. Not only does autonomous thinking lead to better decisions, but team members will also have a greater commitment towards decisions they have contributed to, even if they don't fully agree with the decision. Figure 9.3 illustrates a continuum of three decision making approaches we come across when working with

Table 9.3 Potential challenges and team coaching questions to help teams to reflect on the different decision types

Decision type	Typical speech patterns	Potential challenges	Team coaching questions
Simple decisions	"This should be a very straightforward decision"	• Overthinking the obvious • Missing easily accessible information • Amnesia on past decisions	• Do you have all the information you need to make this decision? • Logically, what do you think is the right decision? • Are there any other obvious options? • What can you learn from previous decisions?
Uncertain decisions	"It's hard to know what we should do"	• Team members may view risk differently • Different professional opinions	• What are your available options? • What benefits and risks are associated with each option? • How could you best mitigate each of the risks? • What options best serve your team purpose and goals? • What does your best judgement tell you, given the information you now have?

(continued)

Table 9.3 (Continued)

Decision type	Typical speech patterns	Potential challenges	Team coaching questions
Complex decisions	"Where do we start"	• Fixed team mindset for dealing with complexity • Organizational demand for immediate results • Organizational politics • Professional divergence	• What else can the team do to ensure it has an agile mindset that is at ease in handling paradox, different truths, experimentation, emergent options, and consistent change? • Does the team have all the information and resources it needs to analyse, develop and plan the right processes/approaches to manage complexity? • Is the team allowing enough space for creativity and innovation?
Ambiguous decisions	"It's so hard to know what will happen"	• Chaos and total unpredictability • The past offers little assistance to the future	• What do you have to accept that you will never know for certain? • What does all of your life and professional experience tell you about the best way forward? • What are your gut feelings saying to you? • What is the consequence of not making a decision? • What is the absolute worst case scenario? • What would a future version of yourself advise?

SOURCE Adapted from Bossons et al, 2015

Figure 9.3   Team decision making continuum

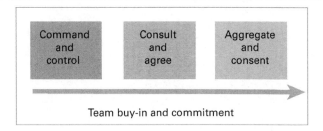

teams: command and control, consult and agree, and aggregate and consent. All three of these may take place simultaneously during the same decision.

Team coaches can help teams to develop an awareness of how they make decisions, as well as consider how they can improve team decision making. Table 9.4 describes each decision making approach, along with the benefits, disadvantages and top tips for each.

Team internal and external processes and rhythm

Have you ever wondered why, despite all our advances in technology, organizational life appears more complicated than ever? We are convinced from our corporate experience and team coaching work that many of these complications come from people not fully collaborating in the work they are trying to do. When we say collaborating, we are talking beyond the boundaries of a team or even the teams within an organization. We are talking about teams across organizations acting together towards a common purpose.

Some team coaches may consider working with processes as something that should be left to experts in process consultancy (see discussion in Chapter 1) or, for example, experts in other ways of working, such as agile coaches. However, we believe that a team coach should be equipped to work with a team on its processes, while at the same time being aware of when it is necessary to bring in other expertise.

Six key areas of the team process that team coaches should help a team consider are:

1 agreeing which teams they need to work with (internal and external);

2 agreeing on the collective challenge and uniting on a common purpose;

3 fully mapping out independencies and where value is gained and lost;

Table 9.4 Benefits, disadvantages and top tips for key decision making approaches

	Command and control	Consult and agree	Aggregate and consent
Description	• Team leader either makes or is heavily involved in all key decisions. • Leader may be: autocratic (ie know nothing else except telling others what to do); reluctantly autocratic (ie aware of their issue and tries to involve others); or blindly autocratic (ie a leader who believes they give autonomy, however, double checks everything).	• Likely to involve lots of formal team discussion and updates based on internal or external expertise. • Team subgroups may be set up. • Despite team involvement, final decision weighting may sit with expert or subgroup in alignment with the team leader.	• Full team share their independent thinking and collectively reach an agreed position. • An agreed position can still include differences of opinion, however, the team reach a collective decision to which everyone 'consents' and agrees to be held collectively accountable.
Benefits	• Potentially quick decision making and clarity. • Can be useful when decisive leadership is required.	• Combines focus and team decision making. • Extremely powerful when the team are fully involved in each decision making step.	• With involvement of each team member, collective intelligence of the team is utilized and buy-in and commitment maximized. • Dissension is given a voice.

| **Disadvantages** | <ul><li>Likely to be viewed by others as controlling.</li><li>Does not utilize the team's collective intelligence.</li><li>Possibility of low team buy-in and commitment.</li><li>Greater possibility of dissension and disengagement.</li></ul> | <ul><li>Too much weight may be placed on expertise.</li><li>Team leader may use expertise to influence the direction of a decision.</li><li>Potential team frustration and lower buy-in, if involved but effectively excluded from key decisions.</li></ul> | <ul><li>Slower decision making.</li><li>Encouraging everyone to share their thoughts can result in more low-level conflict, which requires psychological safety.</li><li>Team may not like it when a command and control decision is required.</li></ul> |
| **Top tips** | <ul><li>Help the team leader become aware of their decision making approach and its disadvantages.</li><li>Potential for one-to-one executive coaching.</li><li>Ask the team leader to consider speaking last.</li></ul> | <ul><li>Despite the influence of experts or subgroups, involve the full team in key decisions (ie view role of experts or subgroups as agents to upskill the full team, so they can make better collective decisions).</li></ul> | <ul><li>Ensure the team is aware of the benefits of what is a slower form of decision making.</li><li>Ensure appropriate time is allowed in forums for discussion and decision making.</li></ul> |

4 negotiating an agreed process that minimizes waste and maximizes rhythm (flow);

5 detailing who needs to do what and when (clarity of roles);

6 measuring progress and accountability.

Story: Developing a team of teams
Contributor: Paul

While working in corporate life, I had the pleasure of being part of a movement towards a team of teams approach. It had the ultimate impact of many teams working as one, without losing their individual team identities.

It started with multiple team representatives coming together and discussing a joint challenge, namely how to get to market more quickly and effectively. Walls were adorned with Post-it notes, as each team shared its key processes, interdependencies, what was helping them do their work and what was holding them back. Importantly, the external client's viewpoint was strongly represented by customer team representatives.

A new 'go to market' process was developed that included agreement on when and what needed to happen internally and externally, and on which weeks and days. There was clarity on what was expected at each stage, who should attend what meetings (in person and virtual), and what work needed to happen in between. A rhythm was created, with each week having key activities everyone was clear on. A process owner acted as a conductor, ensuring the new business rhythm was maintained and the appropriate resources were in place.

As a result, a complex business became easier to run; the speed of decision making improved; clearer roles and responsibilities resulted in people feeling more autonomous despite a more tightly defined process; and process adherence KPIs were used positively to discuss bottlenecks and process improvements. However, the key benefit that helped set a standard for how multiple teams could collaborate was cross-functional teams coming out of their silos and working as one.

Team meetings reinvented

Some team coaches may consider meetings to be outside the remit of a team coaching intervention; however, in our experience it's an area that teams regularly want to improve. While we understand that there may be a desire to focus on what could be considered more important areas, it is difficult to see how a team can be top-performing if it does not hold effective meetings. Most teams we come across struggle with multiple aspects of how they meet. In our opinion, teams should regularly check if they are meeting in the most effective way possible. Supporting this perspective, Hawkins (2017: 109) has commented that 'changing meeting structures and processes is a key part of the coaching process'.

From our experience of working in and coaching teams, some questions we believe a team can benefit from reflecting on include:

1 How does the meeting contribute to your team purpose and goals?

2 What meeting locations could result in new thinking and networking opportunities (eg clients' offices, external and/or novel locations)?

3 How do remote employees need to be supported if video conferencing is being heavily used (eg ensuring employees have appropriate hardware, software and connectivity)?

4 What meeting formats do you use, or have you experimented with, as a team (eg formal meetings, check-in calls, stand-up huddles, virtual, blended physical and virtual, agile meeting methodologies)?

Example: The daily scrum

This is one part of the well-known Agile Scrum Framework. The team meet for a maximum of 15 minutes per day with the scrum master (this could be the team leader) around the team task board either physically or virtually (this could be a team whiteboard displaying key metrics). Team members update the task board, align with each other on tasks and answer three questions. What have you done in the last 24 hours? What will you do in the next 24 hours? And what is getting in your way? (The Agile Mindset, 2019).

---

1 How is energy maintained and created during the meeting (eg use of flip charts, movement and use of breakout spaces, virtual whiteboards/platforms, virtual polls, restricting or eliminating PowerPoint, meetings centred around food)?

2 From the agenda, is it clear what is for discussion, decision making or information sharing? What information can be circulated before the meeting? Does time need to be allowed during the meeting for information review? What outputs are expected?

Example: meetings at Amazon

Jeff Bezos is quoted as saying that Amazon's way of holding meetings is probably the 'smartest thing we ever did'.

In meetings at Amazon, PowerPoint has been replaced by each employee sitting in silence, for up to 30 minutes, reading a pre-prepared memo. Tradition dictates that the authors' names never appear on the memos, as the memos are considered as belonging to the entire team. Memos are written and rewritten, with colleagues improving upon each other's work. The memo sets the context for the forthcoming discussion. Reading the memo silently ensures everyone is prepared for the discussion. Attendees are encouraged to make notes during the reading period. Then the discussion takes place (Locke, 2019).

---

7 Are there 'agreed' meeting behaviours? If not, how can agreements be reached? (NB: this is equally applicable to virtual meetings, eg camera on or off.)

8 In addition to agreed meeting behaviours, how do you ensure everyone's voice is heard and that the same voices do not dominate (eg everyone gets xx time to think independently and xx time to share with the team their thoughts)?

9 Can you track meeting actions and progress using an off-the-shelf technology platform?

10 Did the meeting set-up work as planned (eg room readiness and set-up, flip charts and pens, conference call set-up, video call set-up, and so on)? What could be improved for the next meeting?

Team communication processes

We continually witness many excellent teams who relate well with each other, but derail themselves due to inadequate communication processes. The increasingly global nature of the modern workplace, coupled with a multiplicity of technology communication platforms, has resulted in many teams developing disjointed communication processes that for some teams includes an unofficial 'always on' mindset. Clutterbuck (2007) highlights the need for teams to determine if their communication processes are working. In our experience, the team coach is excellently placed to ask the team:

- Who do you currently communicate with (each other, other teams, internal and external stakeholders, etc) and why is it important?

- For those identified, what is the main purpose of your communications (eg to give or receive information, to consult on a decision, to jointly discuss a shared initiative or problem, or a mixture of each)?

- For those identified, how do you mainly communicate (e-mail, face-to-face, phone, video conference, other technology platforms etc)?

- For each person(s) you communicate with, what are you doing well and what could you do better? How could you find out for sure?

- When you reflect on your team's purpose and goals, what communications should you prioritize for improvement?

The challenges of team ways of working

Focusing on the task at the expense of the future

In our experience, it is not untypical to find teams and organizations focused on a task above all else. This constant focus on 'doing' things has two key issues. Firstly, teams are so busy staying on the hamster wheel, they are failing to take time to look at the big picture of what the future requires of them. Secondly, over time this constant need to think rationally about the task becomes a habit that comes at the expense of building social connections, which it has been suggested are needed to address 'many of the toughest business challenges, like engagement, motivation and productivity' (Hills, 2016: 79). Team coaches need to help teams reflect on how much time they are spending 'doing' things, as opposed to 'thinking' and just 'being' with each other.

Home and remote working: an opportunity and a challenge

There are lots of reasons why a company may want to encourage their employees to work from home for at least some of their week, including office space restrictions, cost reduction programmes, positive environmental impact, productivity gains and work-life balance reasons. During the COVID-19 pandemic in 2020, we witnessed a necessity for working from home. Despite this, there exist mixed opinions among employees and employers about what the right level and approach is for remote working.

In their 2016 study, Gallup (2017) found that 43 per cent of employees had worked from home in some capacity and that 'all employees who spend at least some (but not all) of their time working remotely have higher engagement than those who don't ever work remotely' (p. 154). However, there is a cost. The same report also cited examples of major companies that have scaled back their work-from-home programmes, citing the need to improve teamwork, collaboration and communication.

As team coaches, we would call for balance. Each team and company will need to find its optimum level between facilitating homeworking, with its positive effect on engagement scores, and the need for teams to collaborate and communicate. We would recommend that while teams working virtually should maximize the use of virtual platforms that support collaboration, it is also important to collaborate in person, if feasible.

Common team communication process challenges

In our work with teams, there is a commonality in the issues that teams present regarding communication process challenges. Fortunately, there is also a commonality in the kind of solutions teams come up with. Interestingly, technology features in nearly all the examples, either as the challenge or solution. Table 9.5 illustrates the issues that are constantly reported to us, potential solutions, and our top tips.

Table 9.5   Communication process challenges, potential solutions and top tips

Problems identified	Solutions proposed	Top tips
Over-reliance on e-mail as a communication conduit	Set up shared communication/ collaboration platforms	Agree team behaviours for each platform
Poor meeting behaviours (physical and virtual)	Agree meeting behaviours – acceptable versus unacceptable behaviours	Develop a team charter Refresh on agreed meeting behaviours before the meeting Take time to review meeting behaviours during the meeting Review meeting behaviours after the meeting
Not taking time to speak to each other one-to-one	Create opportunities to connect with team (physically or virtually)	Arrange to go on a walk with a colleague you have to talk to or set up a call

(continued)

Table 9.5   (Continued)

Problems identified	Solutions proposed	Top tips
E-mailing and messaging each other 24 hours per day, 7 days per week	Discuss impact and agree parameters as a team	Working at night or at weekends, save e-mails as drafts and send as per agreed parameters. Also, use delayed send feature available in most e-mail platforms
Social media and smartphones detracting from one-to-one conversations and workflow	Reach a team agreement on appropriate use of social media and smartphones	Develop mobile-free zones/time

---

Using tools and techniques

When applying these tools and techniques, it is essential that the team coach or leader builds connection and psychological safety first. The tools and techniques are offered as a support and guide, that when used should feel natural and in 'flow', with the process and steps behind the tools remaining effectively invisible.

Tools and techniques for developing team ways of working

TOOL 1: Circle of Influence and Concern – Building team proactivity

Why use this tool?

To help teams consider what they can influence within their organizational system and explore what they believe to be outside of their control. This can be very helpful for teams to help prioritize their work and focus on the situations where they can make a difference. The tool can also enable teams to shift negative or limiting mindsets and attitudes to a more positive position.

When to use this tool

- At a stage in the team development when changes are taking place either initiated by the team themselves or imposed from within the organization or external environment.

- When a team is spending a high proportion of their time and energy working on tasks that do not achieve their purpose or improve performance.

Resources required

- Post-it notes or similar.

- Circle of Influence and Circle of Concern model (Covey, 2004) on a flip chart, virtual whiteboard/platform.

How to use this tool

Step 1   Place the 'Circle of Influence' and 'Circle of Concern' model on a large flip chart or virtual whiteboard. Explain the model highlighting the following key points (Covey, 2004: 81-91):

- The model consists of an inner and outer circle. The inner circle refers to the 'circle of influence', whereas the outer circle refers to the 'circle of concern'.

- **'Circle of concern'.** People are concerned about many things, and reactive people tend to try to change all of these things. This can result in a lot of wasted energy because we can only influence a small number of the things we're concerned about. An over-reactive focus on concerns can result in the 'circle of concern' growing at the expense of the 'circle of influence'.

- **'Circle of influence'.** Proactive people focus on the things they can influence and this can result in positive change. What is most within our influence is our own attitude and behaviour, and this should always be our starting point. Ideally, we should be aiming to expand our 'circle of influence'.

Step 2   Ask the team to individually write down all the things that are concerning them at the moment, that are getting in the way of their performance. One concern per Post-it note (if working virtually use an annotate or virtual Post-it note function on a virtual platform).

Step 3   Team members all place their 'concerns' on a flip chart or virtual whiteboard/platform.

Step 4   The team then groups the concerns into key topics/themes.

Step 5   Ask the team to now decide if they can influence the concerns. If they decide they can, then it gets placed in the 'influence' circle. If it is something that no one in the team can influence, it is placed in the 'concern' circle.

Step 6   As a team, view the outputs in each circle and discuss where the team believe they should place the most energy and attention, on concerns or influence.

Step 7   Team to now agree on the top three areas they believe will make the greatest difference in achieving their team's purpose and performance goals.

Step 8   Agree what the next steps should be and capture actions.

Top tips for team coaches

It can be helpful to give some real-life examples of how teams you have worked in or with have expanded their circle of control by working together as a collective.

Time required

Approximately 45 minutes.

TOOL 2: Creating Common Ground – Valuing difference

Why use this tool?

Often we experience differences of opinion in team meetings or when working together to make decisions. This tool can help team members to consider other points of view, to help move towards a common aligned approach.

When to use this tool

At any stage of a team meeting or decision making process to understand different perspectives and value diversity of thought.

Resources required

A means to note down your thoughts.

How to use this tool

Step 1   Individually think about some of the following questions to help explore what other team members are thinking and their perspective on the situation:

- What is our overall purpose that we are trying to achieve?
- What common ground is there?
- How can I help them feel good about this?
- What do you think are their real concerns about this issue?
- What other pressures are they under right now?
- How can I help them to reframe the situation?
- What triggers are they experiencing?
- What are they triggering in me?
- How will this different opinion be helpful to the team?
- How would I view this differently if I focus on the person rather than the situation?

Step 2   Capture the responses.

Step 3   Reflect on the responses and consider – what can you do to help the team find common ground? Capture actions.

Step 4   Consider – what will you do next?

Top tips for team coaches

This tool can be used for individual team members or you can use it with the full team during a meeting. Ask the team to pause and consider these questions regarding a member of the team who they are having difficulty finding common ground with.

Time required

Approximately 20 minutes.

TOOL 3: Pause and Reflect – Improving decision making

Why use this tool?

Many teams struggle to make effective decisions when it comes to more challenging or controversial topics. There are different models for decision making and multiple dynamics taking place when we are working in teams, which can make it hard for teams to agree on the best collective decision.

When to use this tool

At any stage of a team meeting or decision making process to enable the team to stop and reflect on the effectiveness of their decision making.

Resources required

Undistracted time for the team to discuss their decision.

How to use this tool

Step 1   Brief the team that they will have the opportunity to discuss a real decision that they need to make.

Step 2   Ask the team to agree on the subject of the decision and explain that they will have 30 minutes to discuss the topic. Contract with the team that the team coaches observe the team in action and will pause the discussion during the 30 minutes for the team to review and reflect on their decision making. At that point, the team coaches may well give them feedback.

Step 3   Allow the team to discuss their decision whilst the team coaches observe.

Step 4   After around 15 minutes or at an appropriate time the team coaches will request the team to pause. Ask the team to consider:

- What is working well?
- How effective is their decision making?
- What is getting in the way of decision making?
- What could they do differently?

Step 5   Offer any feedback and observations to the team that they haven't already surfaced.

Step 6   Discuss with the team – what will their approach be now?

Step 7   Allow the team to continue and pause again if there is a further need to review and reflect.

Step 8   Finally, review and reflect on what worked well and what could be improved. Discuss key learnings and capture actions.

Top tips for team coaches

- It is important to clearly contract on the role of the team coach during this exercise.
- You may want to share approaches to decision making with the team, as explained earlier in this chapter. During the pause, it may be helpful for the team to consider which style of decision making they are adopting and where they are on the decision making continuum, eg at the authority end, consensus or somewhere in the middle.

Time required

45–60 minutes.

TOOL 4: The Five Whats Model – Effective decision making

Why use this tool?

Helping teams to review and reflect on their decision making can be a powerful way to identify what is working well and how the team can become more effective.

When to use this tool

- At any stage of team development where teams require a different way to think and talk about decision making.
- With teams where decision making was identified as a key area of development or improvement.

Resources required

- Decision making questions.
- Flip chart paper and pens, virtual whiteboard/platform.

How to use this tool

Step 1 Explore some examples of the following questions with the team:

- When have they made a successful collective decision? What did that look like? What made it successful?
- When did they not achieve the decision they hoped for? What got in the way? What was missing?

Step 2 Talk the team through 'The Five Whats Model' explaining each step.

Step 3 As a team, ask them to think of a decision that didn't go well. Split the team into subgroups and ask them to review the decision using 'The Five Whats Model'. Share the blank decision making template either on a flip chart or virtually. Give the subgroups around 20–30 minutes to review. Ask the subgroups to capture their answers.

Step 4 Bring all the subgroups together and discuss their answers to the five questions.

Step 5 The whole team to review – what did they learn about their decision making?

- What is working well?
- What are the areas for improvement?

Step 6 Team to review and discuss – how can they use this model to help them with their decision making in the future?

Step 7 Ask the team to commit to some decision making rules and hold them to account going forward. Capture actions.

Top tips for team coaches

- It may be helpful to share an example of how you have used the decision making model and talk through each question and response.

Tool 4a The Five Whats Model

Question	Areas to consider	Questions to explore further
1. What is the decision?	• Who should be making this decision? • What will a good decision look like?	• What is the goal for this decision? • How will we know if we make a good decision? • Who is impacted by this decision? • Should we be making this decision? • Who else do we need to involve?
2. What options are there available?	• What can we do? • What else can we do? • What else can we do?	• If we had no constraints, what could we do? • What is the cost if we do nothing?
3. What actions will we commit to?	• What do we need to deliver? • What needs to be put in place to make sure we can deliver?	• Who do we need support from?
4. What is the plan?	• How will we monitor progress?	• Who has the accountability for this decision? • Who has the responsibility for delivering the plan?
5. What is the learning for the future?	• How will we learn for the future?	• What went well during the decision making process? • What will we do to avoid errors in future?

Tool 4b   The Five Whats Model – review

Question	Response	What did we do well?	What could we improve?
What was the decision?			
What options were considered?			
What actions were committed to?			
What was the plan?			
What is the learning for the future?			

- The model can be used to review and reflect on previous decisions and to look at decisions that the team are currently making or due to make in the future.

Time required

60 minutes

TOOL 5: 'The Hamster Wheel' – Reflecting on short- and long-term activities

Why use this tool?

Many teams we work with spend a large proportion of their time on operational activities and the day-to-day work of the team. Much less time is given to developing their purpose, strategic goals and looking further ahead.

When to use this tool

- Where it would be helpful for the team to review team processes, meetings and ways of working.
- If the team are spending time mainly focusing on the day-to-day rather than working on the strategic direction.

Resources required

- Flip chart paper and pens, virtual whiteboard/platform.
- Post-it notes or annotate feature on a virtual platform.

How to use this tool

Step 1 Explain the idea of the metaphor of 'The Hamster Wheel'. The hamster wheel describes the idea that teams and individuals can sometimes keep running in circles, going faster and faster with a sense that the motion is the important factor. Often, however, they keep going and don't make progress. Stepping off the wheel helps the team and individuals to review, reflect and focus on the long-term strategy.

Tool 5   The Hamster Wheel

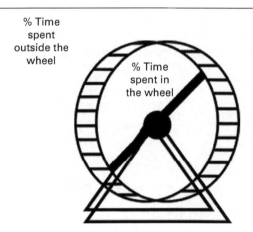

% Time spent outside the wheel

% Time spent in the wheel

Step 2 Place the flip chart with the wheel on the wall/floor or display virtually. Ask each team member to capture the following on two Post-it notes or annotate on a virtual platform:

- What percentage of their time do they think the team are spending in the hamster wheel?
- What percentage of their time do they think the team are spending outside the hamster wheel?

Step 3   Ask the team to review the wheel and discuss:

- What percentage of time do they think they should be spending where, to achieve their purpose and strategic objectives?

Step 4   Split into subgroups (use breakout rooms if working virtually) and consider:

- What are the top activities that are keeping them in the wheel?
- What are the top activities that they should be focusing on outside the wheel?

Step 5   Subgroups to share with the whole team their thoughts and agree what actions they will take to achieve the ideal percentage for the team (eg team processes and meetings structure).

Capture actions.

Top tips for team coaches

- This simple exercise can be used in different ways, eg it may be enough to ask the team to reflect on the percentage of time spent inside and outside the wheel to create new insights.
- 'The Hamster Wheel' can also be used for individual team members, to reflect where they spend their time and then to consider what impact that has on the team.

Time required

30–40 minutes.

TOOL 6: Voice of the Customer – Developing an agile mindset

Why use this tool?

To enable teams to adopt an agile mindset by putting the customer first and hearing what they need now or in the future. This will help the team to ensure that their team processes, principles and ways of working are established to meet the customer needs.

When to use this tool

At any stage of a team's development.

Resources required

Hearing from 'real' customers.

How to use this tool

Step 1　Before the team coaching session, ask the team to consider how they can bring the customer into the room or go out and speak to the customer.

Step 2　Team to arrange a conversation with the customer or customers and enquire:

- What do you need from us that you are not getting now?
- What frustrates you about how we work?
- If we were to make your life easier, what would enable this?
- What would exceptional service look like to you?
- What could we do to achieve this?
- If you think of the future, what else will you need?
- What can we do to make that a reality for you?
- What other suggestions do you have?

Step 3　Thank the customer. Team to consider what they have heard and review:

- What do they need to do differently?
- What are the options to achieve this?
- What actions will they take?
- Who will be accountable for these?
- How will they monitor and review the actions?
- When will this happen?
- How will the team keep the voice of the customer in the room?

Step 4　Team to commit to final actions.

Top tips for team coaches

- It is important for this exercise that the team are hearing from a 'real' customer. Other options to connect with the customer can be via video conference, conference calls or visiting the customer's premises.

- Another option is joint exploration workshops with a customer, where both parties explore their experience of each other and possible improvements. Team coaches are ideally placed to help lead such sessions.

Time required

45–60 minutes.

Reflecting on team ways of working

- Think of a high-performing team you worked in. What effective ways of working did they adopt?

- How does your team make decisions? What works well? What can be improved?

- How could you collaborate more with teams outside of your function, area or organization to form a powerful collective?

- How well do you communicate with stakeholders, customers etc? How could this be even better?

- How can you find out what customers, stakeholders etc want from your team?

- What agile processes does your team currently use? What else could be helpful?

Team transformation 10

What do teams need to do to become transformational?

Defining transformation

Reflect for a moment on what transformations have taken place in your life. Which ones were forced, and which ones were chosen? What are you still trying to transform? What transformation efforts have you temporarily or permanently abandoned? What are the similarities in successful transformations? What are the similarities in unsuccessful transformations? If you are like most people, your life will be a story of successful and unsuccessful transformations and multiple examples of what could be described as a work in progress.

As this chapter will illustrate, transformation is as much a journey as it is an act. We will discuss key areas that we believe, if given focus, can result in transformation journeys of worth, for individuals, teams and organizations.

The psychology behind transformation

To transform or not

As humans we either exploit or we explore (Bossons *et al*, 2015). When we are in exploit mode, we are in a state of contentment and comfort. We exploit what we find around us. We are in relative control. However, to grow and experience new things we must learn how to explore. Learning to explore includes risks that must be navigated. Sayings such as, 'there is no gain without pain' resonate. The reality of our existence is a constant journey of metaphorically staying near our cave, exploiting what is convenient and comfortable, and crossing the river to explore opportunities for growth, learning and adventure.

Throughout this book we have discussed the challenges humans face when making decisions, especially those concerned with the longer term. It is evident that for humans to transform, they need something bigger to help them overcome their tendency to make decisions that benefit their short-term comfort. At a foundational level, purpose, vision and goals (Chapter 4), an identity to aspire to (Chapter 5) and values to guide them, as well as beliefs to sustain them (Chapter 6), can all play a role in helping people to transform. However, to become truly transformational they also need a mindset that wants to continually transform, grow and learn.

Developing a transformational, learning and growth mindset

In Chapter 6, when discussing how beliefs affect our mindset, we referenced the work of Dweck (2012, 2015, 2016), who has popularized the idea of a growth mindset and a fixed mindset. Working with students, Dweck discovered that if you could change a student's mindset, you could increase their level of achievement. She discovered that students who believed their intelligence could be developed (a growth mindset) outperformed those who believed their intelligence was fixed (a fixed mindset). However, in an article entitled 'What Having a "Growth Mindset" Actually Means', Dweck (2016) discussed her concern that the idea was being oversimplified and outlined three common misconceptions:

1 **I already have it, and I always have.** She highlights that it is not an either/or situation. We all have a mixture of fixed and growth mindsets. She notes that a 'pure growth mindset doesn't exist' (Dweck, 2016: 2). This corresponds with our proposition that transformation is about being on a journey. It is about an upward trajectory, with its ups and downs.

2 **A growth mindset is just about praising and rewarding effort.** Highlighting this as untrue and that outcomes do matter, she states 'it's critical to reward not just effort but learning and progress' (Dweck, 2016: 3). Self-reflection, which was referred to in Chapter 2 as essential for a team coach's 'way of being' is equally as important for anyone wishing to develop a transformational mindset.

3 **Just espouse a growth mindset, and good things will happen.** Referring to companies who make grand mission and value statements, she asked, 'what do they mean to employees if the company doesn't implement policies that make them real and attainable?' (Dweck, 2016: 3). Without plans and action, words only are meaningless for individuals who wish to develop a transformational mindset.

The good news is that Dweck's research has demonstrated that we can grow our brains, become intellectually stronger and achieve improved outcomes. Bossons *et al* (2015), writing about neuroplasticity (how the brain can change itself), have stated that 'if we are sufficiently motivated, there is little that we cannot choose to learn' (p. 70). To create the new neurons required for learning, it is suggested we need to regularly acquaint ourselves with new environments and new experiences, as well as exercise (van Praag *et al*, 2000). That the brain changes is a literal statement, with research by Woollett and Maguire (2011) demonstrating structural brain changes in London taxi drivers, when they had to learn, practise and be tested on what is referred to as 'The Knowledge'. However, despite our amazing human capability to keep learning new things at any stage of life, it is easy to find reasons not to take action. Dweck (2016) has highlighted how our 'fixed mindset' persona can show up, speaking into our mind thoughts that make us feel threatened and defensive. She highlights the need to learn how to talk back to that fixed persona, persuading it to collaborate as we pursue challenging goals.

Unlocking our innate creativity

If you ask a room full of people how many of them can draw, nearly everyone will say no. Fifteen minutes later, after watching and drawing along with Graham Shaw's (2015) TEDx talk entitled 'Why people believe they can't draw - and how to prove they can', most people will change their answer to a yes. We might not all be Picasso, but we can all learn how to draw. At the end of his TEDx talk, Shaw asks the audience, 'How many other beliefs and limiting thoughts do we all carry around with us every day?' He further asks, 'and if we did challenge those beliefs, what else would be possible for us all?'

Similarly, if you ask a room full of people how many of them are creative, most people, even after completing the drawing exercise, will say they are not. However, this too is a limiting belief. The reality is each human being is blessed with their own spark of creativity, that most spend their life suppressing. The world is full of potential artists that have never painted, musicians who have not discovered their instrument and poets who have yet to find their pen. Ryan and Deci (2000), the proponents of Self-Determination Theory, have stated that 'from birth onward, humans, in their healthiest states, are active, inquisitive, curious, and playful creatures, displaying a ubiquitous readiness to learn and explore' (p. 56). McGregor and Doshi (2015), who have developed the research of Deci and Ryan in the context of the workplace, have found that play (being motivated by the actual work itself) is the number one intrinsic motivator as to why humans work. We are each born to create, and the workplace should be our playground. Unfortunately, most work is structured in ways that limit individual creativity and therefore individual potential.

So how can we encourage individuals to produce creative work? The Componential Theory of Creativity (Amabile, 2012; Amabile and Pillemer, 2012) has highlighted four psychological components, each viewed as necessary for creative work to take place. Three of the components are associated with the individual, while the fourth is concerned with the environment in which the individual operates. The four components have been described as:

1 **Domain-relevant skills.** Expertise, technical skill, and innate talent in the relevant domain of work – such as product design or electrical engineering.

2 **Creativity-relevant processes (originally called creativity-relevant skills).** Cognitive style and personality preferences that include openness to risk-taking and taking new perspectives, a tolerance for ambiguity, and the self-discipline to keep generating new ideas. In addition, skills in using creative thinking techniques and methodologies are highlighted.

3 **Intrinsic task motivation.** This is about the passion and motivation to undertake a task because of the interest, involvement, challenge or satisfaction derived. This contrasts with extrinsic motivating factors such as bonuses, surveillance, competition, evaluation, or requirements to do something in a certain way.

4 **Social environment.** Also referred to as the work environment, this is the only external component. While the social environment impacts each of the other components, its impact on a person's motivation is viewed as most significant. The more an environment supports intrinsic motivational factors, the greater the creativity.

Given the four components presented, it is not surprising that it has been suggested that too much attention is paid to the idea of the creative person and innate factors, as opposed to the crucial role of the social environment, which supports learning and creativity (Amabile, 2018).

In summary, human beings are capable of amazing feats if they adopt a transformational, learning and growth mindset, but to become all that we are capable of being we also need to be supported by the right social environment. Given the vast amount of our lives we spend at work (see Table 8.1 in Chapter 8), we would suggest that organizations play a significant role in determining the extent to which an individual regresses or flourishes.

The importance of transformation for organizations

How can organizations become transformational?

For an organization to be transformational, it requires much more than words. Eckel *et al* (1998: 4) have stated that 'transformation: alters the culture of the institution, by changing select underlying assumptions and institutional behaviours, processes, and products; is deep and pervasive, affecting the whole institution; is intentional; and occurs over time.' Given this list, it may not be surprising that most weeks the news will feature some organization that has failed to transform itself in the face of a rapidly changing environment. It is likely that by the time an organization has decided to transform, it may already be too late. Transformation should not be something you do, it should be something you are. Organizations need to have a transformational mindset – a mindset that permeates every person in the organization.

From our experience, organizations that best illustrate this mindset are those that:

- Live and breathe a compelling purpose that adds real value to its multiple stakeholders and is about more than just making money.
- Care about delivering on their goals, including financial security and longevity. They care about costs as well as income. They take a long-term view of investments.
- Have a clear vision that guides their thinking. Everyone understands the strategic intent of the organization and is encouraged to make decisions that are aligned to this intent.
- Have organizational values that genuinely drive behaviours, starting with the CEO and board. They understand that organizational culture is the sum of everyone's behaviours.
- Have employees who feel a sense of personal alignment to the purpose, vision and values of the organization.
- Provide opportunities for employees to express their own identities and tell their own stories.
- Remain close to their stakeholders and have an unquenchable thirst to know what people are thinking, irrespective of how difficult the message may be. They are obsessive about two-way communication.

- Select and develop leaders that not only inspire followership, but also have the desire and diligence to manage.

- Understand and support the value of collaboration instead of competition, within teams, between teams and between organizations (where legally possible).

- Continually seek the right balance between the organizational processes required for scale and efficiency, and the need for a transformative and agile mindset.

- Are obsessive about growing and learning, not just as an organization, but every individual within.

- Do not talk about diversity and inclusion narrowly, but embrace the fullness of diversity (eg diversity of thought, neurodiversity, age, gender, background).

- Understand the psychology of why and how people work and subsequently implement policies that support human flourishing (eg developing a culture of coaching individuals and teams).

- Measure and track more than finances (eg client satisfaction, employee engagement, psychological safety, team effectiveness, employee well-being, diversity and inclusion).

This list is based on our experience of leading teams and coaching in some of the world's top-performing companies. It is also informed by research, much of which has been referred to in this book. Nevertheless, we do not live in a perfect world. With the task appearing so daunting, we believe that team transformation can help organizations in their journey to becoming truly transformational.

Developing team transformation

We believe that transformational teams offer organizations one of the most effective ways of ensuring they themselves are transformational. For a team to be transformational, we would suggest there are four key elements a team should embrace (see Figure 10.1). These include team learning, team creativity and innovation, team inclusion and diversity, and team well-being.

Team learning

A meta-analysis on one-to-one coaching studies has demonstrated that, in addition to improvements in performance and results, coaching helps

Figure 10.1   The key elements of team transformation

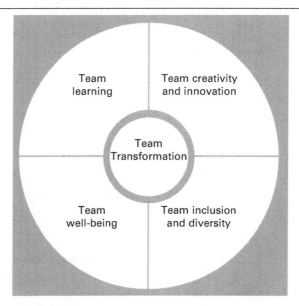

coachees to learn and develop (Jones *et al*, 2016). Our own experience of team coaching would strongly suggest that it offers both individuals and teams these same outcomes. Some of the earliest models of team coaching emphasized the importance of team learning (Hackman and Wageman, 2005; Clutterbuck, 2007), and while expressed using different terms, this has continued to be emphasized in approaches to team coaching (Thornton, 2010; Hawkins, 2011, Peters and Carr, 2013; Hauser, 2014). In our own definition of team coaching, we used the terms 'new thinking' and 'collective potential' when reflecting on the importance of team learning.

Team learning has been described as 'a relatively permanent change in the team's collective level of knowledge and skill, produced by the shared experience of the team members' (Ellis *et al*, 2003: 822). Significantly, when a team learns together, not only do they perform better, but individuals grow more rapidly than they would have otherwise (Senge, 2006). Edmonson (1999) has demonstrated how psychological safety (discussed in Chapter 8) also contributes towards team learning, which in turn leads to improved team performance.

So how can team coaches maximize team learning? Thornton (2016: 65–80) has highlighted eight factors (see Table 10.1) that are helpful to consider when thinking about how people learn in groups.

Table 10.1 How team coaches can maximize team learning

Factors	How team coaches can maximize team learning?
Connectedness and Belonging	When individuals feel safe in a group, they are more open to learning. The team coach has a key role in creating this safety.
Interpersonal Learning	It has been suggested that the learning that can take place between individuals when in groups cannot be equalled. The team coach should highlight to the team the learning opportunity that team coaching offers.
Competition, envy and admiration	While envy can be destructive, it is suggested that when handled well, it can be transformative.
Idealization and emulation	It is important for the team coach to help the team move from the idealization of team members, the team coach or the team itself, towards admiration, which is considered a more positive platform for learning.
Practising courage and freedom to act	Over time, team members are likely to act with greater courage than they would in other settings. This offers an excellent opportunity for experimentation and learning to take place.
Witnessing and being witnessed	Saying things that only previously existed in our head, in front of witnesses, can be extremely powerful.
Encouragement	Teams offer an excellent platform for members to encourage and support one another on their learning journeys.
Group performance coaching	Team members can benefit from helping each other. We believe that encouraging a culture of peer coaching can act as one of the strongest legacies of a team coaching intervention. Clutterbuck (2014: 280) has suggested that with the right conditions in place, 'much of the coaching may also take place between peers within the team.'

SOURCE Adapted from Thornton (2016)

Story: The transformative power of different boards learning and collaborating together
Contributor: Lucy

I was working with a board from a large global business. The board identified that the organization needed to rethink its service strategy and wanted some external input. They believed that they could learn a great deal from companies in the retail and airline sectors about exceeding customer expectations.

We contacted two other well-known companies who had a reputation for excellent customer service. We initially arranged external exchanges with the other boards to get to know each other's businesses, understand the brand, the approach to customer service, and build connections. We then asked each business what key strategic challenges they wanted new insight on and asked them to agree on two strategic questions that they could work on together with the other businesses.

As a result, the two teams worked together on the service strategy for the large global business and came up with new and different approaches to exceeding service. In addition, the global business introduced the ideas across the entire UK business. The results of this initiative demonstrate the usefulness of working with teams we would not normally be in contact with.

Team creativity and innovation

While creativity and innovation are often used interchangeably, they are technically different. Creativity is defined as 'the ability to create' (Merriam-Webster.com) compared to innovation, which is defined as 'the introduction of something new' (Merriam-Webster.com). For the purposes of this section, we will focus on creativity. Helpfully, Hirst *et al* (2011) have described creativity in the context of work as 'an outcome that derives from addressing work challenges' (p. 625).

Following a study of 95 groups, Taggar (2002) has suggested adding team creativity-relevant processes to Amabile's componential theory (discussed earlier in this chapter). The study found that in effective groups, members engage in creativity-supporting behaviours that establish a social environment conducive to creativity. They also note the importance of processes to moderate the relationship between aggregated individual creativity and group creativity. In other words, a group needs processes that allow every voice to be heard, as well as processes that help the group create together.

Research specifically regarding the team context has further built on Amabile's componential theory. Hirst *et al* (2009) discovered a positive relationship between a team learning orientation and team creativity. They also discovered that an individual learning orientation only contributed to team creativity when team learning orientation was high. A team committed to team learning is therefore essential for a team to be creative. In addition, Hirst *et al* (2011) discovered that a team will be more creative when it includes individuals who are open to their competence being judged by others, decentralizes decision making across the team, and when it has less bureaucracy.

Using this research, a team can ask itself the following questions to ascertain if it has a team environment that fosters creativity:

- Do our agreed team behaviours support and encourage individuals to share ideas?
- Do we have processes in place that ensure everyone's voice is heard?
- Do we have processes in place that facilitate the group creating together (eg idea generation, problem-solving techniques, methods for synthesizing ideas)?
- Do we have a team learning orientation?
- Do we have enough people in our team who are open to having their ideas and competence judged? How can we encourage those who do not?
- Do we have the power to make decisions as a team, versus decision making power residing in particular individuals?
- Is our creativity being held back by too much bureaucracy and if so, what can we do to change this or limit its impact?

Team inclusion and diversity

We are both privileged to be involved in pioneering different inclusion and diversity initiatives in organizations, that include female participation in the professional services sector (Lucy) and neurodiversity in the science, technology, engineering and mathematics (STEM) sectors (Paul). It is notable that most diversity initiatives take place at an organizational level; however, we see the need for these initiatives to be systemic. To have the desired impact, inclusion and diversity initiatives should take place at an organizational, team and individual level. It could be surmised from the research and discussions on identity (Chapter 5) and relatedness (Chapter 8) that it is at the level of the team where the benefits of diversity will be most realized. We are therefore of the view that teams that wish to be transformational should not be sitting back waiting for their organization to take the lead. While executive and senior teams carry significant organizational influence, there is still much that every team can do to develop a more diverse team and hence workplace.

In Figure 10.2 we have proposed three areas that teams should look at to review their progress with regards to inclusion and diversity. We have broken diversity down into three segments: what (gender, age etc); who (professional status, capabilities etc); and how (personality preferences, neurodiversity etc).

It can be useful for teams to ask themselves the following questions:

- Using the what, who and how model, how diverse are we as a team?
- Where do we have opportunities to make improvements?
- What could be the benefits if we make these improvements?
- What can we proactively do to become more diverse?
- How will we measure progress?

Figure 10.2   The what, who and how of team inclusion and diversity

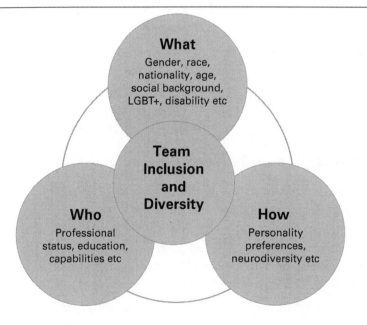

Story: Building better teams through embracing neurodiversity

Contributor: Paul

I was working with the senior team in a large government body. It was our third session together and a strong level of psychological safety had been established. During this session, I shared with the team some of the work I have been doing in the area of neurodiversity. The purpose of telling the story was to challenge the team to reflect on what they were doing to embrace neurodiversity.

During one of the subsequent breakout sessions, a discussion took place that literally transformed lives. One member of a team, who was on the autistic spectrum, discussed openly with their boss and team that they were in a role that they should not be in. The role they were currently in was causing distress to the team member, the team leader and the team as a whole. During the discussion, the team leader suggested a possible role change that might better respect the team member's natural strengths. The team member and the team agreed. It was as if everyone knew something needed to change but nobody had wanted to talk about it. There was an excitement at the table after the exercise. It felt like a weight had been lifted.

A thank-you note a few days later described the positive impact of the changes for the team member, the leader and the team.

Team well-being

Similar to inclusion and diversity, most wellness initiatives are run at an organizational level. Berry *et al* (2010) have suggested that the benefits of workplace wellness programmes include: reduced absenteeism; improved productivity; higher morale; increases in employee pride, trust, and commitment; and a more vigorous organization. Likely to be more relevant to the United States, they note that savings on healthcare costs alone result in an impressive ROI. Vital (2019) has suggested that it is not about adding more programmes; rather, it is about examining the wellness culture, which has been described as 'one in which employee health, happiness, and well-being are prioritized' (Greenwald, 2018: 32).

Table 10.2 Team wellness – how can we support each other in mind, body and spirit?

Mind – building our mental resilience	Body – looking after our physical health	Spirit – being who we are meant to be/best possible version of self
Emotional well-being initiatives (eg self-agility, relationships, communications)	Health awareness (eg impact of daily habits – smoking, drinking, snacking, poor nutrition)	Connecting to individual, team and organization purpose
Mental health first aid (eg champions) and support platforms (eg counselling/addiction services)	Health checks (eg weight, diabetes, blood pressure, heart health)	Opportunities to develop deep human connectedness and support channels
Inclusion and diversity awareness training and support to make changes	Medical support (eg medical access support, medical insurance)	Developing role of playfulness/joy (eg role improvization, autonomy, creativity)
Financial management training (eg banking, saving, debt, pensions)	Physical activity encouragement (eg voluntary tracking, walk-to-talk and walk-and-talk, classes, team sports)	Developing community connectedness aligned with team values (eg school)
Personal effectiveness and ways of working initiatives (eg travel times, work – life balance, working from home)	Physical activity infrastructure (eg work gym, outdoor walkways)	Developing environmental/nature connectedness (eg campaign support)
Leadership capability development (eg developing high support/high challenge leadership/zero bullying)	Posture awareness and infrastructure (eg back health, seating support)	Encouraging individual expression and diversity (eg sexuality, neurodiversity)

Behavioural change support including individual, peer and team coaching	Energy awareness and support (eg bad habit awareness, sleep education)	Developing/showing appreciation for different belief systems and faiths
Family support initiatives (eg bereavement, neurodiversity support)	Nutrition and dietary awareness (eg cookery classes, peer support initiatives)	Encouraging individuals to pursue learning opportunities aligned to their values (eg education)
Team resilience training (eg reflexivity, mindfulness techniques/classes)	Nutrition support (eg workplace healthy eating infrastructure/healthy eating options)	Developing options for sabbaticals/secondments aligned to individual values
Workspace indoor and outdoor improvements (eg quiet room, plants, landscaped walkways))	Regular assessments to ascertain impact of work on physical health, track progress and inform planning	Celebration of individual team member strengths/successes, as well as collective team strengths/successes

While little is written about teams and wellness programmes, Koster (2016), in their profiling of the wellness programme run by a large-scale marketing and advertising software company, highlighted how a 'rewards for wellness activities programme' offered extra rewards for activities completed as a team. They noted how teams had positively embraced the programme, with benefits including community initiatives completed together and deeper connections.

In the absence of programmes such as that outlined by Koster (2016), we believe there is an opportunity for teams to take charge of their own wellness. This may include encouraging and supporting each other to partake in wellness initiatives run by the organization, or it could include wellness initiatives the team instigate themselves. Such team initiatives offer an excellent opportunity for teams to partner with other stakeholder teams both within and outside their organization. We would propose that if a team wants to be truly transformational, they need to look after their mind, body and spirit. In Table 10.2 we have outlined 30 ideas that a team can consider. Tool 5, later in this chapter, will illustrate how a team can use the ideas presented here to improve individual and team wellness.

The challenges of team transformation

'We are too busy to become a transformational team'

One of the main challenges we keep coming across when team coaching is teams who describe themselves as too busy. This is sometimes evidenced by the difficulty of getting the team together for calls, virtually and for in-person team coaching sessions. We normally find that when the team does get together, they are usually able to be 'present', despite their busyness.

The reality is transformation will not take place unless it is given time. Imagine trying to learn, be creative, support team inclusion and diversity activities, and attend to team well-being, without feeling you have enough time. If a team wants to become transformational, it needs to prioritize the activities that support team transformation.

Organization cultures that do not support team transformation

If a team operates in a culture that encourages competition within and between teams, has incentives that mainly reward individuals, is obsessed with results and figures above all else, has a 'blame' culture or 'cover yourself' culture, pays lip service to areas such as purpose, vision, values, inclusion and diversity and well-being, or offers teams little meaningful autonomy, then no matter how great a team is, they are likely to struggle to become transformational. We have witnessed teams who have successfully operated against the organizational grain, but this is more an exception than the rule. Teams need to be supported by their organizational culture, or at a minimum be given the autonomy to find their own path.

Tools and techniques for developing team transformation

> ## Using tools and techniques
>
> When applying these tools and techniques, it is essential that the team coach or leader builds connection and psychological safety first. The tools and techniques are offered as a support and guide, that when used should feel natural and in 'flow', with the process and steps behind the tools remaining effectively invisible.

TOOL 1: Fresh Thinking Model – Building team innovation

Why use this tool?

It is critical for teams to continuously improve and grow. Encouraging a positive culture where everyone has an opportunity to voice their ideas is essential. This tool enables teams to explore their ideas, whether they are completely new or an adaptation of a previous idea.

When to use this tool

- At any stage of team development.
- With teams that wish use a 'fresh thinking' technique to continuously improve.

- With teams to work on how to sustain and develop the changes the team have made.

Resources required

Flip chart paper and pens, virtual whiteboard/platform.

How to use this tool

Step 1   Ask the team why it is important for them to continuously improve – what does this require? To continuously improve, one of the many things we need to do is think creatively.

Step 2   Briefly explain the Fresh Thinking model that has been inspired by and adapted from the thinking of Nick Einhorn, a member of The Magic Circle. The model is based on the principle that many ideas in business are developed from one initial idea that is then expanded on. The innovation model consists of three main phases:

Phase 1   Copy Paste Adapt   Taking an idea and adapting it

Phase 2   Major Shift   Making a shift on the same level

Phase 3   Blue Sky   Brand new ideas

Adapted from Einhorn (2008).

Step 3   Team coach to share an example and demonstrate with an organizational related example where possible.

Tool 1   Example of applying the 'Fresh Thinking' model to an airline innovation

Existing Situation	Passengers all check in at desks
Copy Paste Adapt	Alternative electronic check-in and seat allocation at airport, bags to bag drop
Major Shift	Online check-in and seat allocation, bags to bag drop
Blue Sky	Online check-in and bags picked up at departure from home and arrive at destination. Chauffeur service door to door for first class passengers.

Step 4   Team activity – split into three groups. Each group to apply the Fresh Thinking model to a current real topic. Group 1 to work on 'copy paste adapt', group 2 on 'major shift', and group 3 on 'blue sky'. Give each

group 10 minutes to come up with ideas and capture them either physically or virtually. If working virtually use breakout rooms.

Step 5   Ask the groups to place the captured ideas up on the walls or share on a virtual platform. Each group then moves onto the next phase of reviewing each other's work – group 1 reviews the outputs captured by group 2, group 2 reviews the work of group 3, and group 3 reviews the work of group 1. Each group to add further ideas in different coloured pen. After five minutes rotate the groups again so that every group gets an opportunity to work on each phase.

Step 6   Full team to review each of the captured ideas in turn, asking each other questions to help clarify.

Step 7   Ask the team to tick the top three ideas that they feel could make the biggest difference to this team and the organization.

Step 8   Review the votes and agree on the top three ideas that the team want to keep working on.

Step 9   Team to agree on next steps for the three ideas and capture actions.

Step 10   Final debrief:

- What did the team learn from using this innovation model?
- How could they use this to improve their innovative thinking?
- What will they do next?
- What are their commitments?

Top tips for team coaches

- This tool could also be used during business-as-usual meetings with the team, to help stimulate new ideas.
- We recommend encouraging the team to stand up to help create energy and momentum. Even if working virtually, encourage the team to move in whatever way is possible.
- It is important to contract that no idea is a bad idea so everyone should be heard.
- Each group should use a different colour of marker/annotation pen during the exercise. This allows the team and groups to easily track who has contributed what to each of the phases.

Time required

45 minutes.

TOOL 2: Outside In – Fostering new ideas

Why use this tool?

Teams can become complacent and fail to continue to keep innovating and growing. In a complex and volatile world, developing new thought is vital to help teams respond to what is needed for both the present and the future.

When to use this tool

- At any stage of team development.
- With teams to help them to generate ideas from outside their organization or environment.

Resources required

- An outside area that is ideally a new/stimulating environment.
- Flip chart paper and pens, virtual whiteboard/platform.

How to use this tool

Step 1   Before the team coaching workshop, ask the team to consider:

- What areas do they need to develop new ideas on?
- Where would be the best place for them to get these ideas?
- If they had no constraints where would they go?

Capture their thinking on these questions. If necessary offer some ideas and in partnership agree on the place, environment or location for them to visit. If working virtually, the team should agree on a similar location to visit virtually (eg most leading museums offer virtual tours).

Step 2   Team to visit the location, eg an art gallery, museum, a market, gardens. If working virtually one team member can take the virtual tour and share their screen or each team member could complete the tour separately. During their visit, the team are to think about the area they identified as needing new ideas. Ask them to think about:

- What do they notice?
- What ideas come to mind?

This should happen over 1–2 hours.

Step 3 After the visit, bring the team together. Split into subgroups (or virtual breakout groups) and ask them to discuss:

- What did they observe that would inform the topic area?
- What new thoughts were triggered?
- What ideas occurred to them?

Subgroups to capture their observations, new thoughts and new ideas. Allow 30 minutes for this step.

Step 4 Bring the team together and ask them to share outputs from all the subgroups. Help the team capture key themes. This should take approximately 10 mins.

Step 5 Team to split again into subgroups (or virtual breakout groups) and from what they have observed and discussed, agree on the top three to five ideas they would like to progress.

Step 6 Team to regroup as one and agree on an overall three to five ideas they want to take forward. Team to capture the next steps and actions.

Top tips for team coaches

Using a metaphor can also be a powerful way to connect the team to the environment. For example, if they were visiting gardens, the plants could represent new growth areas for the organization and team; the stream, obstacles that might get in the way; and the bridge over the stream, ideas on how they may overcome the obstacles. Using such metaphors can help the team to develop new ideas and thinking.

Time required

3–4 hours or half a day.

TOOL 3: The Disney Model – Harnessing team creativity

Why use this tool?

Helping teams to harness their creativity around a problem or idea can trigger new thinking and actions. This tool helps teams to look at the problem or idea from three different perspectives:

- What could they do?

- What challenges might they face?
- What is realistic?

When to use this tool

- For teams that want to generate new thinking or test out an idea together.
- When a team needs to think creatively about solutions to a problem they are facing.

Resources required

- Ideally three different rooms, or if that isn't feasible three different areas (or virtual breakout rooms).
- Find graphics and images to represent the thinking styles – 'dreamer', 'realist' and 'critic' – placing one set of images in each room. If working virtually, pre-prepare images or use the image library available on more advanced virtual platforms.

How to use this tool

Step 1   Explain that this tool has been adapted from Walt Disney's strategy for creativity, which he was rumoured to use with his team for testing film ideas (Capodagli and Jackson, 2006).

An outline of the Disney Model

Walt Disney is renowned for being a creative innovator in the cartoon industry. Apart from his boundless energy, there were specific elements in the way he organized his creative workforce that tended to guarantee creative outcomes. When working on the early full-length cartoons that made his name – *Snow White*, *Pinocchio*, *Bambi* and *Fantasia* – he used a revolutionary approach to keep his staff coordinated in their thinking on a particular project.

He moved the ideas around three rooms, which each had a different function:

Room 1. The place where dreams were dreamed, ideas were spun out, no restrictions, no limits – every sort of outrageous creative hunch or idea was freely developed.

Room 2. Here the dreams from room 1 were coordinated and the storyboard created as events and characters fitted into a sequence. (The idea of the storyboard – now ubiquitous – was a Disney invention.)

Room 3. The 'sweatbox' – a small room under the stairs where the whole crew would critically review the project to date, with no constraints in place. The process was safe because it was the project, not a particular individual that was being criticized.

Tool 3   Example questions for the Disney creativity strategy

The Dreamer (what)	The Realist (how)	The Critic (why)
• What do we want to do? • Why are you doing this? • What is the purpose? • What are the benefits? • How will we know when we've got it? • Where will this take us in the future? • What will that be like? • What do we want to consider as options? • Which of these do we want to explore?	• How do we do this? • What specifically needs to happen to implement our idea? • How will each phase be implemented? • Who is involved? • When will each phase be completed? • Where do we need to do this?	• Why are we doing this? • What are the chances of this working? • How do all the elements fit together? • What seems unbalanced? • What will get in the way of this working? • What parts do not fit with the overall objective? • How realistic is this in the time frame? • Why is this necessary?

Then the idea would return to room 1 to allow for the work on the project to continue. The cycle always involved the three rooms. The outcome was that either an idea did not survive room 3 and was abandoned, or it would meet with silence in room 3, which indicated it was ready for production.

Step 2   Set up three different rooms, or areas within a room, to represent the three different states of creativity – 'the dreamer', 'the realist' and 'the critic'. If working virtually use breakout rooms.

Step 3   Ask the team to agree on what problem or idea they want to work on.

Step 4   The team move to the 'dreamer' state/room. Ask the team to explore the 'dreamer' state using the prompt questions, while thinking about what could be possible if no restrictions were in place. For the prompt questions, see example questions provided and capture key discussion points.

Step 5   Next, the team move to the 'realist' state/room. They now explore how they could make the idea happen using the prompt questions. Ask the team to capture the key discussion points.

Step 6   Next, the team move to the 'critic' state/room. They now critically explore the work they have completed on the idea so far, using the prompt questions to critique their ideas. Ask the team to capture the key discussion points.

Step 7 Finally, the team reviews the discussion points and agrees on how they will take this idea forward. They may also decide it is not viable to progress.

Top tips for team coaches

As an alternative to moving rooms or areas, you could use different seating areas if the room is large enough. The key point is to create movement between each of the three stages.

Time required

45–60 minutes.

TOOL 4: The Voice of the Future Generation – Thinking to the future

Why use this tool?

Helping teams to think about the legacy they leave behind is key to building a sustainable future. This tool focuses the team on putting themselves in the shoes of the future generation, to consider what they will need.

When to use this tool

At any stage of team development.

Resources required

Chairs placed in a circle with one chair in the middle. If working virtually, draw a semi-circle on a virtual whiteboard/platform and annotate who is sitting where. Also, draw one chair in the space between the two ends of the semi-circle.

How to use this tool

Step 1 Ask the team to arrange their chairs into a semi-circle with one chair in the space between the two ends of the semi-circle.

Step 2 Explain to the team that this chair represents the future generation of tomorrow. Ask one of the team to sit in the chair of the 'future generation'.

Step 3 The team then ask the team member questions to explore:

- What do they need from the team?
- What legacy does the team need to leave?

- How does the current work of the team impact them in the future?
- What needs to be different?
- What can help create a more sustainable future?

Step 4   Other team members should now swap in and out of the 'future generation' chair.

Step 5   Review and reflect. The team should consider what they have heard and what the key messages were.

Step 6   Next, the team consider the key messages and ask themselves, what do they need to do to ensure they leave a positive legacy? Capture actions.

Step 7   From reviewing the actions, the team agree on the next steps.

Top tips for team coaches

If the team is focused on the here and now it may take a little time to get them into the future state. Some suggestions to help them are to show a video, share an article about the future of work or a sustainable future. Alternatively, ask the team to split into pairs and go for a walk outside and think together about what might be needed from them in the future. If breaking into pairs while working virtually, either put the pairs into break-out rooms or ask them to phone each other. If they phone each other, encourage the pairs to go for a walk while talking to each other.

Time required

30–45 minutes.

TOOL 5: Team Wellness – Assessing team energy and health

Why use this tool?

For teams to perform at their best they need to be healthy in mind, body and spirit. Assessing and measuring their mind, body and spirit wellness will help identify whether the team is in good health and areas they need to pay attention to.

When to use this tool

At any stage of team development.

Resources required

- Team Wellness assessment template.
- Copies of Table 10.2 'Team wellness – how can we support each other in mind, body and spirit?'
- Flip chart paper and pens, virtual whiteboard/platform.

How to use this tool

Step 1   Explain to the team what constitutes team wellness, talking through the mind, body and spirit team wellness model (Table 10.2):

- Mind – building our mental resilience.
- Body – looking after our physical health.
- Spirit – being who we are meant to be/the best possible version of ourselves.

Step 2   Team members to use the Team Wellness assessment and first mark where they think they are on the three buckets, 1 being low and 10 being high.

Tool 5   Team Wellness assessment template

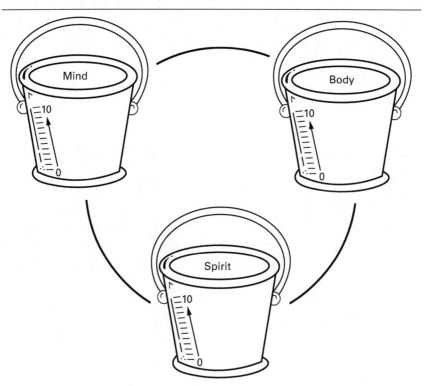

Step 3   In pairs, team members discuss their positive areas and what they need to work on. If working virtually, use breakout rooms or get team members to phone each other.

Step 4   Pairs now explore what they could do to improve their wellness score. Capture actions.

Step 5   Next, the team come back together and complete the Team Wellness assessment, this time scoring the team as a whole. Each team member should reflect and select a team score privately.

Step 6   Using three posters/flip charts or on a virtual whiteboard, show the three buckets and ask each team member to place their team scores for each bucket on the posters, flip charts or virtual whiteboard.

Step 7   Together with the team, work out the average score for each bucket.

Step 8   Discuss and capture ideas on:

- areas that came out as strong and explore what is working well;
- areas that need work and what the team can do to improve these.

Step 9   Team to vote on the top three ideas that could make the biggest difference.

Step 10   Review and agree on the top three ideas.

Step 11   Split into three subgroups. Group 1 takes idea 1, group 2 takes idea 2, and group 3 takes idea 3. Each group explores actions and next steps. If working virtually, use breakout rooms. Capture the actions on flip charts or virtual whiteboard.

Step 12   Ask the subgroups to place the captured ideas up on the walls (or share on a virtual platform). Each group to move onto the next idea – group 1 moves to idea 2, group 2 moves to idea 3 and group 3 moves to idea 1. Ask the subgroups to read the ideas and add any further suggestions. Finally, ask the subgroups to move on again – group 1 to idea 3, group 2 to idea 1, group 3 to idea 2.

Step 13   The team review all three sets of outputs and agree on the actions, who will champion each action, and how the team will review progress.

Top tips for team coaches

- The Team Wellness assessment can be used for both the individual and the team or either.

- When voting in step 9, it can be useful to get team members to first vote privately, with each team member then revealing their selected choices at the same time.

- When working in subgroups (steps 11–13) it can be useful for each subgroup to use a different colour of marker/annotation pen during the exercise. This allows the team and subgroups to easily track who has contributed what.

Time required

45 minutes to complete both the individual and team wellness assessments.

TOOL 6: Team Learning – Sharing learning and knowledge

Why use this tool?

To help the team to focus on how they can share knowledge and learn from one another. This simple tool can help to deepen the connection and learning between team members.

When to use this tool

At any stage of team development.

Resources required

No specific resources.

How to use this tool

Step 1   Explain that this tool can help team members to explore what they can learn from each other and share helpful ideas.

Step 2   Team members split into pairs (if virtual use breakout rooms). Each member of the pair shares with the other:

- How their colleague contributes to the team's success.
- What I can learn from you is…
- One idea can I offer you is…

Each team member should capture their learning and actions.

Step 3 New pairs are then established and the same questions are answered.

Step 4 Continue changing pairs until everyone has been paired with each other or until appropriate to end the exercise.

Top tips for team coaches

It can be helpful to have the pairs share while walking along together outside or in a creative space.

Time required

Approximately 30 minutes.

Reflecting on team transformation

- How would you describe your transformation mindset?
- How open are you to new thinking as a team?
- How does your environment enable creativity and innovation?
- How can you create the right environment for team creativity and innovation?
- In what ways can you bring external thinking into the team?
- How do you ensure team learning takes place?
- What can you do to share more of your learning as a team?
- How diverse is your team?
- How could you improve the diversity in your team?
- What is the one thing you need to do to transform your well-being?
- How does and can the team support each other in mind, body and spirit?
- What team (in your organization or another) would you like to work with on a joint challenge and what could you do to make this happen?

Conclusion 11

What does the future require of team coaching?

Imagining the future

Imagine, for a moment, a world where world leaders truly collaborated. A world where global agreements on trade, health, environment and security were more commonplace. A world where national, corporate and individual self-interest are more easily set aside. We believe the principles and practices of team coaching have much to contribute to our future world. With the future in mind, this conclusion will discuss several areas under the four headings of collaboration, building meaningful connection, the changing nature of work, and the professionalization of team coaching. We will offer our perspective of what team coaching needs to do to continue in its development and impact.

The urgent need for collaboration

How we collaborate as individuals, teams and within and between organizations has been a common thread throughout this book. Two of the key themes that have emerged include the following.

The importance of embracing collaboration and thinking systemically

As humans we know we are connected, we know that what we do in one part of the world can have reverberations elsewhere; however, many times we act in self-interest. From a human psychology perspective, our behaviour as humans is explainable. As referred to throughout this book, when we feel threatened, we seek to protect ourselves, those we care for and our resources.

Also, as mentioned in our discussion on how humans make decisions (Chapter 9), we struggle to calculate the value of things in the future. For example, the impact on CO_2 levels in 2050 of a long-haul flight for a family holiday in 2020. Despite the UN stating, 'Climate change is the defining issue of our time' (United Nations, 2019a) and declaring a 'global climate emergency' (United Nations, 2019b), the human race has struggled to agree on the nature of the issue and the response required. Contrast this with the global response in 2020 to COVID-19. Under the advice of the World Health Organization (WHO) nearly every nation-state took a similar course of action. Economies were brought to a standstill as 'self-isolation' and 'social distancing' became new norms. The presence of an invisible but immediate danger united the world to save lives.

Thankfully, there is good news. As a species, when we agree on a common challenge, find a common purpose, discover what needs to be done (Chapter 4), rise above our own group identity (Chapter 5), agree how we want to work and relate with each other (Chapters 6, 8 and 9), we are capable of the most amazing feats. There are examples of where long-term collaboration as a species is making a real difference. For example, globally extreme poverty, hunger, child mortality and child labour are all falling, life expectancy is rising, more people in the world today live in a democracy than at any other point in history, children are spending longer in school, resulting in increasing literacy rates, and access to the internet is increasing (Matthews, 2018). The graphs for each of these trends reveals a radical change for the better.

Story: Why collaboration matters
Contributor: Paul

Without overstating the benefits, I genuinely believe that team coaching and the principles that underpin it can be part of the solution to creating a more collaborative world.

For me this is personal. I grew up as a child during the Northern Ireland troubles and have seen what happens when neighbours stop listening to each other, start making misplaced assumptions, and bring out the worst in each other's human nature.

I watched as people took sides in a conflict without trying to understand perspectives different to their own. It was only when local people were given a supportive framework in which to talk to each other that needs were discussed instead of slogans. Enough trust was built to allow some unlikely relationships to develop.

What to most had seemed impossible became possible. In 1998 the main protagonists reached a peace settlement. While it has never been a perfect peace, there are many people alive today who would not be otherwise. Collaboration matters!

So, what needs to happen? We know when we agree on a challenge, develop a joint purpose and find a common interest, collaboration is never far behind. To begin with, we need to start listening to understand each other's needs. Also, we need to determine what we can agree on, break problems down, accept there are different shades of grey and that paradoxes will always exist. In addition, as a society we can benefit from asking better-quality questions. For example, the UN has estimated that solutions such as reforestation, ecosystem protection and rewilding represent 30 per cent of the opportunity to address climate change yet receive just 3 per cent of the available funding (United Nations, 2019b). In this example, we should be asking, what would be the benefit of increasing funding in this area to help address climate change and protect biodiversity? What common ground can we find?

No matter how hard it looks right now, there is hope. While the challenge can seem daunting, we need to start asking, how can we collaborate better? We look forward to team coaching making the contribution that we are confident it can.

Connecting teams to drive organizational success

Wilke and Thornton (2019) have described organizations as usually consisting of 'complex collections of groupings' (p. 224). Team coaching is excellently placed to help organizations develop what McChrystal *et al* (2015) have described as a 'Team of Teams'. We believe that this 'Team of Teams' approach is necessary to break down the organizational silos referred to throughout this book. To do this team coaches, whether internal or external, need to be working with multiple teams across an organization. When this is not possible, the team coach must explore opportunities with the team they are working with, to uncover the silos and do what they can to break them down. When solely working with isolated teams (eg only working with a board), team coaching is unlikely to have the full impact we know it can.

To maximize its impact, team coaching should reflect not only on how it can work within organizations but also across different organizations. We recall an example of working with a leading manufacturer and a retailer, who were normally attuned to a relationship that could be described as a roller coaster that moves between adversarial and collaborative. After only three-and-a-half hours of exploring their relationship and working together on joint business ideas, the team leaders commented that they had made more progress in this short space of time than in the last three years. Even teams who exist in a world of constant commercial tension can collaborate at a different level. Team coaches are perfectly placed to help teams within and across organizations redefine what it means for teams to truly collaborate.

The power of deeper connection

Throughout this book, we have continually emphasized the importance of human connection and relationships. Some of the key themes that have emerged include the following.

The 'way of being' of a team coach

In Chapter 2 we discussed that for a team coach to do transformational work, they need to have a 'way of being' that allows them to connect with other humans at a deep level and, through the power of this connection, challenge and speak to a team in ways that very few others do. We proposed the 4 Cs of Being: connection, confidence, courage and continuing (Figure 2.3). We emphasized that developing our 'way of being' is a lifelong journey.

The importance of connecting before commencing the work

Throughout the book, there is a continual theme that calls on team coaches to connect and support before commencing the work. Evidence has been presented that described the fragile nature of the human psyche. Even though many may not admit it or even realize, as humans we long for connection above all else. We need to feel appreciated, we need to feel that others can see who we are, we need to feel loved. While these needs can be absent from our conscious minds, they have a way of coming to the surface when we least expect it (see Chapter 8's discussion on how 'the early years' of our life impact on how we relate to each other). Chapter 8 also high-lighted the important research that linked how long we live with both the depth of our social relationships (Holt-Lunstad *et al*, 2010) and strong peer support (Shirom *et al*, 2011). Relationships matter!

For humans to fully flourish, they need to feel safe. We live in a constant state of threat that causes us to move towards our in-groups, exercise our biases and limit our choices. Team coaches need to help those they work with to feel safe. When humans feel safe (see discussions on psychological safety in Chapter 8 and creativity in Chapter 10) they are more inclined to support others, learn faster and create more. Ultimately, they flourish and perform better. However, it is important to remember that, just when you think you have done enough to make people feel safe, something unexpected may occur. Human beings are infinitely complicated. Chapter 8 discussed the re-search by Kluger and DeNisi (1996), who revealed that much of the develop-mental feedback we give to others has a moderate and, in many cases, a negative performance effect. In Chapter 2, when discussing the challenge versus support model adapted from the work of Sanford (2017), we recom-mended that 'team coaches ensure that they have enough connection and support in place, and then challenge'. The influence of Self-Determination Theory (Deci and Ryan, 1985; 2004) also resounds throughout this book with its emphasis on our human needs of relatedness, competence and au-tonomy. The more team coaches can help others to connect with their deep-est human needs in the context of their workplace, the more they will be able to speak truth 'in' the moment.

Connecting to purpose

Chapter 4 discussed that purpose is not only life-giving but also life-fulfilling. Humans are meaning-making machines and without meaning, we wither and disengage (Frankl, 1946). It was discussed that when people find pur-pose in their work and companies, and have a deeper purpose that connects all their stakeholders to something worth doing, they perform better. For teams, a purpose is essential. A team must know why they are together. They must know specifically: why does our work matter? What would happen if this team was not here? What can they do together that they cannot do apart? As a team of two, we have written a book together that we could not have written apart. Our purpose as a team in writing this book is *to help teams within and across organizations collaborate better, to create meaning-ful lasting change.* We believe that team coaching is the discipline that can best fulfil this purpose. The fulfilment of this purpose will result in more successful organizations, more fulfilled and engaged employees and the solving of problems in the world that at the minute seem insurmountable.

The changing nature of work

As we wrote each chapter, the changing nature of the modern workplace and what this means for both team coaching and how teams within and across organizations collaborate, started to become clearer. Some common themes we would like to draw attention to include the following.

The paradox of the individual

Our lives are a paradox of being an individual while having to learn how to behave in groups. Despite having to do both, individualism predominates. At school, we learn in a group setting but we are examined as individuals. When we go to work, we are recruited as an individual and in many cases rewarded for our individual efforts. Furthermore, we are disciplined, promoted and led by individuals. At work, we are then put into a team and we wonder why it is so difficult. For many, the family system is the main place where we learn how to collaborate and this can unknowingly influence our approach to collaboration. The call for collaboration is often outweighed by the need to compete and survive. Eventually, we are sent away on a team-building event or spend a day exploring each other's personality traits. These interventions, while useful, will always struggle to undo years of our natural desire to look out for ourselves. What needs to happen? Firstly, we need greater recognition that our innate need to survive as an individual is reinforced by a lifetime of conditioning. One-day team-building events, while they can be useful at the early stages of a team's life, are unlikely to have a lasting impact. Team coaching offers a strong antidote to the challenges of individualism and short-termism. Secondly, we need to rethink how we recruit, reward and promote. We need to ask how working in teams and collaboration can best be advanced.

Rethinking leadership selection and development

The case for rethinking leadership selection and development is threefold. Firstly, too often we come across accidental or reluctant leaders who openly admit they were promoted for their technical brilliance but have little desire to lead a team. Secondly, when coaching leaders one-to-one, we are struck by how much time is given over to matters relating to their team. And thirdly, it could be argued that the growth in demand for team coaching is indicative that all is not right in how we select and develop our leaders. What needs to happen? When selecting team leaders, greater effort and emphasis need to be placed on a candidate's history, capability and desire to lead others. When considering leadership development, team leadership and team coaching should be incorporated. While we welcome the emphasis on one-to-one coaching that is now core to most leadership development programmes, the importance of the team dynamic needs to be given its required place. We would like to see suitably qualified leaders trained to be team coaches. However, as pointed out in Chapter 2, internally trained team coaches could be best utilized in team coaching teams other than their own. Imagine for a minute what could happen to the leadership capability in an organization if enough leaders were trained to be team coaches. It is unlikely that the team of teams approach called for in this book can ever be possible without enough internal team coaches.

Embracing true diversity

We are living in a world where individual identity is increasingly being celebrated and recognized. While the workplace has become more diverse, there is still room for much improvement. As outlined in Chapter 10, we have both been involved in initiatives to help develop more diverse workplaces – Lucy on gender and Paul on neurodiversity. For example, what parent would not want to see their daughter given an equal opportunity in life? What parent would not want to see their child, who is on the autistic spectrum, appreciated for what they can uniquely bring to the workplace?

From our experience, we would suggest two things need to happen. Firstly, organizations need to start defining diversity in its fullest sense (see Figure 10.2). It needs to move away from just being the responsibility of the HR team. The very best organizations we have worked with have inclusion and diversity teams that are drawn from across the organization. These teams should include board representation along with a diverse range of personnel. Secondly, the inclusion and diversity team should engage the board on what measures are required. Importantly, everyone involved needs to win both the hearts and the minds of the employees. As discussed throughout this book, we believe that teams are best placed to help organizations realize the benefits of a truly diverse workplace.

The technology opportunity

In writing this book, we have tried to imagine what the impact of technology will be on team coaching. Think for a moment: a future where internet connectivity at reliable 5G speeds has become a global commodity; a world where even the most remote outposts are connected through space satellite technology; a world where advanced HD screen technology and the latest audio technology make virtual connectivity feel real; and a world where 3D-projected real-time holograms, virtual reality (VR) and artificial intelligence (AI) become the norm.

How can team coaching get ready? While it is hard to argue against the suggestion that distance coaching can 'diminish the coach's ability to "hear" unconscious communication' (Roberts and Brunning, 2007: 269), team coaching cannot afford to hide behind the challenges. When reviewing the research on one-to-one coaching, Jones *et al* (2016) did not find a significant difference in the outcomes between face-to-face coaching and a blended approach (eg a mixture of face-to-face and other mediums such as telephone and video conference). Today, at a minimum, team coaching should be adopting a hybrid approach. Not only will this provide vendor cost benefits and facilitate greater scaling opportunities, but it will also put team coaching at the centre of designing the future of work. The response of team coaches to the 2020 COVID-19 pandemic provided evidence of what is possible. We hope that this book can further assist coaches to practice both in person and virtually.

However, there are likely to be other opportunities as a result of technology. In Chapter 1, we stated that 'team coaching needs to disrupt itself and that those team coaches who are innovative in how they integrate technology into their work, will lead the future of how team coaching develops'. We look forward to collaborating with other team coaches in designing this future.

The development and the professionalization of team coaching

We are convinced that all the evidence points to team coaching continuing to be the fastest-growing specialism within coaching and one of the greatest opportunities for organizations. Some important areas for discussion include the following.

Team coaching literature and evidence base

While team coaching has rightly been described as 'practice-led' and 'pre-theory' (Jones *et al*, 2019) it has much to do to become empirically validated at the most rigorous level. Nevertheless, team coaching owes much to all those who have pioneered a new way to approach team effectiveness. It has been a privilege to have been able to add to this work. As for the future, as stated in Chapter 1, 'we believe team coaching will not have to wait as long as its successful forebearer to be empirically validated, specifically in the context of organizations'.

Team coach training

The growth of team coaching has been supported by multiple team coaching training providers, with programmes ranging in duration from a few days to a year (part-time). Some examples include: Team Coaching International, who claim to be the first coaching company to offer a team coaching certification, the Certified Team Performance Coach™; the long-running Academy of Executive Coaching Systemic Team Coaching® Certificate that acts as an entry level into a Systemic Team Coaching Diploma; the Team Coaching Studio's Certificate and Diploma in Team Coaching; and the 'Creating the Team Edge' team coaching accreditation developed by Lucy in 2015. In addition, leading business schools are also increasingly contributing, with programmes such as Hult Ashridge's Team Coaching for Consultants, and the Henley Business School's Professional Certificate in Team, Board and Systemic Coaching Programme, which we are both privileged to be lead tutors on. As the demand for team coaching grows, we expect the supply of programmes from coaching training providers, and increasingly from leading business schools, to increase.

The professionalization of team coaching

De Haan (2019) has commented that 'executive coaching has now become a true profession' (p. 1). While team coaching has a long way to go, we believe the journey has started and will accelerate over the forthcoming years. An essential part of this journey is the work by the professional coaching bodies on team coaching competencies. At the time of writing, a visit to the websites of some of the main coaching bodies such as the International Coach Federation (ICF, 2020), European Coaching and Mentoring Council

(EMCC, 2020) and the Association for Coaching (AC, 2020) reveals very little obvious mention of team coaching. Nevertheless, from our own experience, we know that team coaching and its professional development is very much on the agenda of the leading coaching bodies. This is evidenced through conference agendas, working parties, and the focus on team coaching competencies (Widdowson *et al*, 2020), all of which we have been privileged to be involved in.

Team coaching – living its values

While the competitive spirit between practitioners, academia, training providers, business schools and professional coaching bodies is to be expected, we are of the view that team coaching needs to work to a higher ideal: the ideal of collaboration.

With a developing literature, a widening base of training providers and increasing attention from the professional coaching bodies, it is not surprising that Clutterbuck *et al* (2019: 2) claim that team coaching is 'gradually assuming distinct professional characteristics'.

Final thoughts

We sincerely hope that this book has fulfilled its purpose 'to help teams within and across organizations collaborate better, to create meaningful lasting change'. We hope it has offered fresh perspectives that can help inform team coaches, coaches, HR professionals, organizational consultants and leaders about the potential of team coaching when building top-performing teams. We trust that it has provided a practical guide to team coaching that can help improve collaboration and drive organizational success.

While this book has been written with an organizational lens, we are extremely aware that teams exist in every part of our lives, be it family or community. We are confident, based on our own reflections, that much of what we have written can benefit any team. As for this team, Lucy and Paul, it has been an absolute joy to work together. We have lived the principles of this book, in particular that connection comes before the work itself. This book has been a journey for which we are grateful to so many. Thank you for being part of that journey.

REFERENCES

AC (2012) AC Coaching Competency Framework Revised June 2012 [online] Available at: https://cdn.ymaws.com/www.associationforcoaching.com/resource/resmgr/Accreditation/Accred_General/Coaching_Competency_Framewor.pdf (archived at https://perma.cc/6C6G-QB93) [Accessed 28 December 2019]

AC (2020) The Association for Coaching Website [online] Available at: https://www.associationforcoaching.com/ (archived at https://perma.cc/3PW9-6F7B) [Accessed 15 February 2020]

Adkins, B and Caldwell, D (2004) Firm or subgroup culture: Where does fitting in matter most? *Journal of Organizational Behavior: The International Journal of Industrial, Occupational and Organizational Psychology and Behavior*, 25 (8), pp 969–78

Aeron, S and Pathak, S (2012) Relationship between team member personality and team cohesion: An exploratory study in IT industry, *Management and Labour Studies*, 37 (3), pp 267–82

Aeron, S and Pathak, S (2017) Personality, conflict and performance: Exploring predictive relationships, *IUP Journal of Organizational Behavior*, 16 (2), pp 35–54

Ainsworth, M D S *et al* (1978) *Patterns of Attachment: A psychological study of the strange situation*, Erlbaum, Hillsdale, NJ

Amabile, T M (2012) Componential theory of creativity, *Harvard Business School*, 12 (96), pp 1–10

Amabile, T M (2018) *Creativity in Context: Update to the social psychology of creativity*, Routledge, New York and London

Amabile, T M and Pillemer, J (2012) Perspectives on the social psychology of creativity, *The Journal of Creative Behavior*, 46 (1), pp 3–15

Anca, C and Aragón, S (2018) The 3 types of diversity that shape our identities, *Harvard Business Review,* 24 May, 2018

Anderson, M C, Anderson, D L and Mayo, W D (2008) Team coaching helps a leadership team drive cultural change at Caterpillar, *Global Business and Organizational Excellence*, 27 (4), pp 40–50

Argyris, C (1980) Making the undiscussable and its undiscussability discussable, *Public Administration Review*, 40 (3), pp 205–13

Aziz, A (2019) The power of purpose: Milton Friedman is rolling in his grave, *Forbes* [online] Available at: https://www.forbes.com/sites/afdhelaziz/2019/08/23/the-power-of-purpose-milton-friedman-is-rolling-in-his-grave/#569706d7532d (archived at https://perma.cc/4P8J-FHZY) [Accessed 31 October 2019]

Babiak, P and Hare, R D (2006) *Snakes in Suits: When psychopaths go to work*, Regan Books, New York

Bachkirova, T (2011) *Developmental Coaching: Working with the Self*, McGraw-Hill Open University Press, Maidenhead

Balmer, J M (2008) Identity based views of the corporation: Insights from corporate identity, organisational identity, social identity, visual identity, corporate brand identity and corporate image, *European Journal of Marketing*, **42** (9/10), pp 879–906

Bandler, R and Grinder, J (1975) *The Structure of Magic 1: A book about language and therapy*, Science & Behaviour Books, Palo Alto

Barbour, P J and Bourne, D (2020) Developing sociality in a post-conflict Northern Ireland: An application of the perceiver element grid, *Journal of Constructivist Psychology*, DOI: 10.1080/10720537.2020.1808867

Baumeister, R F, Ainsworth, S E and Vohs, K D (2016) Are groups more or less than the sum of their members? The moderating role of individual identification, *Behavioral and Brain Sciences*, **39**

Beck, K *et al* (2001) Manifesto for Agile Software Development [online] Available at: https://agilemanifesto.org/ (archived at https://perma.cc/3D9A-2C8X) [Accessed 2 January 2020]

Bender, L *et al* (2012) Social sensitivity and classroom team projects: An empirical investigation, in *Proceedings of the 43rd ACM technical symposium on Computer Science Education*, February, pp 403–08, ACM

Bercovitch, J (2009) Mediation and conflict resolution, in *The Sage Handbook of Conflict Resolution*, ed J Bercovitch, V Kremenyuk and I W Zartman, pp 340–57, SAGE, London

Berne, E (1964) *Games People Play: The psychology of human relationships*, Penguin, UK

Berry, L, Mirabito, A M and Baun, W (2010) What's the hard return on employee wellness programs? *Harvard Business Review*, December, pp 2012–68

Bion, W R (1961) *Experiences in Groups and Other Papers*, Routledge Taylor and Francis, London & New York

Boniwell, I (2012) *Positive Psychology in a Nutshell: The science of happiness*, McGraw-Hill Education, UK

Boss, R W (1983) Team building and the problem of regression: The personal management interview as an intervention, *The Journal of Applied Behavioral Science*, **19** (1), pp 67–83

Bossons, P, Kourdi, J and Sartain, D (2012) *Coaching Essentials: Practical, proven techniques for world-class executive coaching*, 2nd edn, Bloomsbury Academic, London

Bossons, P, Riddell, P and Sartain, D (2015) *The Neuroscience of Leadership Coaching: Why the tools and techniques of leadership coaching work*, Bloomsbury Publishing, London

Bowlby, J (1958) The nature of the child's tie to his mother, *International Journal of Psychoanalysis*, **39**, pp 350–73

Bradley, B H *et al* (2012) Reaping the benefits of task conflict in teams: The critical role of team psychological safety climate, *Journal of Applied Psychology*, **97** (1) pp 151–58

Brennan, K A, Clark, C L and Shaver, P R (1998) Self-report measurement of adult attachment: an integrative overview, in *Attachment Theory and Close Relationships*, eds J A Simpson and W F Rholes, pp 46–76, Guilford Press, New York

Brewer, M B (2011) Identity and conflict, in *Intergroup Conflicts and their Resolution: A social psychological perspective*, ed D Bar-Tal, Psychology Press, New York

British Association of Social Workers (2016) The autism employment gap [online] Available at: https://www.basw.co.uk/resources/autism-employment-gap-too-much-information-workplace (archived at https://perma.cc/ZEE9-HVQ6) [Accessed 1 April 2020]

Brown, P T, Meyler, J and Swart, T (2009) Emotional intelligence and the amygdala: Towards the concept of the limbic leader in executive coaching, *NeuroLeadership Journal*, **2**, pp 67–77

Burke, R J (2006) Why leaders fail: exploring the darkside, *International Journal of Manpower*, **27** (1), pp 91–100

Burlingame, G M, McClendon, D T and Alonso, J (2011) Cohesion in group therapy, *Psychotherapy*, **48** (1), p 34

Burr, V, King, N and Butt, T (2014) Personal construct psychology methods for qualitative research, *International Journal of Social Research Methodology*, **17** (4), pp 341–55

Business Roundtable (2019) Statement on the Purpose of a Corporation [online] Available at: https://opportunity.businessroundtable.org/wp-content/uploads/2019/08/BRT-Statement-on-the-Purpose-of-a-Corporation-with-Signatures.pdf (archived at https://perma.cc/Z33E-SV9F) [Accessed 31 October 2019]

Campbell, L (2017) We've broken down your entire life into years spent doing tasks. You spend 33 years of your life in bed, *Huffington Post* [online] Available at: https://www.huffingtonpost.com.au/2017/10/18/weve-broken-down-your-entire-life-into-years-spent-doing-tasks_a_23248153/ (archived at https://perma.cc/D9Z3-TEMV) [Accessed 31 October 2019]

Capodagli, B and Jackson, L (2006) *The Disney Way, Revised Edition: Harnessing the management secrets of Disney in your company*, McGraw Hill Professional

Carr, C and Peters, J (2013) The experience of team coaching: A dual case study, *International Coaching Psychology Review*, **8** (1), pp 80–98

Carton, A M, Murphy, C and Clark, J R (2014) A (blurry) vision of the future: How leader rhetoric about ultimate goals influences performance, *Academy of Management Journal*, **57** (6), pp 1544–70

Cavanagh, M (2006) Coaching from a systemic perspective: A complex adaptive conversation, in *Evidence Based Coaching Handbook: Putting best practices to work for your clients*, ed D R Stober and A M Grant, pp 313–54, John Wiley & Sons, Inc, New Jersey

Childs, R (2012) Coaching with FIRO Element B, in *Psychometrics in Coaching: Using psychological and psychometric tools for development,* ed J Passmore, pp 345–60, Kogan Page, London

Cilliers, F and Greyvenstein, H (2012) The impact of silo mentality on team identity: An organisational case study, *SA Journal of Industrial Psychology*, **38** (2), pp 75–84

Clutterbuck, D (2007) *Coaching the Team at Work*, Nicholas Brealey Publishing, London

Clutterbuck, D (2014) Team Coaching, in *The Complete Handbook of Coaching*, 2nd edn, ed E Cox, T Bachkirova and D Clutterbuck, pp 271–84, Sage, London

Clutterbuck, D and Megginson, D (2012) Coach maturity: An emerging concept [online] Available at: https://www.davidclutterbuckpartnership.com/wp-content/uploads/Coach-maturity.pdf (archived at https://perma.cc/5VQ7-BQF5) [Accessed 27 December 2019]

Clutterbuck, D *et al* (2019) Introduction, in *The Practitioner's Handbook of Team Coaching,* ed D Clutterbuck *et al*, pp 1–8, Routledge, London and New York

Clutterbuck, D (2019) Towards a pragmatic model of team function and dysfunction, in *The Practitioner's Handbook of Team Coaching*, ed D Clutterbuck *et al*, pp 150–60, Routledge, London and New York

Clutterbuck, D (2020) *Coaching the Team at Work: The definitive guide to team coaching,* 2nd edn, Nicholas Brealey, London and Boston

Cohen, J D, McClure, S M and Yu, A J (2007) Should I stay or should I go? How the human brain manages the trade-off between exploitation and exploration, *Philosophical Transactions of the Royal Society B: Biological Sciences*, **362** (1481), pp 933–42

Collins, C G and Parker, S K (2010) Team capability beliefs over time: Distinguishing between team potency, team outcome efficacy, and team process efficacy, *Journal of Occupational & Organizational Psychology*, **83** (4), pp 1003–23

Collins, J C and Porras, J I (2005) *Built to Last: Successful habits of visionary companies*, Random House

Covey, S R (2004) *The Seven Habits of Highly Effective People*, Simon and Schuster, London

Cummings, T G and Worley, C G (1997) *Organization Development and Change*, 6th edn, West Publishing Co, St Paul, MN

Damasio, A (2000) *The Feeling of What Happens: Body, emotion and the making of consciousness*, Vintage, London

David, S and Congleton, C (2013) Emotional agility, *Harvard Business Review*, November Issue

Davies, B and Harré, R (1990) Positioning: The discursive production of selves, *Journal for the Theory of Social Behaviour*, **20** (1), pp 43–63

Decety, J (2011) Dissecting the neural mechanisms mediating empathy, *Emotion Review*, **3** (1), pp 92–108

Deci, E L and Ryan, R M (1985) The general causality orientations scale: Self-determination in personality, *Journal of Research in Personality*, **19** (2), pp 109–34

Deci, E L and Ryan, R M (eds) (2004) *Handbook of Self-determination Research*, University of Rochester Press

De Haan, E *et al* (2010) Clients' critical moments of coaching: Toward a 'client model' of executive coaching, *Academy of Management Learning & Education*, **9** (4), pp 607–21

De Haan, E *et al* (2016) A large-scale study of executive and workplace coaching: The relative contributions of relationship, personality match, and self-efficacy, *Consulting Psychology Journal: Practice and Research*, **68** (3), pp 189–207

De Haan, E (2019) *Critical Moments in Executive Coaching: Understanding coaching process through research and evidence-based theory*, Routledge

De Haan, E, Gray, D E and Bonneywell, S (2019) Executive coaching outcome research in a field setting: A near-randomized controlled trial study in a global healthcare corporation, *Academy of Management Learning & Education*, **18** (4), pp 581–605

Delizonna, L (2017) High-performing teams need psychological safety: Here's how to create it, *Harvard Business Review*, 24 August

De Mello, A (1990) *Awareness: A de Mello spirituality conference in his own words*, Zondervan, Michigan

Dilts, R (1990) *Changing Belief Systems with NLP*, Meta Publications, Capitola, CA

Drake, D B (2008) Finding our way home: Coaching's search for identity in a new era, *Coaching: An international journal of theory, research and practice*, **1** (1), pp 16–27

Drake, D B (2009) Evidence is a verb: A relational approach to knowledge and mastery in coaching, *International Journal of Evidence Based Coaching and Mentoring*, **7** (1), pp 112

Druskat, V U and Wolff, S B (2001) Building the emotional intelligence of groups, *Harvard Business Review*, **79** (3), pp 80–91

Duhigg, C (2016) What Google learned from its quest to build the perfect team, *New York Times Magazine*, **26**, 2016

Du Nann Winter, D (2006) Moving from the clenched fists to shaking hands: Working with negative emotions provoked by conflict, in *Working for Peace: A handbook of practical psychology and other tools*, ed R MacNair, Impact Publishers, Atascadero, Calif

Dunaway, M M (2013) IS learning: the impact of gender and team emotional intelligence, *Journal of Information Systems Education*, **24** (3), pp 189–202

Dutton, J E, Debebe, G and Wrzesniewski, A (2000) A social valuing perspective on relationship sensemaking, Working paper, University of Michigan, Ann Arbor

Dutton, J E, Roberts, L M and Bednar, J (2010) Pathways for positive identity construction at work: Four types of positive identity and the building of social resources, *Academy of Management Review*, **35** (2), pp 265–93

Dweck, C (2012) *Mindset: How you can fulfil your potential*, Ballantine Books, New York

Dweck, C (2015) Carol Dweck revisits the growth mindset, *Education Week*, 35 (5), pp 20–24

Dweck, C (2016) What having a 'growth mindset' actually means, *Harvard Business Review*, 13, pp 213–26

Eckel, C C and Grossman, P J (2005) Managing diversity by creating team identity, *Journal of Economic Behavior & Organization*, 58 (3), pp 371–92

Eckel, P, Hill, B and Green, M (1998) On change: En route to transformation, an occasional paper series of the ACE Project on leadership and institutional transformation, American Council on Education, Washington, DC

Edmondson, A C (1999) Psychological safety and learning behavior in work teams, *Administrative Science Quarterly*, 44 (2), pp 350–83

Edmondson, A C (2012) *Teaming: How organizations learn, innovate and compete in the knowledge economy*, Jossey-Boss, San Francisco, CA

Edmondson, A C and Lei, Z (2014) Psychological safety: The history, renaissance, and future of an interpersonal construct, *Annual Review of Organizational Psychology and Organizational Behaviour*, 1 (1), pp 23–43

Einhorn, N (2008) Presentation on the Copy, Paste, Adapt approach, Tube Lines leadership development programme, September 2008

Eisenberger, N I, Lieberman, M D and Williams, K D (2003) Does rejection hurt? An fMRI study of social exclusion, *Science*, 302 (5643), pp 290–92

Ellemers, N et al (2013) Feeling included and valued: How perceived respect affects positive team identity and willingness to invest in the team, *British Journal of Management*, 24 (1), pp 21–37

Ellis, A P et al (2003) Team learning: Collectively connecting the dots, *Journal of applied Psychology*, 88 (5), pp 821–35

EMCC (2015) EMCC COMPETENCE FRAMEWORK V2 September 2015 [online] Available at: https://emcc1.app.box.com/s/4aj8x6tmbt75ndn13sg3dauk8n6wxfxq (archived at https://perma.cc/S69H-WLPX) [Accessed 28 December 2019]

EMCC (2020) European Mentoring & Coaching Council Website [online] Available at: https://emccuk.org/ (archived at https://perma.cc/3CQ6-P5X2) [Accessed 15 February 2020]

Fenton, A and Krahn, T (2007) Autism, neurodiversity and equality beyond the 'normal', *Journal of Ethics in Mental Health*, 2 (2), pp 1–6

Filipkowski, J, Ruth, M and Heverin, A (2018) *HCI & ICF: Building a coaching culture for change management*, Human Capital Institute publications

Finlay, L (2008) Reflecting on 'reflective practice', *Practice-based Professional Learning*, Paper 52, The Open University

Forsyth, D R (2014) *Group Dynamics*, 6th ed, Wadsworth Cengage Learning, Belmont CA

Frankl, V E (1946) *Man's Search for Meaning*, Random House Group, London

Fransen, K *et al* (2015) Believing in 'us': Exploring leaders' capacity to enhance team confidence and performance by building a sense of shared social identity, *Journal of Experimental Psychology: Applied*, **21** (1), pp 89–100

Fredrickson, B (2009) *Positivity*, Harmony

Gallup (2017) State of the American Workplace [online] Available at: https://www.gallup.com/workplace/238085/state-american-workplace-report-2017.aspx (archived at https://perma.cc/GPX4-KAXH) [Accessed 31 October 2019]

Gersick, C J (1988) Time and transition in work teams: Toward a new model of group development, *Academy of Management Journal*, **31** (1), pp 9–41

Gersick, C J (1989) Marking time: Predictable transitions in task groups, *Academy of Management Journal*, **32** (2) pp 274–309

Gillette, J and McCollom, M (1990) *Groups in Context: A new perspective on group dynamics*, Addison-Wesley

Gilligan, J (1996) *Violence: Reflections on a national epidemic*, Vintage Press, New York

Goleman, D (2006) *Emotional Intelligence*, Bantam

Goleman, D (2013) *Focus: The hidden driver of excellence*, Bloomsbury, London

Grant, A M (2007) Past, present and future: The evolution of professional and coaching psychology, in *Handbook of Coaching Psychology: A guide for practitioners*, ed S Palmer and A Whybrow, pp 23–39, Routledge Taylor and Francis, London & New York

Greenwald, A (2018) Living and working well, *TD: Talent Development*, **72** (8), pp 32–37

Gully, S M *et al* (2002) A meta-analysis of team-efficacy, potency, and performance: Interdependence and level of analysis as moderators of observed relationships, *Journal of Applied Psychology*, **87** (5), pp 819–32

Hackman, J R (2011) *Collaborative Intelligence: Using teams to solve hard problems*, Berrett-Koehler Publishers, San Francisco

Hackman, J R and Wageman, R (2005) A theory of team coaching, *Academy of Management Review*, **30** (2), pp 269–87

Hagerty, B M *et al* (1993) An emerging theory of human relatedness, *Image: The Journal of Nursing Scholarship*, **25** (4) pp 291–96

Hain, D, Hain, P and Matthewman, L (2011) Continuous professional development for coaches, in *Supervision in Coaching: Supervision, ethics and continuous professional development*, ed J Passmore, pp 298–332, Kogan Page, London

Hall, L M and Belnap, B P (2004) *The Sourcebook of Magic: A comprehensive guide to NLP change patterns*, 2nd edn, Crown House Publications Ltd, Bancyfelin

Hardingham, A *et al* (2004) *Coach's Coach: Personal development for personal developers,* Chartered Institute of Personnel and Development, London

Hardy, G E and Barkham, M (1994) The relationship between interpersonal attachment styles and work difficulties, *Human Relations*, **47** (3), pp 263–81

Harms, P D (2011) Adult attachment styles in the workplace, *Human Resource Management Review*, **21** (4), pp 285–96

Harms, P D and Spain, S M (2015) Beyond the bright side: Dark personality at work, *Applied Psychology*, **64** (1), pp 15–24

Harvard Business Review (2015) The Business Case for Purpose [online] Available at: https://hbr.org/resources/pdfs/comm/ey/19392HBRReportEY.pdf (archived at https://perma.cc/8KEY-KVW5) [Accessed 31 October 2019]

Hastings, R and Pennington, W (2019) Team coaching: A thematic analysis of methods used by external coaches in a work domain, *International Journal of Evidence Based Coaching and Mentoring*, **17** (2), pp 174–88

Hauser, L L (2014) Shape-shifting: A behavioral team coaching model for coach education, research, and practice, *Journal of Psychological Issues in Organizational Culture*, **5** (2), pp 48–71

Hauser, L L (2018) Team coaching operating system (TCOS): The intersection of evidence-based research and Gestalt principles, *Gestalt Review*, **22** (2), pp 208–25

Hawkins, P (2011, 2014, 2017) *Leadership Team Coaching: Developing collective transformational leadership*, 1st, 2nd and 3rd edns, Kogan Page, London

Hawkins, P (2012) *Creating A Coaching Culture: developing a coaching strategy for your organization*, McGraw-Hill Education, Maidenhead

Hawkins, P and Smith, N (2013) *Coaching, Mentoring and Organizational Consultancy*, 2nd edn, Open University Press, Maidenhead, UK

Hawkins, P (2019) Systemic team coaching, in *The Practitioner's Handbook of Team Coaching*, ed D Clutterbuck *et al*, pp 36–52, Routledge, London and New York

Hawkins, P and Turner, E (eds) (2019) *Systemic Coaching: Delivering value beyond the individual*, Routledge, London and New York

Hazan, C and Shaver, P R (1990) Love and work: An attachment-theoretical perspective, *Journal of Personality and Social Psychology*, **59** (2), pp 270–80

Heron, J (1999) *The Complete Facilitator's Handbook*, Kogan Page, London

Hills, J (2016) *Brain-Savvy Business: 8 principles from neuroscience and how to apply them*, Head Heart and Brain

Hirst, G, Van Knippenberg, D and Zhou, J (2009) A cross-level perspective on employee creativity: Goal orientation, team learning behavior, and individual creativity, *Academy of Management Journal*, **52** (2), pp 280–93

Hirst, G *et al* (2011) How does bureaucracy impact individual creativity? A cross-level investigation of team contextual influences on goal orientation–creativity relationships, *Academy of Management Journal*, **54** (3), pp 624–41

Hogan, R, Curphy, G J and Hogan, J (1994) What we know about leadership: Effectiveness and personality, *American Psychologist*, **49** (6), pp 493–504

Holt-Lunstad J, Smith, T B and Layton, J B (2010) Social relationships and mortality risk: a meta-analytic review, *PLoS Medicine*, **7** (7), p.e1000316

Hubble, M A *et al* (2010) Introduction, in *The Heart and Soul of Change: Delivering what works in therapy*, 2nd edn, ed B L Duncan *et al*, pp 23–46, American Psychological Association, Washington, DC

Hullinger, A M and DiGirolamo, J A (2018) *The Coaching Journey*, International Coach Federation

Hurley, T J and Staggs, J (2012) Using archetypes in coaching, in *Psychometrics in Coaching: Using psychological and psychometric tools for development*, ed J Passmore, pp 277–90, Kogan Page, London

ICF (2016) International Coach Federation and PricewaterhouseCoopers ICF Global Coaching Study: Executive Summary [online] Available at: https://coachfederation.org/app/uploads/2017/12/2016ICFGlobalCoachingStudy_ExecutiveSummary-2.pdf (archived at https://perma.cc/W9MG-GEGG) [Accessed 21 August 2019]

ICF (2019) Updated ICF Core Competency Model October 2019 [online] Available at: https://coachfederation.org/app/uploads/2019/11/ICFCompetencyModel_Oct2019.pdf (archived at https://perma.cc/5RV9-782R) [Accessed 28 December 2019]

ICF (2020) International Coach Federation Website [online] Available at: https://coachfederation.org/ (archived at https://perma.cc/3BGZ-WDDS) [Accessed 15 February 2020]

Implicit Association Test (2011) [online] Available at: https://tandis.odihr.pl/handle/20.500.12389/21557 (archived at https://perma.cc/Z9JG-6SZN) [Accessed 2 January 2020]

Ingham, H and Luft, J (1955) The Johari Window: A graphic model for interpersonal relations, *University of California Western Training Lab*

International Finance Corporation (2014) Conflicts in the Boardroom Survey – Results and Analysis, [online] Available at https://www.ifc.org/wps/wcm/connect/topics_ext_content/ifc_external_corporate_site/ifc+cg/resources/ guidelines_reviews+and+case+studies/conflicts+in+the+boardroom+-+survey+2013 (archived at https://perma.cc/XZD5-Q732) [Accessed 31 October 2019]

Jones, J M, Dovidio, J F and Vietze, D L (2013) *The Psychology of Diversity: Beyond prejudice and racism*, John Wiley & Sons

Jones, R J, Napiersky, U and Lyubovnikova, J (2019) Conceptualizing the distinctiveness of team coaching, *Journal of Managerial Psychology*, **34** (2), pp 62–78

Jones, R J, Woods, S A and Guillaume, Y R (2016) The effectiveness of workplace coaching: A meta-analysis of learning and performance outcomes from coaching, *Journal of Occupational and Organizational Psychology*, **89** (2), pp 249–77

Kaczmarek, S, Kimino, S and Pye, A (2012) Board task-related faultlines and firm performance: A decade of evidence, *Corporate Governance: An International Review*, **20** (4), pp 337–51

Kahn, W A (1990) Psychological conditions of personal engagement and disengagement at work, *Academy of Management Journal*, **33** (4), pp 692–724

Kahneman, D (2011) *Thinking, Fast and Slow*, Penguin Books, UK

Kantor, D (2012) *Reading the Room: Group dynamics for coaches and leaders* (Vol. 5), John Wiley & Sons, San Francisco, CA

Katzenbach, J R and Smith, D K (1993a) *The Wisdom of Teams: Creating the high-performance organization*, Harvard Business School Press, McGraw-Hill Inc, Boston, Massachusetts

Katzenbach, J R and Smith, D K (1993b) *The Discipline of Teams*, Harvard Business Press, Boston, Massachusetts

Kegan, R and Lahey, L L (2009) *Immunity to Change: How to overcome it and unlock potential in yourself and your organization*, Harvard Business Press

Kelman, H C (2004) Reconciliation as identity change: A social psychological perspective, in *From Conflict Resolution to Reconciliation,* ed Y Bar-Siman-Tov, pp 111–24, Oxford University Press, Oxford

Kim, Y J *et al* (2017) What makes a strong team?: Using collective intelligence to predict team performance in League of Legends, in *Proceedings of the 2017 ACM Conference on Computer Supported Cooperative Work and Social Computing*, February, pp 2316–29, ACM

Kline, N (1999) *Time to Think: Listening to ignite the human mind*, Hachette, UK

Kline, N (2015) *More Time to Think: The power of independent thinking,* Ward Lock, London

Kluger, A N and DeNisi, A (1996) The effects of feedback interventions on performance: A historical review, a meta-analysis, and a preliminary feedback intervention theory, *Psychological Bulletin*, 119 (2), pp 254–84

Koster, K (2016) 'Rethinking WELLNESS', *Employee Benefit News*, 30 (10), pp 14–16

Kozlowski, S W and Ilgen, D R (2006) Enhancing the effectiveness of work groups and teams, *Psychological Science in the Public Interest*, 7 (3), pp 77–124

Kriek, H S and Venter, P (2009) The perceived success of teambuilding interventions in South African organisations, *Southern African Business Review*, 13 (1), pp 112–28

Kroll, C and Shea, C (2018) The Agile Evolution, it's more than process, *Workforce Solutions Review*, 9 (2), pp 22–25

Lanz, K (2016) Team coaching, in *Excellence in Coaching: The industry guide*, 3rd edn, ed J Passmore, pp 313–26, Kogan Page, London

Lau, D C and Murnighan, J K (1998) Demographic diversity and faultlines: The compositional dynamics of organizational groups, *Academy of Management Review*, 23, pp 325–40

Law, H (2007) Narrative coaching and psychology of learning from multicultural perspectives, in *Handbook of Coaching Psychology: A guide for practitioners*, ed S Palmer and A Whybrow, pp 174–212, Routledge Taylor and Francis, London & New York

Lawrence, P and Whyte, A (2017) What do experienced team coaches do? Current practice in Australia and New Zealand, *International Journal of Evidence Based Coaching and Mentoring*, 15 (1), pp 94–113

Leahy, V and Mia, A (2019) Working with multicultural groups in organizations: Issues of power and difference, in *The Art and Science of Working Together: Practising group analysis in teams and organisations*, ed C Thornton, pp 170–80, Routledge, London

Leary-Joyce, J and Lines, H (2018) *Systemic Team Coaching*, AoEC Press

Lee, C, Farh, J L and Chen, Z J (2011) Promoting group potency in project teams: The importance of group identification, *Journal of Organizational Behavior*, 32 (8), pp 1147–62

Lee, G (2003) *Leadership coaching: From personal insight to organisational performance*, Kogan Page Publishers, London

Lencioni, P (2002) *Five Dysfunctions of a Team: A leadership fable*, Jossey-Bass, San Francisco

Lewin, K (1945) *Resolving Social Conflicts*, Harper and Row, New York

Lewin, K (1947) *Frontiers in Group Dynamics: Concept, method and reality in social science: social equilibria and social change*, Tavistock

Linley, P A *et al* (2010) Using signature strengths in pursuit of goals: Effects on goal progress, need satisfaction, and well-being, and implications for coaching psychologists, *International Coaching Psychology Review*, 5 (1), pp 6–15

Litchfield, R C *et al* (2018) When team identity helps innovation and when it hurts: Team identity and its relationship to team and cross-team innovative behavior, *Journal of Product Innovation Management*, 35 (3), pp 350–66

Locke, T (2019) Jeff Bezos: This is the 'smartest thing we ever did' at Amazon [online] Available at: https://www.cnbc.com/2019/10/14/jeff-bezos-this-is-the-smartest-thing-we-ever-did-at-amazon.html (archived at https://perma.cc/JEM6-DNU9) [Accessed 5 January 2020]

MacLellan, L (2019) Responsible capitalism is not a form of millennial pandering, Quartz at work [online] Available at: https://qz.com/work/1691365/business-roundtable-statement-on-purpose-of-companies-goes-back-to-the-future/ (archived at https://perma.cc/E22N-2WYD) [Accessed 31 October 2019]

Made by Dyslexia (2017) Connecting the dots [online] Available at: https://madebydyslexia.org/assets/downloads/connecting_the_dots_2019.pdf (archived at https://perma.cc/9PNV-MVHZ) [Accessed 1st April 2020]

Mann, C (2015) The 6th Ridler Report: Strategic trends in the use of executive coaching. Presentation 1st December 2015 [online] Available at: https://www.associationforcoaching.com/resource/resmgr/Research/6th_ridler_report_-_joint_ic.pdf (archived at https://perma.cc/C6TH-PC9B) [Accessed 15 December 2016]

Mannix, E and Neale, M A (2005) What differences make a difference? The promise and reality of diverse teams in organizations, *Psychological Science in the Public Interest*, 6 (2), pp 31–55

Martin, E R (2006) Team effectiveness in academic medical libraries: A multiple case study, *Journal of the Medical Library Association*, 94 (3), pp 271–78

Mathieu, J *et al* (2008) Team effectiveness 1997–2007: A review of recent advancements and a glimpse into the future, *Journal of Management*, 34 (3), pp 410–76

Matthews, D (2018) 23 charts and maps that show the world is getting much, much better: These are bleak times — but a lot of things are improving [online] Available at: https://www.vox.com/2014/11/24/7272929/global-poverty-health-crime-literacy-good-news (archived at https://perma.cc/23BZ-6TBP) [Accessed 19 February 2020]

McCann, D (2012) Coaching with teams: Team Management Systems (TMS), in *Psychometrics in Coaching: Using psychological and psychometric tools for development*, ed J Passmore, pp 95–118, Kogan Page, London

McChrystal, G S *et al* (2015) *Team of Teams: New rules of engagement for a complex world*, Penguin Business

McGregor, L and Doshi, N (2015) How company culture shapes employee motivation, *Harvard Business Review*, **11**, pp 1–13

McKee, A (2018) *How to be Happy at Work: The power of purpose, hope, and friendship*, Harvard Business Press

Megginson, D (2013) The Ridler Report (2013) Trends in the use of executive coaching: in collaboration with EMCC UK. Available at: https://www.portfolio-info.co.uk/files/file/ridler-report-2013.pdf (archived at https://perma.cc/BBT2-5QXH) [Accessed 15 April 2017]

Neenan, M (2016) Cognitive behavioural coaching, in *Excellence in Coaching: The Industry Guide*, 3rd edn, ed J Passmore, pp 131–45, Kogan Page, London

Menzies Lyth, I (1989) *The Dynamics of the Social: Selected essays, volume 2,* Tavistock

Merriam-webster.com, definition of 'belief' [online] Available at: https://www.merriam-webster.com/dictionary/belief (archived at https://perma.cc/N97H-QWQ7) [Accessed 17 October 2019]

Merriam-webster.com, definition of 'creativity' [online] Available at: https://www.merriam-webster.com/dictionary/creativity (archived at https://perma.cc/27GE-KDC7) [Accessed 17 January 2020]

Merriam-webster.com, definition of 'innovation' [online] Available at: https://www.merriam-webster.com/dictionary/innovation (archived at https://perma.cc/T6SR-RXDP) [Accessed 17 January 2020]

Merriam-webster.com, definition of 'system' [online] Available at: https://www.merriam-webster.com/dictionary/system (archived at https://perma.cc/A4TU-DGTG) [Accessed 2 January 2020]

Miller, S D, Duncan, B L and Hubble, M A (1997) *Escape from Babel: Towards a unifying language for psychotherapy practice*, Norton Professional Books

Mitchell, R *et al* (2015) Managing inclusiveness and diversity in teams: How leader inclusiveness affects performance through status and team identity, *Human Resource Management*, **54** (2), pp 217–39

Molenberghs, P (2013) The neuroscience of in-group bias, *Neuroscience & Biobehavioral Reviews*, **37** (8), pp 1530–36

Molleman, E (2005) Diversity in demographic characteristics, abilities and personality traits: Do faultlines affect team functioning? *Group Decision and Negotiation*, **14** (3), pp 173–93

Murphy, C and Sayer, M (2019) Standing on the shoulders of the science of team effectiveness: building rigour into your team coaching design, in *The Practitioner's Handbook of Team Coaching,* ed D Clutterbuck *et al*, pp 75–88, Routledge, London and New York

Mwangi, P G (2019) Is this team tight enough to deliver? *DBA Africa Management Review*, **9** (1), pp 40–51

Norcross, J C (2010) The therapeutic relationship, in *The Heart and Soul of Change: Delivering what works in therapy*, 2nd edn, ed B L Duncan *et al*, pp 133–41, American Psychological Association, Washington, DC

O'Connor, S and Cavanagh, M (2016) Group and team coaching, in *The SAGE Handbook of Coaching*, ed T Bachkirova, G Spence and D Drake, pp 485–504, SAGE Reference, Los Angeles

O'Connor, J and Seymour, J (1990) *Introducing NLP: Psychological skills for understanding and influencing people*, Conaro Press

Passmore, J (2014) *Psychometrics in Coaching: Using psychological and psychometric tools for development*, Kogan Page, London

Peters, J and Carr, C (2013) *High Performance Team Coaching*, Friesen Press, Victoria, BC

Peters, J and Carr, C (2019) What does 'good' look like? An overview of the research on the effectiveness of team coaching, in *The Practitioner's Handbook of Team Coaching*, ed D Clutterbuck *et al*, pp 89–120, Routledge, London and New York

Pisarski, A *et al* (2008) Organizational influences on the work life conflict and health of shiftworkers, *Applied Ergonomics*, **39** (5), pp 580–88

Pittman, C M and Karle, E M (2015) *Rewire Your Anxious Brain: How to use the neuroscience of fear to end anxiety, panic, and worry*, New Harbinger Publications

Polzer, J T and Elfenbein, H A (2003) Identity issues in teams, *Harvard Business School Background Note 403-095*, February 2003

Porter, C O, Gogus, C I and Yu, R C (2011) The influence of early efficacy beliefs on teams' reactions to failing to reach performance goals, *Applied Psychology*, **60** (4), pp 645–69

Price, C and Toye, S (2017) *Accelerating Performance: How organizations can mobilize, execute, and transform with agility*, John Wiley & Sons, Inc, Hoboken NJ

Project Implicit (2019) [online] Available at: https://implicit.harvard.edu/implicit/uk/selectatest.jsp (archived at https://perma.cc/9ENG-J3EX) [Accessed 2 January 2020]

Renshaw, B and Alexander, G (2005) *Supercoaching: The missing ingredient for high performance*, Random House Business, London

Renshaw, B (2018) *Purpose: The extraordinary benefits of focusing on what matters most*, LID Publishing Limited, London

Rico, D F and Sayani, H H (2009) Use of agile methods in software engineering education, in *2009 Agile Conference,* pp 174–79, IEEE

Riess, H *et al* (2012) Empathy training for resident physicians: A randomized controlled trial of a neuroscience-informed curriculum, *Journal of General Internal Medicine*, **27** (10), pp 1280–86

Roberts, V Z and Brunning, H (2007) Psychodynamic and systems-psychodynamic coaching, in *Handbook of Coaching Psychology: A guide for practitioners*, ed S Palmer and A Whybrow, pp 253–77, Routledge Taylor and Francis, London & New York

Rock, D (2008) SCARF: A brain-based model for collaborating with and influencing others, *NeuroLeadership Journal*, **1** (1), pp 44–52

Rogers, C R (1961) *On Becoming a Person: A therapist's view of psychotherapy*, Robinson, London

Rogers, C R (1995) *A Way of Being*, Houghton Mifflin Harcourt

Rogers, J (2016) *Coaching skills: The definitive guide to being a coach*, 4th edn, Open University Press, Maidenhead

Rom, E and Mikulincer, M (2003) Attachment theory and group processes: The association between attachment style and group-related representations, goals, memories, and functioning, *Journal of Personality and Social Psychology*, **84** (6), pp 1220–35

Rosoux, V (2009) Reconciliation as a peace-building process: Scope and limits, in *The Sage Handbook of Conflict Resolution*, ed J Bercovitch, V Kremenyuk and I W Zartman, pp 543–60, Sage, London

Ryan, R M and Deci, E L (2000) Intrinsic and extrinsic motivations: Classic definitions and new directions, *Contemporary Educational Psychology*, **25** (1), pp 54–67

Sandahl, P and Philips, A (2019) *Teams Unleashed: How to release the power and human potential of work teams*, Nicholas Brealey Publishing, Boston

Sandold, D J D (2013) Extending the reach of Basic Human Needs: A comprehensive theory for the twenty-first century, in *Conflict Resolution and Human Needs: Linking theory and practice*, ed K Avruch and C Mitchelle, Routledge Taylor & Francis Group, London and New York

Sanford, N (2017) *Self and Society: Social change and individual development*, 2nd edn, Routledge

Schein, E H (1988) *Process Consultation: Its role in organisational development*, Wesley, London

Schein, E H (1990) A general philosophy of helping: Process consultation, *Sloan Management Review*, **31** (3), pp 57–64

Schein, E H (2013) *Humble Inquiry: The gentle art of asking instead of telling*, Berrett-Koehler Publishers, San Francisco

Senge, P M (2006) *The Fifth Discipline: The art and practice of the learning organization*, Random House Business Books, London

Shapiro, D L (2010) Relational identity theory: a systematic approach for transforming the emotional dimension of conflict, *American Psychologist*, **65** (7), pp 634–45

Shaw, G (2015) TEDx talk: Why people believe they can't draw – and how to prove they can [online] Available at: https://youtu.be/7TXEZ4tP06c (archived at https://perma.cc/8JRK-8LDK) [Accessed 21 January 2020]

Shirom, A *et al* (2011) Work-based predictors of mortality: A 20-year follow-up of healthy employees, *Health Psychology*, 30 (3), pp 268–75

Sheldon, K M *et al* (2004) The independent effects of goal contents and motives on well-being: It's both what you pursue and why you pursue it, *Personality and Social Psychology Bulletin*, 30 (4), pp 475–86

Silvia, P J and O'Brien, M E (2004) Self-awareness and constructive functioning: Revisiting 'The human dilemma', *Journal of Social and Clinical Psychology*, 23 (4), pp 475–89

Sinek, S (2009) *Start with Why: How great leaders inspire everyone to take action*, Penguin Radom House, UK

Smith, E R, Murphy, J and Coats, S (1999) Attachment to groups: Theory and measurement, *Journal of Personality and Social Psychology*, 77 (1), pp 94–110

Spain, S M, Harms, P and LeBreton, J M (2013) The dark side of personality at work, *Journal of Organizational Behavior*, 35 (S1), pp S41–S60

Spunt, R P, Falk, E B and Lieberman, M D (2010) Dissociable neural systems support retrieval of how and why action knowledge, *Psychological Science*, 21 (11), pp 1593–98

Stelter, R (2009) Coaching as a reflective space in a society of growing diversity: Towards a narrative, postmodern paradigm, *International Coaching Psychology Review*, 4 (2), pp 207–17

Stober, D R (2006) Coaching from the Humanistic Perspective, *in Evidence Based Coaching Handbook: Putting best practices to work for your clients*, ed D R Stober and A M Grant, pp 17–50, John Wiley & Sons Inc, New Jersey

Taggar, S (2002) Individual creativity and group ability to utilize individual creative resources: A multilevel model, *Academy of Management Journal*, 45 (2), pp 315–30

The Agile Mindset (2019) Scrum Framework [online] Available at: https://www.theagilemindset.co.uk/scrum-framework/ (archived at https://perma.cc/NEF9-GEWC) [Accessed 4 January 2020]

The Reader's Digest (1947) September

Thong, M (2018) How Agile helps non-technical teams get things done [online] Available at: https://opensource.com/article/18/8/agile-helps-non-technical-teams (archived at https://perma.cc/VE4Z-EB85) [Accessed 15 August 2019]

Thornton, C (2010, 2016) *Group and Team Coaching: The secret life of groups*, 1st and 2nd edns, Routledge, London

Thornton, C (ed) (2019) *The Art and Science of Working Together: Practising group analysis in teams and organisations*, pp 1–44, Routledge, London

Tillett, G and French, B J (1991) *Resolving Conflict: A practical approach*, Oxford University Press, Melbourne

Tuckman, B W (1965) Development sequence in small groups, *Psychological Bulletin*, 63 (6), pp 384–99

Tuckman, B W and Jensen, M A C (1977) Stages of small-group development revisited, *Group & Organization Studies*, **2** (4), pp 419–27

United Nations (2019a) Home, Global Issues, Climate Change [online] Available at: https://www.un.org/en/sections/issues-depth/climate-change/ (archived at https://perma.cc/P6ZU-JCRH) [Accessed 21 February 2020]

United Nations (2019b) Home, Explore Topics, Climate Change [online] Available at: https://www.unenvironment.org/explore-topics/climate-change (archived at https://perma.cc/U4WD-ESVJ) [Accessed 21 February 2020]

Van Nieuwerburgh, C (2017) *An Introduction to Coaching Skills: A practical guide*, 2nd edn, Sage Publications Ltd, London

Van Praag, H, Kempermann, G and Gage, F H (2000) Neural consequences of environmental enrichment, *Nature Reviews Neuroscience*, **1** (3), pp 191–98

Van Vianen, A E and De Dreu, C K (2001) Personality in teams: Its relationship to social cohesion, task cohesion, and team performance, *European Journal of Work and Organizational Psychology*, **10** (2), pp 97–120

Wageman, R (2001) How leaders foster self-managing team effectiveness: Design choices versus hands-on coaching, *Organization Science*, **12** (5), pp 559–77

Wageman, R *et al* (2008) *Senior Leadership Teams: What it takes to make them great*, Harvard Business School Press, Boston MA

Wardhana, A K (2018) Work stress (causes, impacts and solutions): A case study on the Net. Yogyakarta Employees, *Russian Journal of Agricultural and Socio-Economic Sciences*, (4), pp 80–91

Warneken, F and Tomasello, M (2006) Altruistic helping in human infants and young chimpanzees, *Science*, **311** (5765), pp 1301–03

Whitmore, J (2009) *Coaching for Performance: GROWing human potential and purpose, the principles and practice of coaching and leadership*, 4th edn, Nicholas Brealey Publishing, London

Whittington, J (2012, 2016) *Systemic Coaching & Constellations: An introduction to the principles, practices and applications*, 1st and 2nd editions, Kogan Page, London

Widdowson, L J (2017) Creating the Team Edge, Henley Centre for Coaching members' website, Henley Business School, Henley

Widdowson, L J (2018) Understanding team leaders' and team coaches' perceptions of the effectiveness of the 'Creating the Team Edge' framework, MSc Unpublished Dissertation, Henley Business School, Henley

Widdowson, L J and Barbour, P J (2019) Team Coaching: Coaching in Action Guide, The Henley Centre for Coaching, Henley Business School, Henley

Widdowson, L J and Barbour, P J (2020) Systemic team coaching, in *The Coaches' Handbook: The complete practitioner guide for professional coaches*, ed J Passmore, Routledge

Widdowson, L J *et al* (2020) Bridging the team coaching competency gap: A review of the literature, *International Journal of Evidence Based Coaching and Mentoring*, **18** (2), pp 35–50

Wilke, G and Thornton, C (2019) Translucent boundaries, leaders, and consultants: How to work with whole organizations, in *The Art and Science of Working Together: Practising group analysis in teams and organisations*, ed C Thornton, pp 224–36, Routledge, London

Vitale, N (2019) Why total wellbeing? (And why should HR and people teams integrate wellbeing into their cultures?), *Workforce Solutions Review*, 10 (4), pp 19–21

Woollett, K and Maguire, E A (2011) Acquiring 'the Knowledge' of London's layout drives structural brain changes, *Current Biology*, 21 (24), pp 2109–14

Woolley, A W *et al* (2010) Evidence for a collective intelligence factor in the performance of human groups, *Science*, 330 (6004), pp 686–88

Xu, X *et al* (2009) Do you feel my pain? Racial group membership modulates empathic neural responses, *Journal of Neuroscience*, 29 (26), pp 8525–29

INDEX

Figures and tables are indicated by page numbers in *italics*.

4 Cs of being 30–39
360 team diagnostic tool 59

action learning sets 4–5
agile mindset organizations 195–96
Agile Scrum Framework 205
agile way of being 196–97
alliance (strength of the relationship) 32–33
Amazon 206
appreciative feedback 175–76
archetypal practices model 38
Association for Coaching (AC) 259
    coaching competencies 23–24
attachment styles 164
attachment theory 164
    group attachment theory 171–72
attention deficit-hyperactivity disorder 177
autism 176–77
awareness 49, 50
    considerations for awareness in
        organizations 139–40
    defining 133–34
    psychology behind 134–39
    what humans pay attention to 134
    see also team awareness
Awareness-Choice-Execution (ACE) Cycle of
        Change model 135

'Being, Doing and Knowing' model of team
        coaching competency 22–39
beliefs *see* values and beliefs
Bezos, Jeff 206
board identity challenges 96–97
The Body Shop 66

Cancer Research UK 65
challenge versus support model 35
CID-CLEAR model of team
        coaching 45
Clifton, Jim 168
coaching qualifications 19–20
cohesion in groups 32–33, 35, 36
Componential Theory of Creativity
        (Amabile) 225, 230–31
congruence/genuineness 32, *34*
constellations 144

Constellations tool (creating systemic
        awareness) 157–59
countertransference, management of 32
COVID-19 pandemic
    awareness of global connections 139
    impact of remote working on teams 13
    responses to 68, 193
    use of technology at work 257
    working from home 207
Creating Team Edge Profile (CTEP)
        diagnostic instrument 145
Creating the Team Edge framework 14–15,
        46–50
    awareness 49, 50, 133–60
    identity 49, 85–107
    purpose 49, 61–84
    relatedness 49, 50, 161–89
    seven characteristics 49–50
    transformation 49, 50, 222–49
    values and beliefs 49, 108–32
    ways of working 49, 50, 190–221
creativity
    team creativity and innovation 227, 228,
        230–31
    unlocking 224–25

developmental dyspraxia 177
developmental feedback 175–76
Disney, Walt 242–43
diversity
    challenges for teams 95–96
    team inclusion and 227, 228, 231–33
Dweck, Carol 126, 223–24
dyslexia 177

Eco-Systemic Team coaching 45
Einhorn, Nick 238
empathy 32–33
empathy bias 164–65
epilepsy 177
European Coaching and Mentoring Council
        (EMCC) 258–59
    coaching competencies 23–24
executive teams, challenge of a common
        team purpose 72–73
EY 65

facilitation skills 26, 27
feedback 32, *34*
    Feedback Goldfish Bowl tool 180–81
    issues related to 175–76
    performance and 146
    Tell Me tool 182–84
fixed mindset 126, 223–24
Ford, Henry 115
frameworks, models and approaches 41–60
    Creating the Team Edge framework
        46–50
    determining the need for 50–51
    keeping them in perspective 41–42
    review of 45–46
    stage of the team's developmental
        journey 51
    team coaches' views on 43–44
    useful questions for team coaches 50–60
Frankl, Victor 63–64
Friedman, Milton 68
future of team coaching 250–59
    building meaningful connection 253–55
    changing nature of work 255–57
    collaboration 250–53
    connecting teams (team of teams) 252
    connecting to purpose 254–55
    development and
        professionalization 257–59
    embracing true diversity 256
    imagining the future 250
    importance of connecting before
        commencing the work 253–54
    paradox of the individual 255
    rethinking leadership selection and
        development 255–56
    systemic thinking 250–52
    technology opportunity 257
    'way of being' of a team coach 253

goals
    alignment with values 64
    consensus and collaboration
        on 32–33
Golden Circle concept 63
Google 170–71
group attachment theory 171–72
group coaching 4–5
group dynamic processes 137–38
group dynamics 26, 27
group identity
    cohesiveness and survival 86–87
    dangers of 87
groups
    distinction from teams 2–3
    human need to be in and work in 1–2

growth mindset 126, 223–24
Growth Mindset tool 125–27

Hardingham, Alison 35, 37
heroic leader concept 2
High-Performance Team Coaching
        (HPTC) System 46
home working, opportunities and
        challenges 207–08

identity 49
    board identity challenges 96–97
    dangers of group identity 87
    defining 85
    group identity, cohesiveness and
        survival 86–87
    importance for organizations
        87–88
    psychology behind 86–87
    understanding the self 86
    see also team identity
Ikea 66
Implicit Association Test (IAT) 136–37
inclusion, team inclusion and diversity 227,
        228, 231–33
individualism, tension with team
        working 1–2, 3
in-groups 164–65
innovation, team creativity and
        innovation 227, 228, 230–31
International Coach Federation (ICF) 20,
        258–59
    coaching competencies 23–24
interviewing team members 57–59

Johari Window 155–57

King, Martin Luther 72
Kline, Nancy 43–44

leaders
    role in developing a team purpose 69–70
    role in team coaching 20–21
learning groups 4–5
limiting beliefs 224
Logical Levels Model 110–11
Lumina Learning® psychometric tools 145
Lumina Spark® psychometric tool 145

Machiavellianism 175
managers, role in team coaching 20–21
Microsoft 66
models *see* frameworks, models and
        approaches
motivation

intrinsic motivation 64
moving towards reward and away from
    threat 165–66
Myers-Briggs Type Indicator®
    (MBTI®) 145

Nandos 65
narcissism 175
neurodiversity in teams 176–77, 231–33

one-to-one coaching
    contracting 51–52
    in parallel with team coaching 175
organization and team context 26, 29–30
organizational development 26, 29
organizations
    agile mindset 195–96
    becoming a team of teams 195–96, 204
    challenge of 'spoken' versus 'lived'
        values 112–13
    considerations for systemic
        awareness 139–40
    developing an 'agile way of being'
        196–97
    how they can become
        transformational 226–27
    impact of not being aware of the
        system 139–40
    importance of how people relate at
        work 167–68
    importance of identity 87–88
    importance of purpose 65–68
    importance of transformation for 226–27
    importance of ways of working 193–97
    values and beliefs 111–12
    ways of working based on psychological
        needs of employees 193–95
out-groups 164–65

partnering with another team coach, benefits
    and drawbacks 53–54
Performance Edge Partners Limited 46
PERIL team coaching model 45
personal power 37
personality, dark triad of 175
personality psychometrics 147
physical and virtual learning design 26, 28
Pilbeam, David 46
positive regard 32, 34
process consultancy 6
professionalization of coaching 19–20,
    258–59
psychology of
    awareness 134–39
    decision making 192–93

identity 86–87
purpose 62–64
relatedness 163–66
transformation 222–26
values and beliefs 109–11
ways of working 190–93
psychometric tools to increase individual
    self-awareness 59–60
psychopathy 175
purpose 49
    common purpose as a means to unite
        people 64
    finding meaning and purpose in the
        everyday 63
    importance for organizations 65–68
    life-giving power of 63–64
    link with motivation, values, goals and
        well-being 64
    psychology behind 62–64
    the 'why' of 62–63
purpose-driven organizations 65–68
purpose-driven teams 61–84
    benefits of having a team purpose 69
    benefits of having an agreed purpose
        61–62
    challenge of a common purpose in
        executive teams 72–73
    challenges of team purpose 72–73
    collective performance goals 72
    defining purpose 61–62
    developing a team purpose 68–71
    ideal team purpose 71
    ideal team purpose process 71
    importance of context for team
        purpose 70
    need for a team purpose 68–69
    organizational barriers to becoming
        purpose driven 73
    reflecting on team purpose 83–84
    role of leadership in developing a team
        purpose 69–70
    team involvement in developing team
        purpose 70–71
    tools and techniques for developing 74–84
        Developing your 'Why' (why, how
            and what) 74–76
        Getting Creative (developing a
            compelling team purpose) 80–81
        Memorable Object (connecting to
            personal purpose) 76–77
        Purposeful Pictures (sharing personal
            purpose) 77–78
        Team Shield 81–83
        Word Power (developing a compelling
            purpose) 79–80

reflective practice 38
relatedness 49, 50
    a theory of 166
    importance in organizations 167–68
    link with human survival 163
    psychology behind 163–66
    see also team relatedness
relational interpretations, quality of 32
relationships, impact of earliest experiences
            on 163–64
remote working, opportunities and
            challenges 207–08
repair of alliance ruptures 32, *34*

Sands, Sharon 46
Santagata, Paul 170–71
SCARF model 146, 166
self, understanding the notion of 86
self-awareness
    use of psychometric tools to develop
            59–60
    see also awareness; team awareness
Self-Determination Theory (SDT) 163, 224
self-disclosure 32, *34*
Shape-shifting model of team coaching 46
Shaw, Graham 224
Sinek, Simon 74
Stakeholder Mapping tool 178–80
supervision for team coaches 39
support versus challenge model 35
systemic awareness 138–40
systemic practice 26, 27

team awareness 133–60
    assessment or diagnostic tools 145
    catalyst for change 134–35
    challenges 146–47
    defining awareness 133–34
    developing awareness of group
            dynamics 137–38
    developing awareness of our implicit
            bias 136–37
    developing awareness of what happens
            when we communicate 135–36
    developing systemic awareness 138–39
    development of 140–45
    development tools and techniques
            147–60
        Constellations (creating systemic
            awareness) 157–59
        Johari Window (developing deeper
            awareness) 155–57
        The Power of Thoughts (ways to
            reframe our thinking) 159–60

        Stepping into another person's
            shoes (individual and team
            awareness) 152–55
        Support and Challenge (getting the
            balance right) 149–52
        Systemic Awareness (understanding
            team strengths and areas of
            development) 148–49
    group dynamics awareness 140–41,
            142–43
    individual and collective self-
            awareness 140–41, 145
    issues relating to feedback 146
    psychology behind awareness
            134–39
    reflecting on 160
    systemic awareness and
            constellations 140–41, 143–44
    using personality psychometrics 147
    when greater team awareness can do
            more harm than good 146
team building 5–6
team coach contracting, differences from
            one-to-one coaching 51–52
team coaches
    'being' element of a team coach 30–39
    benefits and drawbacks of partnering
            with another team coach 53–54
    characteristics of 8
    coaching qualifications 19–20
    confidence 30, *31*, 35, 37, 43
    connection 30–35, *36*, 43
    continuing 30, *31*, 38–39, 43
    courage 30, *31*, 37–38, 43
    developing team coach awareness
            140–42
    internal or external coaches 21–22
    number and types of professional coaches
            globally 20
    power of 'being' 43–44
    professionalization of coaching
            19–20
    reflective questions 40
    supervision for 39
    team size and number of coaches
            required 54–55
    training 258
    useful questions on frameworks, models
            and approaches 50–60
    views on frameworks, models and
            approaches 43–44
    who can be a team coach 19
    why their 'way of being' is so
            important 19–40

team coaching
  'Being, Doing and Knowing' model of
    competency 22–39
  'being' element 30–39
  characteristics of the team coach 8
  checking that the team and client are
    ready for it 56–57
  competencies 22–40
  contracting for one-to-one interviews
    before starting 57–59
  creating lasting change 9
  defining 7–11
  developing better ways of working 10
  developing new thinking 10
  developing safe and trusting
    relationships 9–10
  distinction from other team
    interventions 4–7
  'doing' dimension (core
    competencies) 23–26
  effectiveness of 13–15
  frameworks, models and approaches
    41–60
  future of 250–59
  helping teams work together, with
    others and within their wider
    environment 9
  ideal team size and number of coaches
    required 54–55
  integration of technology into 13
  key applications from therapeutic
    relationships 31–35, 36
  'knowing' dimension (foundation
    knowledge) 26–30
  length of time an intervention should
    last 55
  literature and evidence base 258
  literature and frameworks 26, 29
  living its values 259
  maximizing collective potential, purpose
    and performance goals 11
  moving towards an empirically tested
    and validated theory 15
  professionalization of 258–59
  reflective questions 18
  role of the leader 20–21
  seven key elements 8–11
  towards mastery 39–40
  type of teams that can benefit from
    it 11–13
  use of team diagnostic tools and
    techniques 57–60
Team Connect 360 diagnostic
  145

team creativity and innovation 227, 228,
  230–31
Team Diagnostic Survey 145
team diagnostics 26, 30
  tools and techniques 57–60
team effectiveness, reflective
  questions 60
team facilitation 6
team identity 85–107
  defining identity 85
  importance of identity for
    organizations 87–88
  psychology behind identity 86–87
  reflecting on 107
team identity challenges 92–96
  board identity 96–97
  destructive intergroup conflict 92–93
  overcoming diversity challenges 95–96
  perils of ignoring team history and the
    wider system 94–95
  strong team identity can harm innovative
    behaviour 94
team identity development 88–92
  creating your team story 92
  importance of common goals 90–91
  importance of finding and being
    yourself 90
  team member differences can strengthen
    team identity 91
  tools and techniques 97–107
    Logical Levels (exploring your team's
      identity) 97–100
    Newspaper Headlines (creating your
      identity) 101–02
    Personal Identity Timeline (exploring
      who I am) 102–04
    Personal Identity Wheel
      (understanding my identity)
      104–05
    Picture this! (exploring identity)
      100–01
    What's your story? (sharing personal
      identity) 106–07
  understanding team identity 89–90
  valuing each team member 91
team inclusion and diversity 227, 228,
  231–33
team leaders
  interviewing 58
  role in team coaching 20–21
team leadership and development
  26, 28–29
team learning 227–30
team member interviews 58

team of teams, organizations as 195–96,
        204
team psychological safety 169–71
team relatedness 161–89
    attachment styles 164
    challenges of 174–77
    conflict resolution 174–75
    defining relatedness 161–62
    development of 168–74
    development tools and techniques
        177–88
        Feedback Goldfish Bowl
            (developing open and honest
            conversations) 180–81
        Making Connections (getting to know
            each other better) 187–88
        Professional Gossiping (appreciating
            the strengths of team
            members) 186–87
        Stakeholder Mapping (understanding
            the strength of team
            relationships) 178–80
        Swimming Pool (discovering your
            place in the team) 184–86
        Tell Me (giving and receiving
            feedback) 182–84
    empathy bias 164–65
    feedback issues 175–76
    gender diversity and 172–73
    group collective intelligence 169, 172–73
    how we relate to other people at
        work 167–68
    importance of team psychological
        safety 169–71
    individual and team personality
        traits 169, 173–74
    in-groups and out-groups 164–65
    managing the dark side of
        personality 175
    model for 168–69
    neurodiversity in teams 176–77
    psychology behind relatedness 163–66
    reflecting on 188–89
    states of relatedness 161–62
    team cohesion and inclusion 169,
        171–72
    team emotional intelligence (TEI) 169,
        172
    unresolved intra-team conflict 174–75
    workplace culture 167–68
team stakeholder interviews 59
team transformation 222–49
    challenges 236–37
    creativity and innovation 227, 228,
        230–31

defining transformation 222
developing a transformational, learning
        and growth mindset 223–24
development 227–36
development tools and techniques
        237–49
    Disney Model (harnessing team
        creativity) 241–44
    Fresh Thinking Model (building team
        innovation) 237–40
    Individual Wellness (assessing energy
        and health) 245–48
    Outside In (fostering new ideas)
        240–41
    Team Learning (sharing learning and
        knowledge) 248–49
    Team Wellness (assessing team energy
        and health) 245–48
    Voice of the Future Generation
        (thinking to the future) 244–45
inclusion and diversity 227, 228,
        231–33
neurodiversity in teams 231–33
psychology behind transformation
        222–26
reflecting on 249
team learning 227–30
team well-being 227, 228, 233–36
to transform or not 222–23
unlocking our innate creativity 224–25
unsupportive organizational
        cultures 236–37
when members are too busy for team
        coaching 236
team values and beliefs 108–32
    challenge of 'spoken' versus 'lived'
        values 112–13
    challenges of 118–19
    defining values and beliefs 108–09
    developing team belief 117–18
    developing team values 113–15
    development of 113–18
    development tools and techniques
        120–32
        Different Truths (challenging our
            team beliefs) 130–32
        Fly on the Wall (observing team
            values and beliefs) 121–23
        Growth Mindset (how our beliefs
            affect our mindset) 125–27
        Immunity to Change (exploring our
            negative beliefs) 127–30
        Living Your Values (understanding
            good and bad day
            behaviours) 123–25

Values Cards (exploring your team's values) 120–21
importance of organizational values and beliefs 111–13
importance of team belief 115–17
importance of team values 113
issue of too much team belief 119
psychology behind values and beliefs 109–11
reflecting on 132
when individual and team values don't align 118–19
team ways of working 190–221
agile way of being 196–97
challenges of 207–09
communication process challenges 208–09
communication processes 198, 206–07
decision making 197–201
defining ways of working 190
development of 197–207
development tools and techniques 209–21
Circle of Influence and Concern (building team proactivity) 209–11
Creating Common Ground (valuing difference) 211–12
The Five Whats Model (effective decision making) 214–17
'The Hamster Wheel' (reflecting on short- and long-term activities) 217–19
Pause and Reflect (improving decision making) 213–14
Voice of the Customer (developing an agile mindset) 219–21
home and remote working issues 207–08
internal and external processes and rhythm 198, 201–04
link between psychological needs and work 190–92
psychology behind ways of working 190–93
reflecting on 221
task focus at the expense of the future 207

team meetings reinvented 198, 204–06
team well-being 227, 228, 233–36
teams
challenge of team performance 3
definition of a team 2–3
distinction from groups 2–3
importance of 1–2
tension with individualism 1–2, 3
technology, integration into team coaching 13
TEDx talks 224
Tesco 65
Tesla 66
Theory of Team Coaching 13
therapeutic relationships, key applications for team coaching 31–35, 36
thinking, system one and system two models 192–93
timescale of team coaching 55
Tourette's syndrome 177
transformation 49, 50
defining 222
importance for organizations 226–27
psychology behind 222–26
see also team transformation

Uber 66
unconditional positive regard 32

values and beliefs 49
alignment with goals 64
changing our values and beliefs 110
defining values and beliefs 108–09
importance for organizations 111–13
in context 110–11
psychology behind 109–11
shaped by human experience 109–10
see also team values and beliefs
Virgin Group 65

Wallis, Glenn 46
ways of working 49, 50
importance for organizations 193–97
see also team ways of working
well-being, link with purpose 64